ADVANCE PRAISE FOR
An Ecological Pedagogy of Joy

"An Ecological Pedagogy of Joy supports exploration of how ecological pedagogy lives in the world and, as such, carries tenets of life writing, Indigenous and literary métissage, and ecological notions of interweaving. Featuring contemporary research while inviting readers to consider the ancestries informing the work, it evidences how pedagogy can be understood as organized around relationality and living inquiry. Scholars and teachers of eco-sustainability, Indigenous and community-based research, and post/qualitative ways of knowing will find this a valuable resource."
—Ellyn Lyle, Dean, Faculty of Education, Yorkville University

"After many years of work, study, and community service, I have learned that the most important guidance that I can provide is to help human beings connect with the many gifts that exist in the place where they live. Guiding people to attend to such sacred ecology insights helps them understand more deeply the multiple and complex ways that we are all unified by what gives us life. This book is a beautiful recounting of this wisdom teaching and also a poignant reminder of the critical need to express gratefulness for these gifts as a fundamental part of what it means to live as a real human being."
—Dwayne Donald, Professor & Tier 1 Canada Research Chair, Faculty of Education, University of Alberta

An Ecological Pedagogy of Joy

Complicated Conversation

A Book Series of
Curriculum Studies

William F. Pinar
General Editor

Volume 59

Jodi Latremouille, Lesley Tait, David W. Jardine

An Ecological Pedagogy of Joy

On Relations, Aliveness and Love

New York · Berlin · Bruxelles · Chennai · Lausanne · Oxford

Library of Congress Cataloging-in-Publication Control Number: 2023027958

Bibliographic information published by the Deutsche Nationalbibliothek.
The German National Library lists this publication in the German
National Bibliography; detailed bibliographic data is available
on the Internet at http://dnb.d-nb.de

Cover design by Peter Lang Group AG

ISSN 1534-2816
ISBN 9781636671673 (hardback)
ISBN 9781636671666 (paperback)
ISBN 9781636670812 (ebook)
ISBN 9781636670829 (epub)
DOI 10.3726/b20711

© 2024 Peter Lang Group AG, Lausanne
Published by Peter Lang Publishing Inc., New York, USA
info@peterlang.com - www.peterlang.com

All rights reserved.
All parts of this publication are protected by copyright.
Any utilization outside the strict limits of the copyright law, without the permission of the
publisher, is forbidden and liable to prosecution.
This applies in particular to reproductions, translations, microfilming, and storage and
processing in electronic retrieval systems.

This publication has been peer reviewed.

An Ecological Pedagogy of Joy

On Relations, Aliveness and Love

Jodi Latremouille, Lesley Tait & David W. Jardine

A Field Guide

Acknowledgments	xi
Giving Thanks	xi
Notes from a Visit with Kehte-aya Bob Cardinal	xii
Gratitude and Permissions	xiv
As We Begin	xvii
On Braiding	xvii

PART I: "ALL STORIES ARE NOT CREATED EQUAL"

To Begin—"All Stories" (Jodi Latremouille, Lesley Tait, & David Jardine)	1
Feasting on Whispers (Jodi Latremouille)	2
"She Loved to Embroider" (Lesley Tait)	6
WAYSTATION I: "Standing Silent in the Sun" (Taylor Nyeste)	24

PART II: AN ECOLOGICAL PEDAGOGY OF JOY

An Ecological Pedagogy of Joy (Jodi Latremouille)	29
Nôhkom's Gloves: A Recollection of "Spirit" and our Family Belongings (Lesley Tait)	37
A Record Year (Jodi Latremouille)	54

viii | *A Field Guide*

"The Open Breath" (Lesley Tait)   66
WAYSTATION II: Logger (Vern Latremouille)   70
"Slower, More Miraculous Returns" I (David Jardine)   80
A Modern Hunting Tradition (Jodi Latremouille)   81

PART III: ENTANGLED

Entangled Relations (Jodi Latremouille & Lesley Tait)   87
WAYSTATION III: Medicines Heal Your Heart (Emilia Tait)   104

PART IV: "TO RE-TEACH A THING ITS LOVELINESS"

Environment (Jodi Latremouille)   125
WAYSTATION IV: A Conversation with David Geoffrey Smith on The Prevenient Givenness of Life (David G. Smith & David Jardine)   127
Birding Lessons and the Teachings of Cicadas (David Jardine)   134
Environment (Jodi Latremouille)   135
WAYSTATION V: "Out of Control" Activism (Sydney Tait)   139
Educational Philosophy (Lesley Tait)   141
WAYSTATION VI: The Joy of Learning: Upsetting What We Know (Gail McNicol-Jardine)   155

PART V: RELATIONS, ALIVENESS, LOVE

And So. Relations, Aliveness, Love (Jodi Latremouille, Lesley Tait & David Jardine)   159
WAYSTATION VII: "Everyone is Hungry": A Conversation with Jackie Seidel about Bees (Jackie Seidel & David Jardine)   175
wahkohtowin   183
Winter (Lesley Tait)   189
A Breath, When the Birds Will Show Us (Lesley Tait)   192

PART VI: SILENT READING

Successful Assimilation (Lesley Tait)   193
WAYSTATION VIII: Mom's Poem (Sheila Ewasiuk)   200
Raising a Reader (Jodi Latremouille)   206
Raising a Writer (David Jardine)   212
WAYSTATION IX: I Provide a Pre-emptive Waystation (Eric Jardine)   214

PART VII: **BREATH AGAIN**

Breath Again (David Jardine)	217
Sharp Exhale: When Will the Birds Show Me? (David Jardine)	219
Remembrances of the Land and Rocks in my Pocket (Lesley)	224
WAYSTATION X: "Hush, child . . ." A Conversation with Kiera and Taylor Nyeste	227
My Forgetting, Their Remembering (David Jardine)	228
More on Whiling Time and Aliveness (David Jardine)	230
wicihitowin	233
sakihitowin	233
Some [Edited] Introductory Words for Two Little Earth-Cousins (David Jardine)	236
WAYSTATION XI: Await (Meredith McLeod)	240
So Where Are We, Now? (Jodi Latremouille, Lesley Tait & David Jardine)	241
My Treasured Relation (Jodi Latremouille)	241

PART VIII: **WHERE DO WE TURN?**

Where do we Turn? (Jodi Latremouille, Lesley Tait & David Jardine)	249
"We Do Know What to Do" (David Jardine)	250
WAYSTATION XII: Heartland (Kiera Nyeste)	258
We are Back in the Place Where We See Our Footsteps in The Grass (Jodi Latremouille, Lesley Tait & David Jardine)	259

References   261

Acknowledgments

Giving Thanks

We begin by acknowledging and giving thanks to all that gives us life.

manitow- Creator

kîsikâwi-pisim- Sun

tipiskâwi-pisim- Moon

We also acknowledge and give thanks to the land and all our relations who sustain and teach us.

Kehte-aya Bob Cardinal of the Maskekosihk Enoch Cree Nation in Alberta has shared many teachings that guide our work. Kehte-aya refers to the heart and also implies mindfulness. Bob often reminds us that the longest journey is from the mind to the heart. Kehte-aya are the wise ones who have made that journey. They are sacred hearted, kind hearted, and compassionate human beings. They have become that way through many years of dedication to traditional wisdom. Two of the authors, Lesley and Jodi, had the privilege to participate in a 2014 University of Alberta graduate course entitled *Holistic Understandings of Learning,* which he co-taught at his teaching lodge with Dr. Dwayne Donald. The three of us are grateful for the many occasions we have had to sit with Kehte-aya Bob Cardinal during the writing of this book. His support and permission to share particular teachings are acknowledged as they occur throughout the book. We would like to give thanks to Dwayne Donald for his support, guidance and encouragement over the past six years. Both of them quietly and consistently remind us to find the spirit in the work, to give thanks and respect to Creator, the sun and the moon, the land, the places we belong to, all of the earthly beings who nourish and give life to everything, and to remember all our relations to whom we are responsible.

Notes from a Visit with Kehte-aya Bob Cardinal

The Sacred Four Directions Teachings guide us to find balance in how we live our lives.

EAST
Bear: Emotional Clarity, Patience, Compassion
Sun

journey from head to heart
a child comes—they feel safe
they are the only ones that know truth
innocence and purity—how do we embrace that?

take it slowly
let it grow first
how could students embrace this—lead them—
let them take it in their own way
and live it for themselves

SOUTH
Grandmother Mouse: Spiritual Knowing, Humbleness, Nurturing, Love, Patience, Innocence
Earth

humbleness
it's a miracle when we get up in the morning
go softly and slowly—walk on Mother Earth
feel that connection
sounds and colour
what are you trying to lift?

WEST
Thunder Being: Mental Strength and Courage, Respect
Water

I like this—no answers—
readers have to figure out for themselves
allow it to travel with the wind, water and sun
there's no ending

some people want to own this
pass it on to people who are willing to listen
look beyond your own life
all languages have a place

recognize spirituality

writing that has that character of staying open
words create our reality, our truth

NORTH
Buffalo: Physical Strength and Courage, Relations, Gifts, Protection, Care
Relations

wind and air moves everything
sun gives blessings
water moves everything, gives life, blessings
earth gives trees and food
what do we keep sacred?

we don't see it but we live it each day

what do we keep sacred?
without wind, air, water, earth, we wouldn't be here
move things in a good way
take the work out into the world

humbleness
gratitude

VISION
Eagle: Unified Understanding, Connection
Balance

re-spiriting

(Kehte-aya Bob Cardinal, oral teachings, March 28, 2019; June 24–28, 2020)

Gratitude and Permissions

We would also like to express our deep appreciation to Eric Jardine, Gail McNicol-Jardine, Sydney Tait, Emilia Tait, Sheila Ewasiuk, Taylor Nyeste, Kiera Nyeste, Vern Latremouille, Meredith McLeod, David G. Smith and Jackie Seidel for their thoughtful Waystations along the paths of the text.

We would like to acknowledge that this project has received funding from the VIU Publish grant.

We are grateful for the generous permissions we have received to use lovely artwork, and to reprint previously published articles and book chapters by the authors.

For artwork and photographs:

> We would like to thank Anita McComas for permission to use the cover painting and another work in the body of the text:
> Anita McComas, Cover painting: "Feeling a Bit Curious."
> Anita McComas, Painting in the text: "Moonlight Reflections."
> For more of Anita McComas' work, see anitamcomas.com.
> We would like to thank Danielle Bertoia for permission to use the photo, entitled "Await."
> All other photographs and images have been provided by the authors or borrowed from our family archives.

For work by the authors previously published in various outlets:

Jodi Latremouille

Latremouille, J. (2014). Feasting on whispers: Life writing towards a pedagogy of kinship. Master of Arts thesis, Faculty of Education, University of Calgary.

Latremouille, J. (2014). My treasured relation. *Online Journal of Applied Hermeneutics*. PID: http://hdl.handle.net/10515/sy5d50gd4.

Latremouille, J. (2015). A modern hunting tradition. *One World in Dialogue: A Peer Reviewed Journal and Focus Newsletter, 3(2),* 1–6. Alberta Teachers' Association Social Studies Council. ©2022 by the Alberta Teachers' Association, 11010 142 Street NW, Edmonton AB, T5N 2R1. All rights reserved. Reprinted with permission. Published 2022.

Latremouille, J. (2016). Raising a reader: Re-memorying through the four directions. *Language and Literacy,* 18(1), 1–11. Language and Literacy Researchers of Canada: the Canadian Society for Studies in Education. http://ejournals.library.ualberta.ca/index.php/langandlit.

Latremouille, J. (2018). Environment. In D. G. Krutka, A. M. Whitlock, M. Helmsing (Eds.), *Keywords in the social studies: Concepts and conversations.* Peter Lang.

Latremouille, J. (2020). An ecological pedagogy of joy. In S. Steinberg & B. Down (Eds.), *SAGE handbook of critical pedagogies.* Sage.

Lesley Tait

Tait, L. (2016). Remembrances of the Land and Rocks in my Pocket. In J. Seidel & D. Jardine (Eds.), *The Ecological Heart of Teaching: Radical Tales of Refuge and Renewal for Classrooms and Communities.* (p. 166–167). Peter Lang.

Tait, L. (2016). Successful Assimilation. In J. Seidel & D. Jardine (Eds.), *The Ecological Heart of Teaching: Radical Tales of Refuge and Renewal for Classrooms and Communities.* (p. 17–18). Peter Lang.

David Jardine

Jardine, D. (1997). "All beings are your ancestors": A bear Sutra on ecology, Buddhism and pedagogy. Originally published in *The Trumpeter: A Journal of Ecosophy. 14*(3), 122–23.

Jardine, D. (1997). American Dippers, Alberta winter strawberries. *Raise the Stakes: The Planet Drum Review.* Originally published in Special issue on "Mainstreaming Watersheds," #27 Summer 1997, page 8. © Planet Drum Foundation, used with permission. P.O. Box 31251, San Francisco, CA 94131. https://www.planetdrum.org.

Jardine, D. (1998). Birding lessons and the Teachings of Cicadas. *Canadian Journal of Environmental Education, 3,* 92–9.

Jardine, D. (2014). Some introductory words for two little earth-cousins. *Journal of Applied Hermeneutics.* Online: http://jah.journalhosting.ucalgary.ca/jah/index.php/jah/article/view/61.

Jardine, D. (2014). This is why we read. This is why we write. *Journal of Applied Hermeneutics.* Online: http://jah.journalhosting.ucalgary.ca/jah/index.php/jah/article/view/64/pdf.

Jardine, D. (2016). "You need accuracy": In appreciation of modern hunting traditions and a grouse's life unwasted. *One World in Dialogue: A Peer Reviewed Journal and Focus Newsletter, 3*(2). Alberta Teachers' Association Social Studies Council. ©2022 by the Alberta Teachers' Association, 11010 142 Street NW, Edmonton AB, T5N 2R1. All rights reserved. Reprinted with permission. Published 2022.

Jardine, D. (2019). "Like Life, it is Hazy" Originally published in *The Planet Drum Pulse,* Winter 2020, page 1, © Planet Drum Foundation, used with permission. P.O. Box 31251, San Francisco, CA 94131. https://www.planetdrum.org.

Jodi Latremouille, Lesley Tait & David Jardine

Latremouille, J., Tait, L., & Jardine, D. (2021). Relations, aliveness, love: Curriculum in the spirit of the Earth. *Oxford Encyclopedia of Curriculum Studies.* W. Schubert & Ming Fang He, eds. Oxford University. DOI: https://doi.org/10.1093/acrefore/9780190264093.013.1278.

understandings, and what is lifted up in the daily choices that we make in teaching through the heart-mind (Joanna Macy, 2014).
5. *PART FIVE: Relations, Aliveness, Love.* We invoke the Cree principles of wahkohtowin, wicihitowin, and sakihitowin to consider the role of knowledge in schools, and how, as the "storytellers of society," teachers might infuse knowledge traditions with wisdom and careful consideration for how those stories are told. Stories help us find out and remember where we are, and thus who we are. We consider the discipline and rigour embedded in remembering over and over that this—what we face today, together with our young ones—is just how the world has *turned out*, and not the way it *must be*.
6. *PART SIX: Silent Reading.* We write about teaching in a colonized and "successfully assimilated" world of "literacy" and "civilization." We write about programs and levels and the panic of "falling behind." We think about ways that literacy might live more expansively. We consider how the interruption of our panics and the renewal of holistic understandings of literacy might bring us back to beautiful books again, to translating water, to our collective curiosity, and to a deeper attentiveness for children and the world. We don't claim that this way of reading the world is *easier,* only that it can be so much *better.*
7. *PART SEVEN: Breath Again.* We recite and re-cite the relations that hold us together. We look for company, we try to sit still, we try to stay alive together in our mutual affection. We argue and conspire over minute details, and notice how we become intertwined, more alive, more responsible—through our words, our facing one another, our living up to each other.
8. *PART EIGHT: Where Do We Turn?* Tiny stones saved in our pockets, gifts, stories, help us learn and re-learn that if we can see our own very smallness in the all-important beating of our hearts and working of our hands in the dirt, well then, we *do* know what to do.

This book invokes a spirit of métissage (Cynthia Chambers, Erika Hasebe-Ludt, Carl Leggo, & Anita Sinner, 2012; Dwayne Donald, 2012; Erika Hasebe-Ludt, Cynthia Chambers, & Carl Leggo, 2009) rooted in woven place-stories, poetic interludes, images, life writing, conversations, and scholarly wanderings. Métissage, as both a philosophical orientation, a form of inquiry, and an ethical teaching practice, brings together a multiplicity of voices. Dwayne Donald (2012) writes that:

> Indigenous Métissage brings place-based ecological interpretations of ethical relationality together to support the emergence of a decolonizing research sensibility that provides a way to hold together the ambiguous, layered, complex, and conflictual character of Aboriginal and Canadian relations without the need to deny, assimilate, hybridize, or conclude. (p. 536)

This work is layered in spiralling, recursive, conflicting and cooperating relations. "Métissage ... offers a textual way to honour this tension" (Dwayne Donald, 2012, p. 534) in a complex and generative community. The writing is "pedagogical rather than prescriptive" (Erika Hasebe-Ludt, Cynthia Chambers, & Carl Leggo, 2009, p. 6), in that it does not provide confident advice or clear, linear answers to our questions, but rather invites wandering reflections and dialogues around possible ways of living well together. It also invites readers to allow themselves to read pedagogically rather than prescriptively. Getting lost is not always a mistake—the place will take care of you.

What could a classroom be like? What images of the living, shared and contested disciplines of knowledge that we have inherited might be most livable, sensible, attracting the young and old together in the work of coming to know and speak and writing and read and listen and search? What might we talk about, and how might we talk—and who gets to talk and who has been silenced, and who benefits from the silencing? What we are interested in is the loop and intersect and summons of earthly living, human and more than, and what then becomes of these schools we've taught in, these studies we've undertaken and children we're raising. Our various voices loop and blend and intersect and summon ancestors, summon our own decades-old writing that seems new when braided right here. Asking all this is asking about our ability to be responsive and responsible to our circumstances, to cultivate a pedagogy that enables us to live well in our places, and to respond to the Earth and its ways:

> âakssissawâato'op. It means that when you visit a place you give that place life [you] honour the presences there and enliven the place with food, drink, respectful relations, and prayers. In return, that place gives life back to you. (Dwayne Donald, personal communication, December 10, 2014)

It is hard work to see that nothing, here, has necessarily gone wrong in this braiding of lives together, even though sometimes things fall apart in our hands, or tangled threads become tough knots that bind instead of caress if we pull too tight. It is hard work to hold back and *look* and *see*. But only with such holding back and displacing the eggs they find there. They are generally called *brood parasites*, leaving eggs behind to be raised by others. Something in the etymology is helpful here: "one who lives at another's expense, person who eats at the table of another. 'Feeding beside,' from *para-* 'beside' + *sitos* 'food'" (Online Etymological Dictionary, hereafter OED).

What we've got in this photo is a mature male junco feeding birdseed to an immature female cowbird, August 3, 2019, Bragg Creek, Alberta, mid-morning. One can safely assume that this female was raised in that junco's nest and that the junco is still doing what needs to be done. Both are active and fulsome in the flurry of other birds swooped nearby.

It is hard work to see that nothing, here, has necessarily "gone wrong" in this braiding of lives together. It is hard work to hold back and *look* and *see*. Even if the recent, unusual influx of cowbirds this year means that species will shift hereabouts, and then, of course, perhaps shift back and forth, there is something just barely legible here, a beckon of living and lives held together. Tense and intense in the relax of the sun. Full of pasts and futures and other human worries and pleasures.

There are braids and threads, asides, intermixing voices and stark single cries and laughs. There is writing that is brand new this morning and some work published in 30 years ago.

What we want to speak of is an ecological pedagogy of joy, one full of relations, aliveness and love, and what we have discovered is that this is not just a matter of talking *about* matters that are different than a large swath of work in education, curriculum, teaching and learning. It is a matter of talking differently, writing differently, reading differently, knowing, doing and being differently, in a way that is itself a metaphorical concord of what we are writing about. And that common accord extends to and issues from doing what we can to live in this accord with all the alertness we can muster. Being alert, paying attention reminds us of teachings from Kehte-aya Bob. miyo waskawewin, he would say. Walk well in the world.

Our book is divided into eight parts. Here are sketches of what is to come:

1. PART ONE: *All Stories are not Created Equal*. The mode of "telling our (unique, individual, personal, important) stories" has become such an unquestioned way of being in the world. We want to approach this orientation with some caution, to look those stories squarely in the face, to uncover what has been assumed, to question our own stories, to wear down good pathways and interpretations. We want to consider *better* possibilities for living together, not just *any* possibilities. We share our stories here in the hopes that the worlds of teaching and living with children might be reimagined and rebuilt, in tethered and tethering relations.
2. PART TWO: *An Ecological Pedagogy of Joy*. We write about the challenge of trying not to fall prey to the ecological dangers of despair, panic, denialism, misplaced optimism, and short-term thinking in the face of our climate reality. Facing our climate crisis squarely and honestly offers possibilities for pedagogical practices of love and joy, intimately connected with our places, cycles and those who reside here with us.
3. PART THREE: *Entangled*. We reflect on well-meaning institutional requirements for ethical research, which in the well-intentioned interests of protection and objectivity, can render the work sterile and even violent. These requirements often lose sight of the necessary intimacy and trust that is built into the work that teachers and researchers do in this interpretive and relational work. Objectivity and subjectivity are not merely intertwined—they are fallacies in a world of relations.
4. PART FOUR: *To Re-Teach a Thing its Loveliness*. We consider meanings of "environment," "resources," "conservation," and who we become in how we know these kinds of things. We think about teaching through holistic

attempting to keep clear (a couple of the etymological origins of the Latin *scola*, root of "school" and "scholar") that we can maintain enough composure and propriety in these "ecologically sorrowful times" (David Jardine, 2015a, p. xv).

What shall we say? And what form of speaking and writing is proper to the fix we are in?

Sensitivity to and panic over our current ecological circumstances can blind us as much as blind ambition. "To be patient in an emergency is a terrible trial." (Wendell Berry, with Bill Moyers, 2013, n.p.) To be patient *at all* is tough enough work. It is no accident that patience is named an aspired to virtue in the bloodlines of European thinking and in that of Buddhism as well, in the stories and teachings shared by Indigenous Elders, and we expect, far beyond those reaches as well. The ecological requirements of the braid are like those of a living topic or topography treated well. If we rush or get distracted, the braid unravels on its own or knots up in our clumsy hands; if we walk without attendant care, or forget the teachings of miyo waskawewin, we will lose our footing or lose our way.

We consider those we cite in this text as those who have journeyed before us. We sometimes repeat references over and over. We do so as a deliberate sort of meditative repetition, a sort of re-reading, re-acknowledgment chant, rather than a passing kind of *Ibidem* "see previous acknowledgement" gesture. Think of this as that junco/cowbird resting back down on the railing again. Or as re-listening to an already well-known and loved piece of music. Or listening to our Elder telling the story of the rock for the fourth time, because there is still more for us to learn.

Look. There they are again. As if for the first time, now braided here, here. A new arrival and a reminder all at once. Just like the inrush of a new class in the fall, or a student's unexpected question, or my own child's unexpected lament can lift up seemingly settled matters and make reconsideration exhilarate. A child can ask a question about place-value or about a Cross Fox seen that morning and it can rattle through old territories, wake up old stories, set off Google searches and come to rest in unexpected places that show the life of the knowledge in which we are immersed: *living* disciplines, *living* fields of knowledge. We notice that children *want* to lean into the rigour, the attendant care and ethical responsibility for these living fields and lives and places. They *want* this study to be real, to be good, to be difficult and careful, worthwhile and life-giving. We've rarely come across students who want the work they do to be trivial and time wasting—unless, of course, they've been taught to expect this and to have their finding the world alluring dismissed in schools. This sort of ecological pedagogy of joy needs good care. And if it is cared for, it "increase[s] in being" (Hans-Georg Gadamer, 2004, p. 40). Carefully watching birds makes watching birds more careful.

This emergent way of thinking, speaking, naming, writing, imagining, bespeaks immediately the presence of children. This is why we three, as teachers and parents, hope to provide space for children to lend their voices to pedagogy, spaces within which to rear the young, to listen with love to the ancestors, to think carefully enough to make our way into a future that is inevitably more theirs than ours:

> Some people are beginning to try to understand where they are, and what it would mean to live carefully and wisely, delicately in a place, in such a way that you can live there adequately and comfortably. Also, your children and grandchildren and generations a thousand years in the future would still be able to live there. That's living in terms of the whole fabric of living and life. (Gary Snyder, 1980, p. 86).
>
> Ancient knowledges are able to be (re)cognized within contemporary contexts because these knowledges are living knowledges—they exist and are relevant now, in this time, they are not relics of some forgotten past. (Sandra Styres, 2017, p. 83)

Look, the peas have ripened again and there is comfort to be had in seeing those Ravens side-glancing over the compost. Again. Such repetition is no more or less than a chance to become familiar through reappearance and reacquaintance, through staying put a bit, and trying to remember, collecting oneself, and circling back upon familiar well-worn pathways. We hope these reminders, asides and trials provide readers with a sort of alternate text that fills out kinship relations to the main text. Even if they are not, or not always read, a reader's eye can't help but notice that there are soils underfoot when sticking to the main path and pondering the sky. We have also decided to deliberately use the full first name of the authors we cite in these footnotes. Family names are full of ancestral tracelines, but, as John Caputo points out, "obligations require proper names" (John Caputo, 1993, p. 201). We feel obligated to these authors, Elders and relations that we are citing, and we want to acknowledge that sense of obligation. Last names refer back to ancestries and family relations, communal and even often contested histories, whereas first names may highlight the importance of the role each of us grows into within our communities, as well as the unique gifts we each bring to this work.

As We Begin | xxv

On Naming
Jodi Latremouille

Ursula Le Guin (1985) writes about a reversal of the Biblical story of Adam naming "woman" as well as the animals. In this story Eve "Unnames" the animals as a freeing gesture, to hand back the names that were arbitrarily imposed upon them by humans without the animals' consent. These named ancestries and roles may help us enter honestly into good relations with others.

There are, however, some instances where these first names are too hard to retrieve. That in itself is a strange fix we find ourselves in. We provide a standard reference list at the end of the book that collects and sorts our obligations in a strange but admittedly efficient way—alphabetically. Nothing wrong with efficiency well-thought-through and kept to its proper measure. But we cannot avoid pointing out how rich and abundant is the history and consequence *of this very schooled commonplace of alphabetization* (see Ivan Illich & Barry Sanders, 1988). It, too, is full of hidden braids and has rich and abundant undergrowth and causes and conditions and consequences.

ABCs
David W. Jardine

As for learning your ABCs, as for this most mundane of classroom events, so hides the *alpha*, and the *beta* like a murmuring coil. *Of course* it is not just a name. It never is:

Prior to the 12th century in Europe, references were given before the cited text. This was not a matter of "authorizing" the citation to follow, but of allowing readers to call to memory the images and topographies of the work about to be cited, so that the reader might be ready to "hear" its reminders (Mary Carruthers, 2005, p. 100). References given prior to citations gave readers a chance to prepare themselves properly and adequately for the words that followed. (David Jardine, 2012, p. 163–4)

Indigenous teachings, too, are braided in the practices of saying up front who we are and where we are from. "When a story is told, thousands of ancestors and unborn children come into the room" (Lesley Tait, personal communication, March 28, 2019).

We have had the company of friends, relations, children and Elders in the braiding of this book. The spirit of our young ones also flows through this work. We have invited our children to contribute photos, to wonder about images, to bring our work to bear with their new, requiring and response-able arrivals. The Waystations are written and inspired by our children, along with friends and relatives of us and this work. These Waystations are places to stop for a while. Or places to skip to or skip over or both. These folks share with us the joy of thinking, of working, of carefulness and intense attention to our living circumstances and the places we inhabit.

To even imagine, here, now, introducing this book to you—readers, companions in the company of cowbirds and juncos and ravens and moons—that we are up to this task is both our clear-headed declaration and the locale, of course, of our repeated failings.

And yet, here we are, proposing an ecological pedagogy of joy, one full of relations and aliveness and love.

Here we are:
Calling up to the creators;
we are here, we are here.
(Judson Innes, 2016, p. 110)

We are calling downwards, too, into the deep soils and waterstreams, into the heats of compost overturns.

So, in speaking of an ecological pedagogy of joy, we aspire to *pedagogical writing*. At its heart, pedagogy heralds the arrival of new life here in our midst (David G. Smith, 1999, p. 140). Our children will have something to say about what we have heretofore understood to be the givens in our lives, in theirs and in our ways of understanding the Earth. Pedagogy thus requires "keeping the world open" (Mircea Eliade, 1968, p. 139) to this arrival. Such an open world is not literally simply what it is. It is not constituted by objective self-identity, where A=A. It is not simply a given. It has to be made and remade, read and re-read, written and re-written, learned and unlearned and relearned, remembered and forgotten and remembered again. Breathed and borne and sometimes unbearable. It is a *living* Earth, this world, animate, full of spooks and spirits, multiple voices. Such a world is open to becoming understood otherwise, to *becoming* otherwise.

Such a world is interpretable. It is *enterable*, full of portals and ways. Or, inversely put, this is how we depend on the child, for the (re-)opening of the world. "The child" is a herald of an interpretable world. Of a living world.

Our children are not us, but they are.

> *Lesley:* I listen to the Elder's story
> of the rock for the fifth time.
> I hear it differently this time,
> because I am not the same person I was.

Just imagine. A pedagogy premised on an unresolvable, that is, on an *inability* to unbraid these threads or braid them once and for all—interweaving and criss-crossing.

We still bear the child in us:

> We cannot seek quick and easy solutions because there are none. (Senator Murray Sinclair, 2017)

It is the "memory of ways" (Wendell Berry, 1983, p. 73).

> The primary medium for seeking to understand life, *Niipaitapiiyssin*, and for coming to know [*Mokaksin*] *Ihtsipaitapiiyo'pa* [Source of Life] is through kinship relations. (Betty Bastien, 2004, p. 106)

So, in the end, time to get lost in the wilds a bit, dip in, circle back, whatever seems right. This might help sum up this book in the meanwhile, but no more or less than that cowbird and junco with which we began.

These two birds, both, breath the air that we, here, you, here, breath. And my perhaps-misplaced grief over the spilt junco egg cracked on the ground that we can imagine with great sorrow is also well-spent in relief of the rocks and soils it hits, taste on the tongue of animals come by—life lost and life gained in one fleet gesture. Just like me (David), this morning, blueberries. August 10, the air gone cold in an old, familiar way. Seasons. Turns. Melancholy.

Part I

"All Stories are Not Created Equal"

To Begin—"All Stories" I
Jodi Latremouille, Lesley Tait & David Jardine

> All stories are not created equal. Some can rally against understanding, just as others promote it; some can encourage healing, just as others keep problems festering. But why should we be surprised that something as basic as the narrative impulse should bring with it all the complexities and contradictions of life itself? (Will Hermes, 1997, n.p.)

Our lot is such that we cannot often or easily or definitively or adequately tell the difference between stories that hide or occlude, and ones that shed light. The disguise can give away secrets. The light casts shadows and relieves them all at once, in one curved gesture of shed. The heartfelt can honestly deceive. One person's reading the story back to me shows that it has a hither side, that a place is an abstraction siphoned off from its multifarious inhabitants, each of whom read and re-read.

Feasting on Whispers I: "An Intimate Reciprocity"
Jodi Latremouille

There is an intimate reciprocity to the senses; as we touch the bark of a tree, we feel the tree touching us; as we lend our ears to the local sounds and ally our nose to the seasonal scents, the terrain gradually tunes us in in turn. The senses, that is, are the primary way that the earth has of informing our thoughts and of guiding our actions. Huge centralized programs, global initiatives, and other 'top down' solutions will never suffice to restore and protect the health of the animate earth. For it is only at the scale of our direct, sensory interactions with the land around us that we can appropriately notice and respond to the immediate needs of the living world. (David Abram, 1996, p. 268).

Top/Down, In/Out. Sartre/Aoki
David W. Jardine

From an old and creaky self-publishing thing, something about tongues being boneless:

Whereas a church spire inspires me to lift up my eyes to the heavens above, entering a tea room inspires in me something different. The entrance to the ceremonial room, by the very way it is built, urges me to incline my body and to bow, bringing me closer to the earth those textured layers of humus allow buds of tea trees to leaf. The savouring of the tea allows me to touch again this earth that cradles and nourishes both my body and soul. During the Tea ceremony, I come to respect the fullness of silence, and I become aware of how silently I participate in the constituting of that silence. And in that silence, I experience being-one-with-the-earth. (Aoki, 1987, p. 67).

We have been schooled into aspirations that draw our eyes upward, or, more horrifying, inward into the seductive Cartesian allure of self-presence:

In *Nausea*, Jean-Paul Sartre's fingertips are no longer flesh of the same Earth as the tree he touches; they are no longer flesh at all. His fingertips are only his reflective self-awareness of that touching:

Geneson: So when Sartre.....goes to the tree, touches the tree trunk and says, "I feel in an absurd position. I cannot break through my skin to get in touch with this bark, which is outside me," the Japanese poet would say.....?

Snyder: Sartre is confessing the sickness of the West. At least he is honest. The [poet] will say, "But there are ways to do it, my friend. It's no big deal." It's no big deal, especially if you get attuned to that possibility from early in life. (Snyder, 1980, p. 67).

Something is awakened here that is beyond the nightmare of self-presence and its ensuing exhaustion. It is a "call to be mindful of our rootedness in earthy experiences." (Aoki, 1987, p. 67).

But more: such a call can best be heard "if you get attuned to that possibility from early in life." Attunement. But also pedagogy. The possibility of touching the Earth, this attunement, is rooted (perhaps also uprooted) early in life. (David Jardine, 1992a, p. 173–4)

To Begin—"All Stories" II
Jodi Latremouille, Lesley Tait & David Jardine

A story can be the very locale of manipulation, self-deception or illness, the thing that holds illnesses in place, that holds wounds open and unhealing.

Or great joy and wonder and precisely that hale whole breath that can mend relations and still the nerves of animal bodies and bird scatters.

All Beings Are Your Ancestors: A Bear Sutra on Ecology, Buddhism and Pedagogy I

David Jardine

"Transforming according to circumstances, meet all beings as your ancestors" (Hongzhi Zenjii, 1991).

Just spotted a year-old black bear crossing HWY. 66 @ McLean Creek, heading north.

From a distance, struggling at first to resolve its colour and lowness and lopey canter into dog or cat likenesses as it stretched up to the side of the road and across and suddenly slowed into distinctive roundhumpness . . . bear!

Stopped and watched him amble up the shalysteep creekedge. Wet. Greenglistening. Breath arriving plumey in the damp and cold after days of heat waves . . . been 33 degrees C. and more for 4 days running in the foothills of the Rockies west of Calgary. Here, roaming in the edge between prairie and forest, between flatlands and hills and mountains—here, when summers break, they tend to break deeply.

Cold rain. Cold.

It is so thrilling to not be accustomed to this sort of experience, to have it still be so pleasurable. Bear. His presence almost unbelievable, making this whole place waver and tremble, making my assumptions and presumptions and thoughts and tales of experiences in this place suddenly wonderfully irrelevant and so much easier to write because of such irrelevance.

To Begin—"All Stories" III

In this book, we are trying to elaborate the experience of an *ecological pedagogy of joy*, an idea that Jodi first spoke and wrote (Jodi Latremouille, 2020) and that now encurls us three with hope and a desire to say what we can about what we've witnessed firsthand, inside and outside of school. Love, affection, curiosity, living fields of living relations and the deep breaths of discover, care, sorrow and study.

We are teachers.

We are parents.

We are dirt-beings and sky beings and water beings and air. Earth beings. Fellows of Ravens and bears who, with us, quite literally and quite figuratively, conspire whispered oxygen with Lodge Pole Pine trees and their kin, who sense the ominousness of what surrounds, what our species has done, what we might now do. A while back, David Smith sent David a newspaper photo of a kneeling man grinning over the corpse of a grizzly bear, gun in hand, taking some weird pleasure, some weird satisfaction or fulfillment, in having wrought irreverent death at a safe distance.

David Smith's message-line in the email was "sometimes I'm ashamed of my species." It's not about the killing. It's not about the hunting. It's about trophy-consciousness.

And then again, sometimes not. And then again, our lot is the tough work of finding out the difference, here, now, in these circumstances that are ours and that are well beyond us as well, tangled up in the air and water and soil, the rocks in pockets, tangled in the fire we huddle around to hear the tale as much as the fire that drives dreams of eco-catastrophes.

Guided by Story
Lesley Tait

"Where words and place come together, *there* is sacred" (Scott Momaday, 1997, p. 111).

The world can be rebuilt with stories. Stories hold the entire knowledge of our world. Stories hold the language, the ceremonies, the teachings of the land, the teachings of the ancestors, the science, the medicines, the understanding of time and cycles . . . .all of it held in story. But they are not floating or untethered meant for entertainment. They are entertaining, don't get me wrong. My kids have often sat and listened, completely caught up in a story told by an Elder. But their intention is much more relational. Stories exist in relation to the places and the contexts in which we belong.

I have been taught by story, I have been corrected by story, and I have been guided by story.

Feasting on Whispers II: Grandmother Stories
Jodi Latremouille

According to Keith Basso, a cultural and linguistic anthropologist and Professor Emeritus at the University of New Mexico until his death in 2013, members of the White Mountain Apache tribe take great pleasure in reciting the native names of places within the Cibecue Valley, in Navajo Country, Arizona. They repeat these place-names because, as one Apache Elder states, "those names are good to say" (David Abram, 1996, p. 155). This reminds me of my elderly Grandma Gertie who likes to sit me down and go through old photo albums every time I visit her in her tiny assisted-living apartment at the other end of town.

"Look, that's me as a young woman with my younger brothers and sisters. I helped look after the littlest ones. See here, that's your grandpa Lou on our wedding day. Oh, he was handsome. He built that cabin, there, see? There's your Aunt Marie and your Uncle Nathan. They ran that fishing camp with your mom and dad. They really worked hard, running that fishing camp."

> "Yes, grandma, I remember."
> the tradition of the 'agodzaahi
> she will feel the "arrow" story make her ill
> and weak as it penetrates her
> skin.
> The story will then work
> outwards from within,
> making her desire to "re-place herself,"
> to live right.
> 'agodzaahi (*that which has happened*) story (Keith Basso, 1996, p. 156)
> "The place, it is said, will
> keep 'stalking' her" (p. 158–9)
>   Grandmother, I am shot with arrows.
> 'agodzaahi

"She Loved to Embroider" I
Lesley Tait

My late grandmother Joyce Ewasiuk was born in 1926 in a delightful brick row house at 6 Grange Close Southampton, England to a very proper English mother and a quiet, gentle father. Her entire life, she moved through the world with a sense of wonder and a flair for the dramatic. Every passerby was a mysterious stranger begging to be followed, every rose bush merely a hurdle over which to soar and every bridge was simply an invitation to dive into the river below.

To Begin—"All Stories" IV (Jodi Latremouille, Lesley Tait & David Jardine)

What shall we do? The latest neologism helps and harms all at once: *solastalgia* (Glenn Albrecht, Gina-Marie Sartoire, Linda Connor, Nick Higginbotham, Sonia Freeman, Brian Kelly, Helen Stain, Anne Tonna, & Georgia Pollard, 2007). The distress, fear, anxiety and disorientation we experience in these perilous earth-times. How we *feel*. Seems like a good place to start, but a terrible place to end up: now that it has become a medically recognized pathological condition:

> *James Hillman*: I'm outraged after having driven to my analyst on the freeway. The fucking trucks almost ran me off the road. I'm terrified, I'm in my little car, and I get to my therapist's and I'm shaking. My therapist says, "We've gotta talk about this." My thin skin and my frailty and vulnerability. We convert my fear into anxiety—an inner state. [We] don't work on what that outrage is telling you about potholes, about trucks, about Florida strawberries in Vermont in March, about burning oil, about energy politics, nuclear waste, that homeless woman over there with sores on her feet (James Hillman & Michael Ventura, 1992, p. 12)

> Going 'inwards' and curing myself of my woes over the world leaves the world behind and, in fact, *makes it worse* precisely through the withdrawal of my affection and concerted action. (David Jardine 2016a, p. 165)

It is too easy to then turn towards my sorrowing "self" in the very same act of self-centredness that got us into this spot in the first place:

> *Michael Ventura:* You're not saying that we don't need introspection, an introspective guy like you?
> *James Hillman:* Put this in italics so that nobody can just pass over it: *This is not to deny that you do need to go inside*—but we have to see what we're doing when we do that. By going inside we're maintaining the Cartesian view that the world out there is dead matter and the world inside is living. (James Hillman & Michael Ventura, 1992, p. 12)

Here is where a sort of Buddhist[/ecological] topspin on this idea can help. If we simply let go of that "Cartesian view" then going "out" into the world, say, of

> schooling and its dependent co-arisings [or the world of bears or fires or smoke or stories inherited from grandmothers] is going out into that field-fabric *of my very self* that arose and still arises in the sway of schooling [and foothills and snowy near-solstice portends]. Risking sounding too 1967 about this, "going out," properly done, *is* "going inside," [but it is] *going inside of the fabric of which I am a fold.* It is just like how caring for the watershed in the Foothills *is* caring for my "self" and loving the world, quite literally, *as* my very self, not just loving the world *as well as* myself. (David Jardine, 2016a, p. 165)

The title of James Hillman and Michael Ventura's collection of interviews explains too much and too little all at once: *We've Had a Hundred Years of Psychotherapy and the World's Getting Worse.*

The tale of an ecological pedagogy of joy must somehow "break open," (Hans-Georg Gadamer, 2004, p. 360) "break forth," (p. 458) and reveal hidden hints of "reciprocity" (Hans-Georg Gadamer, 1984, p. 323) underneath the numbing surfaces of familiarity and contempt and distraction and exhaustion. The phenomenologically undeniable experience of *solastalgia* threatens, in its own way, to be its own trap, encasing us in the very sort of self-regarding withdrawal that gives rise to the conditions that cause it. Cause become effect becomes cause.

The refuges offered by the tales we might tell must be allowed to do their dirty work of freeing us from a too encased and embroiled understanding of ourselves out, instead, into the wild, unforeseen dependent co-arisings of our earthliness. Latin, *fugere*, to be free from, to dispel a spell, to flee:

> Insight is more than the knowledge of this or that situation. It always involves an escape from something [Latin *fugere*] that had deceived us and held us captive. Thus, insight always involves an element of self-knowledge and constitutes a necessary side of what we called experience in the proper sense. Insight is something we come to. It too is ultimately part of the vocation of man—i.e., to be discerning and insightful. (Hans-Georg Gadamer, 2004, p. 360)

The purpose of proposing an ecological pedagogy of joy is not to proffer yet another locale of somnolence. It is, instead, a locale pitched on a knife-edge: What shall we tell the children? What are *they* trying to tell *us* without trying, without telling? What shall we teach? What needs learning? To what shall we aspire? How do we deeply aspire amidst the smoke?

How did we get caught up in all this earthly portend? How did we forget so easily and with such self-satisfaction? Why is the catch so sticky, so stuck, so mesmerizing? Why won't they listen? Why can't I hear? What have I done? Where have I been?

In this practice, the subtleties start to come up. One becomes kind of world-weary. You go through a stage where you just look at this world and think it's crazy! "I'm living in a madhouse! Society is nuts!" And you think "No! Not this again! Don't they ever learn? Do we have to go through this again?" If you attach to world-weariness, you attach to just another thing. (Ajahn Sumedho, 2010, p. 95)

The teacher, like the parent, the elder, the wee one, stands along this sharpedge which must move like moon tides and we with it, pulled by this child and this, attentive, wary, opening the world to interpretation all over again, and over again.

"No! Not this again!"

Feasting on Whispers III: "Languages and Melancholies Continued"
Jodi Latremouille

Hush...

I wanted to know why these languages and melancholies continued to dominate, after all the great examples of teaching and learning that I knew to exist, not only in my childhood experiences, but also in every school that I had ever taught in. Although my experiences in the classroom gave me a glimpse into the possibilities for meaningful learning, I continued to feel distressed by the dominant stories of education: cynical staffroom conversations; the business language of accountability and time-on-task; and the media's disrespect for educators as well as youth. I did not like to see how these stories affected those most intimately involved in the work of education.

To Begin—"All Stories" V
Jodi Latremouille, Lesley Tait & David Jardine

Yes, this again. Don't be disappointed that you have to take another breath.

Weird and haunting, this neurasthenia (Kevin Aho, 2018; David Jardine, 2019). This is no pathological trouble. It is verging insight. It doesn't need medication. It is medicine.

To what extent is it our self-involved aspirations that have got us into trouble in the first place? What story, then?

We will wind our way around three life-affirming and life-sustaining Cree ideas: wahkohtowin, wicihitowin, and sakihitowin, too quickly translated as relations, aliveness and love. We are searching, here, for keys that will help break certain spells under which we all seem cast.

Feasting on Whispers IV: "Whispers Trailing"
Jodi Latremouille

> Now she stands in front of her classroom, reaching for this ineffable sense of kinship with things, pointing and hoping, not for explanations, but for the right kinds of questions, for what calls for questions. (Michael Derby, 2015, p. 1)

> *a question . . .*

What might education be when it is seen as abundant, convivial, enmeshed in those whispers trailing back/from/into/within worlds of relations?

> *and a question. . .*

What happens when the stories we tell of education are grounded in rich histories, live topics, real people, and earthly potentialities?

To Begin—"All Stories" VI
Jodi Latremouille, Lesley Tait & David Jardine

What of the sorrow of stories that have outlasted their tell, lost their trick? What of stories that bears tell back to us about what we've done, about how we've embroidered, what braids we've dropped without knowing it, what braids bind us underneath the "cool and calm of efficient teaching and excellent time-on-task ratios" (David G. Smith, 1999, p. 140) and how these, too, are braids that bind tighter that breath itself, some days.

Embroider. "Perhaps by influence of *broiden*, irregular alternative Middle English past participle of **braid** (v.)." (OED).

Stories that bear tell-back, that bears tell-back.

All Beings Are Your Ancestors: A Bear Sutra on Ecology, Buddhism and Pedagogy II

David Jardine

Bear's making this whole place show its fragility and momentariness and serendipities.

Bear's making my own fragility and momentariness show.

That is what is most shocking. This unforeseeable happenstance of bear's arrival and my own happiness are oddly linked. This "hap" (Joel Weinsheimer, 1987, p. 7–8) hovering at the heart of the world.

My own life as serendipitous, despite my earnest plans. Giddy sensation, this.

Like little bellybreath tingles on downarcing childgiggle swingsets.

Felt in the *tanden* (Katsuki Sekida, 1976, p. 18–19, 66–67) in Walking Meditation (Thich Nhat Hanh, 1995).

Breath's gutty basement. Nearby, the lowest Chakra tingles with an upspine burst to whitesparkle brilliance just overhead and out in front of the forehead.

In moments like this, something flutters open. Shifting fields of relations bloom. Wind stirs nothing. Not just my alertness and sudden attention, but the odd sensation of knowing that these trees, this creek, this bear, are all already alert to me in ways proper to each and despite my attention. Something flutters open, beyond this centered self.

With the presence of this ambly bear, the whole of things arrives, fluttered open.

To Begin—"All Stories" VII
Jodi Latremouille, Lesley Tait & David Jardine

What stories should we tell, then? What lines of words, which trails of following and beckon? The good news and bad news turn out to be the same, here. We can only discover what a path offers by taking it and drawing you along with us.

"She Loved to Embroider" II
Lesley Tait

It was with that certain lack of trepidation and an understanding that her life was to be lived without fear and regret that she decided to brave the air raids sirens of WWII and head out to a community dance in hopes of meeting a handsome soldier. Normally, air raid sirens yelping over the entire city sent everyone scrambling for shelters stationed throughout the city. Two friends, however, were determined to make their way to the dance where many young and hopeful soldiers were bound to be. The trick to travelling during an air raid is the duck, count and run maneuver. As my grandmother described it to me, one must hide in the nearest doorway and count to ten after the last shell was heard, thus ensuring all shrapnel had landed. Then one was to take off at a near sprint to the next doorway.

Hide, count and run, hide, count and run.

This must all be done while wearing your very best outfit and trying not to become too sweaty so as to avoid ruining your hair or face, lest those handsome soldiers be scared away.

It was at this dance that she would meet her eventual husband, Victor Ewasiuk, a Canadian Soldier.

To Begin—"All Stories" VIII
Jodi Latremouille, Lesley Tait & David Jardine

At this dance, why isn't learning uproarious in its pleasures? An ecological pedagogy of joy. Even when the news is troubling, there is joy to be had in knowing what is real, finding your way around, looking for the accurate swing of things:

We ought to be like elephants in the noontime sun in summer, when they are tormented by heat and thirst and catch sight of a cool lake. They throw themselves into the water with the greatest pleasure and without a moment's hesitation. In just the same way, for the sake of ourselves and others, we should give ourselves joyfully to the practice. (Kunzang Pelden, 2007, p. 255)

Feasting on Whispers V: "Welcome to the Feast"
Jodi Latremouille

A feast (n.) c.1200, is a "religious anniversary characterized by rejoicing" (rather than fasting), from Old French feste (12c., Modern French *fête*) "religious festival; noise, racket," from Latin *festa* "holidays, feasts," or *festus* "festive, joyful, merry" (OED)

The notion of a feast lends a sense of abundance—not of unearned or excessive abundance, but of harvest time, celebration, to hard work and sharing. A feast conjures up images of celebration, repeating rituals. Every fall, my organic produce delivery service, Footprints Harvest, and a local restaurant called Brambles Bakery, team up to host a "Fall Harvest Dinner." At this event, parties are not permitted to book a private table. Local farmers are invited to sit and eat with customers, everyone mingling together at long, familial tables. Courses on the set menu are brought out in a seemingly chaotic yet carefully planned sequence, as the family of cooks and volunteer servers in the kitchen scramble to co-ordinate homemade loaves, fresh greens, roasted vegetables and the highlight of the evening, a whole roast pig. Strangers become friends over the course of an evening as they pass the communal platters along, reach across the table for a piece of homemade sourdough to sop up the sauce on their plates, and split the last serving of apple crumble from the final plate to travel around the table, dividing up the crumbs carefully and fairly.

Conversations rise and fall in time with the appearance of new delicacies—in appreciation, in excitement, in nourishment. Farmers testify to the trials and successes of the season, as their neighbors listen and feast on the evidence. The Latin, *convivium* (a feast), is the ancestor of **convivial**, "to carouse together." This derives from com—"together" + *vivere* "to live" (Online Etymology Dictionary). This feastly evening sends folks off into the crisp autumn evening with full bellies and a new friend or two.

All Beings Are Your Ancestors: A Bear Sutra on Ecology, Buddhism and Pedagogy III

David W. Jardine

All Beings are your Ancestors. The feary sight of him, teaching me, reminding me of forgotten shared ancestries, forgotten shared relations to Earth and Air and Fire and Water.

That strange little lesson having to be learned again: that he has been here all along, cleaving this shared ancestry, cleaving this shared Earth of ours, making and forming my life beyond my "wanting and doing," (Hans-Georg Gadamer, 2004, p. xxviii) beyond my wakefulness and beyond my remembering.

It is not so much that this bear is an "other" (Paul Shepherd, 1996) but that it is a relative, which is most deeply transformative and alarming to my ecological somnolence and forgetfulness. It is not just that I might come awake and start to remember these deep, Earthy relations.

It is also that, even if I don't, they all still bear witness to my life.

Relations. Who would have thought? Coming across one of us that I had forgotten.

Coming, therefore, across myself as also one of us. Such a funny thing to be surprised about again. In the face of this Great Alert Being, I, again, become one of us!

Great Alert Being, this bear. Great Teacher. His and my meaty bodies both of the same "flesh of the [Earth]" (David Abram, 1996, p. 66–7; see David Abram & David Jardine, 2000, p. 167–77) rapt in silent conversations

Where, my god, have I been? And what have I been saying, betraying of myself and my distraction.

"She Loved to Embroider" III
Lesley Tait

My grandmother used to write stories. Stories about who she was and why she was who she was. Stories that have become my gift. These stories have allowed me to know my grandmother. Know her thoughts, her worries, her joys and her life.

After the war and after my grandfather had returned to Edmonton, my grandmother began her own journey. Train from Southampton to London, train from London to Liverpool, H.M.S. Letitia from Liverpool to Halifax and a final train ride from Halifax to Edmonton. All in all, 24 days.

It was in Edmonton, in a two-room attic, that she began her life as a wife and mother. There was a total of four homes and three sons. These three sons bestowed a total of 8 grandchildren, of which I count myself one.

Each story was presented to me with the pomp and circumstance of a visiting Royal. At the time, I didn't understand the gifts being bestowed to me. I didn't understand that my grandmother knew her time with me was limited. I would never have the chance to know her as an adult, as a mother myself and as a grandmother years from now. She was giving me a chance to find her, to understand her and to be given life lessons and understanding when she was no longer here herself. She was giving me herself.

As an aging adult with children grown and gone, my grandmother found herself with too much time on her hands and a hankering for a little mischief. It was then that she discovered clogging, painting, bartending, modelling, skit performing and writing. As entertaining as each was, it was the crafting of a well-made story that captured her sense of wonder.

As writing became a large focus in her life, she helped found a group still in existence: The Northgate Writing Society. This group of older adults has met every Friday for the past 26 years. They sit in round, with a fabric loom occupying the corner, and tell their stories. They weave stories of war, of childhood, of love, of loneliness, of grandchildren and of each other.

I reached out to the continuing and new members of the society to ask if they would be open to the idea of me spending some time with them.

They welcomed me and invited me to Edmonton for a conversation and lemon meringue pie.

I approached the building weighed down by permission forms, ethics applications and thoughts of doubt. Just outside the door sat a sturdy wooden bench with wrought iron rails. It was the sort of bench meant for conversation about the latest weather change or a quick catch up with a friend who you had not seen in a while.

I sat.

I gathered my nerves.

Yet here, engraved on the back is what had called me. "This bench is dedicated to Joyce Ewasiuk for her unending devotion to the Northgate seniors." Here I was about to enter into something that was full of her echoes.

Feasting on Whispers VI: "A Feast for the Intellect"
Jodi Latremouille

American (and Canadian) public schools often operate as service-oriented places of management. William Pinar (2012, p. 42) argues for the fundamental shift that is required, whereby "curriculum theorists . . . invite public school teachers to reoccupy a vacated 'public' domain, not simply as 'consumers' of knowledge, but as active participants in conversations they themselves will lead." In this shift from curriculum (noun: a course to be run) as a commodified service to be rendered, to currere (verb: a path) as an invitation into a "complicated conversation" (p. 47), he is opening up spaces within which learning can become more rigorous, intellectual, and . . . nourishing. William Doll (2002, p. 24) describes this curriculum reconceptualization as a "shift from Erasmus' hierarchy of limited subjects [to] Rabelais' abundant 'feast for the intellect'." To conceive of education as a feast, an abundant meal, a celebration that exists in ritual, is to ask us how we shall live together "in the context of an ongoing conversation which is never over, yet which must be sustained for life together to go on at all" (David G. Smith, 1988, p. 27). How shall we feed each other in these abundant conversations, in such a way that makes "communion - community- possible." (Laurel Richardson, 2001, p. 37).

All Beings Are Your Ancestors: A Bear Sutra on Ecology, Buddhism and Pedagogy IV

David W. Jardine

This bear ambles in the middle of all its Earthly relations to wind and sky and rain and berries and roadsides and the eons of beings that helped hone that creek edge to just those small pebbly falls under the weight of his paws:

Even the very tiniest thing, to the extent that it 'is,' displays in its act of being the whole web of circuminsessional interpenetration that links all things together. (Keiji Nishitani, 1982, p. 150)

The whole Earth conspires to make just these simple events just exactly like this:

Within each dust mote is vast abundance (Hongzhi Zenji, 1991, p. 14)

This is the odd butterfly effect (James Gleick, 1987, p. 17) fluttering in the stomach.

This, too, is the profound co-implication of all beings that is part of ecological mindfulness—that each being is implicated in the whole of things and, if we are able to experience it from the belly, from each being a deep relatedness to all beings can be unfolded, can be understood, can be felt, can be adored, can be praised in prayerful grace, a giving thanks (Gary Snyder, 1990, p. 175–85). Lovely intermingling of thinking and thanksgiving (see Martin Heidegger, 1968).

So the thrill of seeing this bear is, in part, the exhilarating rush felt in seeing it explode outwards, emptying itself into all its relations, and then retracting to just that black bear, now an exquisite still-spot ambling at the center of all things. And more than this:

The center is everywhere. Each and every thing becomes the center of all things and, in that sense, becomes an absolute center. This is the absolute uniqueness of things, their reality. (Keiji Nishitani, 1982, p. 146).

Like breath exhaled outwards and then drawn in deep draughts. This inwardness and outwardness of emptiness (Sanskrit: *sunya*; Japanese: *ku*)—each thing is its relatedness to all things, reflecting each in each in Indra's Netted Jewels and yet each thing is always just itself, irreplaceable. Smells of the forests of mid-August and the sweetness of late summer wild flowers. Winey bloomy blush. Intoxicating.

All Beings are your Ancestors.

"She Loved to Embroider" IV
Lesley Tait

My grandmother, Joyce Ewasiuk, has been sitting on my bookshelf for a long time. Getting arthritic and watching me walk past her countless times beckoning me to come and get to know her again.

Reading her stories allows me to hear her voice again, full of its usual wit and sarcasm. They help me to find her, to visit her, to feel her touch. Reading her life's work is a practice of immersion. I can see the exasperation on her mother's face as she finds her way into trouble again. Sloshing water all over the stage in an over the top presentation of Macbeth's witches while stationed inland during an evacuation. Causing passengers on a dull train ride to Farham heart palpitations when she, a spy, was sure she had apprehended a Nazi.

Something happens to me as I read her words. They become intertwined with the fabric of my being. These words carefully wrap themselves around my neurons, heart muscles and the bones of my body, ensuring their survival, her survival with me. I share a story now, so that you too may get to know her, and in turn come to know me as well:

Joyce Ewasiuk (1988):

Now that I'm older, I can understand my grandmother's stubbornness to run to the safety of the bomb shelter. She never came downstairs until she was well corseted, her nose powdered, and her hair in a neat bun. She must've been horrified at the indignity of not only coming downstairs but leaving the house in her nightgown. I'm sure that, if given a choice, she would have preferred to die in her bed rather than suffer the further humiliation of squeezing through that narrow shelter door.

Four bunks were issued to the shelter, but as I was the only person to sleep on a bunk, one was removed to enable the adults to sit up straight and in more comfort. Although water dripped between the ridges of the corrugated iron, the shelter was fairly cozy. It was heated and lit by an enormous paraffin lamp that once held a place of honor in Nanny's parlor. It was gloriously ugly, decorated with maroon scrolls and gold angels ... One night, mother handed a tea tray into the shelter. It was covered with a lace cloth and her best china and silver. She had even included the sugar tongs. The last time I'd seen the China it was being packed and placed under the stairs for safekeeping:

"Vicar coming for tea, Mabs?" laughed my father.

"Oh, Mabel, your best china. It will get broken," said Nanny.

"I thought I'd bring a little civilization into this rat hole," said mother. "Anyway, if the house goes, I'll have a souvenir, and if we go, who will care.

From then on, except for a larger cup for my father, we always had our tea in the shelter on our best China.

(Excerpt from "Time for Tea" By Joyce Ewasiuk, 1988, p. 100)

Feasting on Whispers VI: "Squeaky, Perhaps Barking Voices"
Jodi Latremouille

These writings are a feastly offering. There may be some funny citations, some strange, unusual, squeaky, perhaps barking voices. They are the voices of my friends, my colleagues, my sister. They are my cousins, the landscapes of my youth, and my dog named Buster. Sometimes, I even fancy myself on a first-name basis with the elder philosophers in my field.

From the Array of Stalks Sutra
David Jardine

Teachers, your teachers. Ours:

".... they protect .... they show ....they instruct .... they reveal ..... they guide ...
Remembering this, you will weep" (cited in Tsong-Kha-Pa, 2004, p. 83).

"Recollect your teacher's kindness in accordance with this statement. Personalize it by replacing 'they' with 'these teachers'." (p. 83)

Many long-gone yet still whispering to me, *patient, waiting for me.* Tsong-Kha-Pa citing from the *Ten Teachings Sutra*:

"Develop the following ideas with respect to your teachers, I have wandered for a long time, and they search for me." (p. 83)

My teachers are all around me. "Everything around us teaches" (Tsong-Kha-Pa, 2000, p. 151).

Feasting on Whispers VII: "The Fall Harvest Dinner Cannot Guarantee"
Jodi Latremouille

This is not a quick tour I am taking in a classroom, in a life. I am a visitor in these places, these locales, these words; I have a responsibility to treat them well. The whispers of places—the more-than-human world, texts, colleagues making their way in their own work—remind me: we inhabit these places together. The Fall Harvest Dinner cannot guarantee that everyone will enjoy every dish, nor can it pretend to prevent all contamination of the food being shared so heartily amongst the guests.

And yet, we hope that it will nourish us.

All Beings Are Your Ancestors: A Bear Sutra on Ecology, Buddhism and Pedagogy V
David Jardine

Hey, bear!

If we are to meet all beings as our ancestors, we must also meet all those very same beings as our descendants. This odd, fluid, difficult, shifting edge point between the ancestors and the descendants is where our humanity lives.

This is "the empty field" (Hongzhi Zenjii, 1991) that opens and embraces. It is also the lifespot of teaching and learning and transmission and transformation. There are many Great Teachers. All praise to bear and his subtle gift.

Bragg Creek, Alberta, August 8–10, 1997

"She Loved to Embroider" V
Lesley Tait

Her pale hand no longer possessed the strength it once did. Perhaps she sat in that chair by the fire counting down her days. Perhaps she knew recovery was no longer an option for her. What does one feel when they know? When they truly understand that time and life is a finite thing?

As each hand slowly unwrapped her gift, she knew what we wanted from her, what we needed. We may have to let her go, but we were not done hearing her tales. She was a collection of stories. We wanted more.

My grandmother was not comfortable with tears, but here, with the gift in her hands, even she could not stop them from rolling down her aged face.

A laptop. Please grandma, tell us more.

I read her stories to find a way to visit the echoes she has left behind. I become the precocious child who found herself at odds with her mother's Victorian understandings. I am the emigrant to Canada travelling by train alone, pregnant and full of both fear and excitement. I am the new mother in a new country who writes home with feelings of adventure mixed with a touch of regret. I am the old women who has maintained her spirit and still finds herself involved in the occasional mischief. I am she and she is I.

David: I remember you describing in our class years ago, of the train arriving and . . ….? Does this sound familiar? Is this writ out somewhere? Did I imagine this?

Ahh yes. That was my grandmother. She came across from England as a war bride. Pregnant and naive. They (an entire boat of war brides) travelled from Southampton to Canada by boat. I even have the old menus from the trip. I also have many of the "artefacts" she kept from the journey. Once they arrived, they travelled across Canada stopping at major cities dropping off the brides to the waiting families.

In Regina, one friend had inadvertently married an Indigenous soldier. I guess everyone looks the same in uniform. When she arrived in Regina, his entire family was there dressed in their best regalia and on horseback. They were thinking about impressing her. The story goes that she came to the edge of the train, saw her husband and his family and promptly turned around and would not get off the train. Something about "not signing up for this."

She loved telling that story. Now she was also a storyteller. Meaning she loved to embroider. I don't think she ever wrote that one down, but I vividly remember her telling it on many occasions.

Feasting on Whispers VIII: "A Word on Whispers"
Jodi Latremouille

A recent e-mail exchange with a dear colleague, Rajan Rathnavalu:

JODI (Latremouille): Rajan, do you remember the other day in class when you said that if 'something needs to proclaim itself loudly, there is something fundamentally wrong with it'?

RAJAN (Rathnavalu): Yes, I remember.

In 1999, the year I ordained as a monk, I started teaching meditation classes at the U of T. I remember a conversation with a friend who helped sponsor the classes. We were walking by an aerobics class that had music playing loudly in the background. He said something to the effect that, "When we can't hear our own rhythms, we need the external to be louder." These are my words, but they express his general sentiment.

I think I was remembering this space when I heard about the Eyes High pep rally. Propaganda often seems to come through loudspeakers. A mind that is conscious of the ways of the world doesn't need exaggeration . . . as it has the proper measure of things.

There is a time to speak the truth loudly, but that often seems to arise in contexts where people aren't listening. I tend to think that speaking softly indicates a respect for the listener—that they have the capacity to "get it" without having to be hit over the head with the idea.

Further, I think good educators often will leave a lot unspoken. When students have to work for things, there is an inner learning dynamic that helps carry the meaning further and more deeply.

When we find ourselves speaking "loudly," I tend to believe that it is we ourselves who aren't listening. We haven't connected to the space the student is in, so we're trying to impose a particular reality (ours) when in fact, the student isn't ready for this. But they generally are ready for something—it's our job as educators to tune into these inner rhythms and meet them in a way that is meaningful.

(Rajan Rathnalavu, personal communication, March 28, 2014)

WAYSTATION I
"Standing Silent in the Sun"
Taylor Nyeste

Sometimes I wish I could photosynthesize so that just by being, just by shimmering at the meadow's edge or floating lazily on a pond, I could be doing the work of the world while standing silent in the sun.
— Robin Wall Kimmerer, 2013, p. 176

To Begin—"All Stories" IX
Jodi Latremouille, Lesley Tait & David Jardine

So, an ecological pedagogy of joy, rife with tales told, embroideries and bears and breath and such. And an admission that we are always laced up, always and only between this breath and the next, this generation and its ascends and descends, between bear and tree and compost pickings.

"The End of Its Tether"
David Jardine

Tether. "Figurative sense of 'measure of one's limitations' is attested from 1570s" (OED):

The ego today is a "mind at the end of its tether." All it can do is leave itself open to the possibility of grace and to a renewal which might then take place in its absence. In the *absence of ego* and into its emptiness an imaginal stream can flow. (James Hillman & Sonu Shamdasani, 2013, p. 62)

> Great moon,
> eagle moon,
> goose moon,
> frog moon
> Tethered
> Here
> (Lesley Tait)

Ego-absence will feel first like ego-weakness; the solutions will seem to regress rather than to advance the problem into new terrain. But at this moment of transition we cannot advance until we have first retreated enough inward and backward so that the [emergent images] can catch up with us. (James Hillman & Sonu Shamdasani, 2013, p. 62)

Feasting on Whispers X: "Little Voices in our Ears"
Jodi Latremouille

Our teachers are the raucous merry-making of a festive occasion, but they are also those little voices in our ears, those warm, rising murmurings in our hearts, that remind us that the celebration is fleeting and that we had better sit up and pay attention.

David Jardine aside:

Owl moon

"We cannot bring healing to the split...

Owl.

...without [their] cooperation since it is from them that we are split." (James Hillman, 2005, p. 62)

To Begin—"All Stories" X (Jodi Latremouille, Lesley Tait & David Jardine)

Ties bind, but they are our only recourse of finding ourselves loosed and freed for their whispered demands. In other words:

> Ambivalence, rather than being overcome. . . . . may be developed within its own principle. It is a way in itself. *Ambivalence is an adequate reaction* to these whole truths. The way is slower, action is hindered, and one fumbles foolishly in the half-light. This way finds echo in many familiar phrases from Lao Tzu, but especially: "Soften the light, become one with the dusty world." (James Hillman, 2005, p. 6)

"Hush, Child"
Jodi Latremouille

hush, child . . .

whisper . . .

So, the other day, my 3-year-old, Kiera, says,
"Mommy, I have a tummyache."
"Oh? What's wrong, dolly?"
Mommy, my brain is trying to say bad things."
And I say, nervously, "Oh? Like what?"
She replies, "It wants to say bad words."
I reply, "What kinds of words?"
She says, "My brain wants to call Buster (our dog)
stupid."
I ask her, "So, what do you do?"
She says, "Well, my heart is trying to be nice, and my brain is trying to be mean."
I am spellbound. I continue. "So, what do you do,
Kiera?"
She says, "I try to get them to stop arguing. I try to
get them to be nice to each other. My brain argues
with my heart and my heart says no!"
I ask her, "Who told you about this?"
She says, "Nobody, I just noticed."

. . .hush

Part II
An Ecological Pedagogy of Joy

An Ecological Pedagogy of Joy I
Jodi Latremouille

> To exist in a state of communion is to be aware of the nature of existence. This is where ecology and social justice come together, with the knowledge that life is held in common. Whether we know it or not, we exist because we exchange, because we move the gift. And the knowledge of this is as crucial to the conditions of the soul as its practice to the body. (Susan Griffin, 1996, p. 151)

As an educator, writer and researcher in a time of ecological crisis, I am often overcome with guilt, hopelessness, panic, despair, misplaced hope in romantic ideals or techno-fixes. And yet, I remain mindful of how my various ill-measured responses may effectively perpetuate and exacerbate ecological destruction and social injustices. bell hooks (2003, p. 169), in an engaged, pluralistic and ethically oriented critical pedagogy, challenges educators to pay attention, "to look and live and find or create the spaces of joy." I wonder how a pedagogy oriented towards ethical ways of knowing and unknowing, writing, and teaching that well up from within, "not out of a sense of duty, but out of a sense of joy" (Dave Foreman, in Derrick Jensen, 2002, p. 10) may heed bell hooks' call, and further extend this spiritual form of impassioned, engaged and loving attention beyond human communities out towards our biotic communities (Rebecca Martusewicz, 2005, p. 331–348). As we re-story our human identity as beings-in-relation (Donna Haraway, 2016) and cultivate our not-knowing, teachers may seek ways to open "our heart-minds" (Joanna Macy, 2014, par. 6) towards more generous, careful, imperfect, loving relations with human and more-than-human communities alike.

"Only beauty can save the planet"

(from James Hillman)

Only beauty can save the planet. Let me explain. Even the strongest combination of guilty feelings, economic reasoning and scientific evidence are not enough to turn the tide so that our planet's life may continue. Nevertheless—and here is where beauty comes in—if you love something, you want it to stay around and stay close, and keep radiantly well. And it is precisely beauty that makes you fall in love. [It] gives you the feeling that what is here is to be treasured and not misused or harmed, and certainly not to be regarded in terms of functional usefulness or economic return, for such is to look at the world as a slave or a whore. (James Hillman, 2006a, p. 192)

Below the ecological crisis lies a deeper crisis of love, that our love has left the world; that the world is loveless results directly from the repression of beauty, its beauty and our sensitivity to beauty. For love to return to the world, beauty must first return, else we love the world only as a moral duty: clean it up, preserve its nature, and exploit it less. If love depends on beauty, then beauty comes first. Separated from beauty, love becomes a duty. Love thy neighbour becomes a moral obligation, almost a commandment, and [separated from beauty] the world's alluring face becomes a temptress. (p. 192)

An Ecological Pedagogy of Joy II
Jodi Latremouille

Following the principles of ecological pedagogy, which is not only a teaching philosophy, but also may be considered a "social and political movement" (Moacir Gadotti, 2003, p. 5, italics in the original text) I seek to respect the principles of the Earth Charter (Earth Charter International Council, 2000) of respect and care for the community of life; ecological integrity; social and economic justice; and democracy, non-violence and peace (Earth Charter International Council, 2000, p. 3–5). As I consider how it is possible to cultivate more measured yet always imperfect responses in these "ecologically sorrowful times" (David Jardine, 2015a, p. xv) I contemplate an ecological pedagogy of joy through a place-based narrative of *Small-Town Stories*, and a poetic remembering of *A Record Year* of climate change in my hometown of Merritt, British Columbia. I end with reflections regarding a heart-mind-ful and place-based pedagogy that is oriented towards pluralistic ways of knowing and connecting with others, an openness to the unknown, and to respectful relations with humans and our more-than-human kin:

> Our knowledge of the world instructs us first of all that the world is greater than our knowledge of it. To those who rejoice in abundance and intricacy, this is a source of joy. To those who hope for knowledge equal to (and capable of controlling) the world, it is a source of unremitting defeat and bewilderment. (Wendell Berry, 1983, p. 56).

Humans are now coming up against hard limits to our life on earth. And yet, we continue to suck up mineral and petroleum resources, belch out toxic waste into poverty-stricken communities, raze rainforests and develop techno-quick-fixes to our problems, while leaving the long-term ecological and social consequences to future generations. This crisis may be understood in terms of four levels of increasing consequence: (1) humans are exceeding carrying capacities around the world through our excessive consumption of resources, population increase, runaway pollution of our sources of life, and degradation of our landscapes; (2) our collective actions are "creating a lack of possibility for future generations and civilizations" in that they are giving rise to repercussions that will extend far beyond our current civilization; (3) runaway rates of extinction are "shredding the fabric of life;" and (4) oxygen production in oceans is decreasing to such an extent that "everything more complex than anaerobic life-forms" will not survive.

Robert Nixon (2011, p. 2) called this creeping trouble "slow violence" because it occurs very gradually and out of the sight of the public.

American Dippers and Alberta Winter Strawberries I
David Jardine

In the seventh month the Fire-star declines,
In the ninth month winter garments are handed out.
The eleventh month comes with the
                        blustering wind;
The twelfth month, with the shivering cold.
                      Without cloak or serge
How are we to see the year out?
From "In the Seventh Month," compiled in the Shih Ching, 7th to 12th century B.C., China (in Wu-Chi Lui & Irving Yuchen Lo, 1990, p. 9).

    The American Dipper is a small black bird, halfway in size between a Robin and a Sparrow, L-shaped with stubby upright tail and head balanced high. These Dippers are common all year long along the Elbow River that winds out of the Rocky Mountains and through Calgary, Alberta. Walked this past winter, in -40-degree winds, along the Elbow and its swirls of ice fog over rare still patches of open water, most of the river steeply hurrying east.

    Dippers. Swim underwater upstream about 10 feet at a go, feeding on water-carried food. Then standing there dipping up and down while waiting for the next dive. Or rush to low water-surface flights full of a distinctive twittery warble. Like the muskrat in the steaming cold beaver pond nearby, remaining here as I leave. Remaining here, -40, what little left low-riding sun setting.

Leaving, under the darkening air-blue arch of what I hope is a gathering Chinook, caught in bitter cold that breaks your bones:

The twelfth month comes with the chopping of ice—clanging stroke after stroke.

The first month comes—we bring ice to the cold-house for storage;

The second month comes—we rise early
And make offering of garlic and lamb.
 In the ninth month comes the severe frost.

(Wu-Chi Lui & Irving Yuchen Lo, 1990, p. 9)

Home, eating freshly bought fresh strawberries. Delicious red juicy-drip taste. Then suddenly grotesquely beautiful. Suddenly out of place. How can these be here? And as these strawberries begin to taste become unbecoming of this place and this cold, I end up feeling out of place as well. Eating these strawberries betrays something of those Dippers and that ice and my living here.

An Ecological Pedagogy of Joy III
Jodi Latremouille

Violence is generally conceptualized as "immediate in time, explosive and spectacular in space, and as erupting into instant sensational visibility" (Robert Nixon, 2011, p. 264) In comparison, slow violence is nearly inconceivable; the long-term consequences fester and ooze, creeping into our soils, air, oceans, communities over generations, garnering much less attention than explosive, sensational, newsworthy events. On October 17, 2009, Maldives president Mohamed Nasheed attempted to bring attention to the devastation of slow violence. He held an underwater cabinet meeting ahead of the 2009 UN climate change conference in Copenhagen. In this sensational "preview of the aftermath" (Randeep Ramesh, 2009). Nasheed hoped to draw attention to the consequences and generational experience of climate change: The Maldives, with a maximum elevation of 2 meters above sea level, will be the first nation to disappear under the ocean as a result of climate change. (Robert Nixon, 2011, p. 4)

The climate refugees around the world experience slow violence already, whether they are ejected from, forced to live and die in, or choose to stay in their war-weary and weather-wrought, degraded and poisoned home-places around the world, are exponentially more affected than the wealthy. These "impoverished resource rebels" (p. 265) experience ecological justice as a multiple commitment: to human rights; to gender equity; to narrowing class divides; to protecting livelihoods and homes. The relative invisibility of these slow violences enables the wealthy elite to "wall off the wealth, raise the walls of denial" (Naomi Klein, 2014, p. 22) against the realities of slow violence. Corporate capitalism continues along its upward free fall of swift growth, the triple myths of endless human progress, of the tenacious pioneering and domineering spirit (next: resource extraction in space!), and of unfettered economic growth in the broken promise of material wealth for all, continue to serve as a self-referential and self-serving rationale for endlessly deferring climate action to the future.

> There is a word in Cree that means "you have gone too far."
> *pastahowin*

The short-term, neoliberal "politics of disposability" (Henry Giroux, 2017, par. 3) builds an illusory wall of security around the wealthy elite, so that they may continue to defer any progressive action that would address the causes and consequences of this slow violence.

American Dippers and Alberta Winter Strawberries II
David Jardine

In the seventh month the Fire-star declines,
In the ninth month winter garments are handed out.
Spring days bring us the sun's warmth.

And the orioles sing.
(Wu-Chi Lui & Irving Yuchen Lo, 1990, p. 9).

I recall growing up in southern Ontario, in what was then a small village crouched between Hamilton and Toronto, just at the west end of Lake Ontario—full of black-orange orioles, singing, and their droopnests branchended on silver maples or Royal Oaks, named like the red-and-white dairy trucks that delivered milk and cheese and butter and eggs.

Undeniable ecological memory stored too deep, it seems, to switch.

Earthy flesh memory born(e) in the body of the child I was raised. We carry memories of where we were born, and the triggers of such memories are themselves bodily:

"In the seventh month the shrikes cry" (p. 10)

And in such a cry is borne part of my self, crying back for the remembering of a seventh month, when strawberries arrived up out of our waiting.

So "bioregions" are not simply places with objectively nameable characteristics. They infest our blood and bones, and become odd, unexpected templates of how we carry ourselves, what we remember of the Earth, and how light and delicate are our footsteps in all the places we walk.

Burlington was, in the 1950s, a market garden area-small 40- to 60-acre farms bursting full and an area with many canning factories and wooden fruit-basket factories (up in Freeman, a once-named crossroad near the rail lines that has since disappeared). Back when such things mattered, Burlington was right at the hinge between the north/south rail route up from the fruit-growing areas of Lincoln County (Vineland, Jordan Harbour, east to Niagara-on-the-Lake) and the east/west rail routes to Toronto, Kingston, and on to Montreal, or west to London and Sarnia or down to Windsor and Detroit. Swimming, 1957, Lake Ontario, off the redbrick Legion Hall parking lot south of Water Street, just after the Aylmer Factory had burped out the leftover bilge of tomato canning, and how this hot-scented red-scummed flotation that made the water flapthick muffled and fly surface buzzy melding into the Polio Scares—1953, me 3 years old, and the summers of nightmare visions of Iron Lungs and no swimming at all.

I remember, growing up in Burlington—then a small village of 4,000, long-since overgrown into the anyplace bedroom of nearby city condensations—having to wait for strawberries.

> In the fourth month, the small grass sprouts.
> In the fifth month the cicadas sing.
> In the eighth month we harvest the field.
> In the tenth month the leaves begin to fall.
> (Wu-Chi Lui & Irving Yuchen Lo, 1990, p. 10)

Their appearance once meant something deeper and more difficult than their obvious bright pleasure-presence to the tongue: about place, about seasonality, about expectation, about era, about arrival, about remembering, about reliance, about resignation and hope and little-kid pleasures, about waiting, about patience and time and its cycles. Strawberries once belonged somewhere and in some whence. They thus placed me, too, somewhere, some while. They thus arrived, not as objects but as bright and brief heralds. As heralds, they were always young, always new and fresh, always delicate and timely, always soon to take leave, leaving grief again at their passing.

An Ecological Pedagogy of Joy IV
Jodi Latremouille

All humans participate to different degrees in the oppression of earth's living systems, including our own human social, physical and psychological living systems; the public education system, too, is deeply complicit in the earth's destruction (see Michael Derby, 2015) I recognize that "the social and curricular fragmentation of a market economy of education" (William Pinar, 2006, p. xvi; see also Amitabh Pal, 2005, p. 5) perpetuates and solidifies the social inequity at the root of the degradation of our communities and biosphere. Through gendered, racialized and economic oppressions and the normalization of violent resource appropriations, our education system promotes and participates wholeheartedly in the deferral of our collective earthly responsibilities:

> In the contemporary neoliberal and ever more corporatized model of schooling, curriculum, and pedagogy at all levels, the destination is the future. This is not an indeterminate or open future that has yet to unfold; rather, it is the future that is known and colonized in advance. It is the future of competition for few

resources, the future of competing to be the winner, to be on top, to be the best, to be excellent. (Jackie Seidel, 2016, p. 70)

Under the spell of this logic, students are cut off from the particularities of their times, places, and communities (David Gruenewald, 2003, p. 620) in favor of abstract futuristic *elsewheres* of the global marketplace. The clear focus in education remains on (impossibly) trying to anticipate the needs of the workplace so that students of *all* nations can successfully compete against *all* other nations in the global economy.

Nôhkom's Gloves: A Recollection of "Spirit" and our Family Belongings I
Lesley Tait

> People receive nourishment from particular places and the inhabitants of those places, as they learn the skills necessary to live in those places. And as they learn and practice the skills necessary to live in that particular place they become who they are. (Cynthia, Chambers, 2008, p. 117)

My mother grew up poor. The kind of poor where 15 kids were raised in a one room school house. The kind of poor where the generosity of others might help you make it through the winter. The kind of poor where you knew better than to ask for things. It's a tough way to start a story, but you have to start where it starts.

My mother was raised by nôhkom Alice Calahoo and nimosôm Roderick Calahoo (chief of Michel First Nation) alongside her 14 siblings on the Michel reserve. They didn't have fancy things. Money went to things that were needed, not things that were wanted.

I grew up poor. Writing that down like that would hurt my parents' feelings. I'm sure of it. They worked hard. Dad had dropped out of high school in Grade 10 to "rally against the man" before finally returning to graduate. Mom graduated from high school and took a year of medical secretary training at NAIT. Dad got a job with the government and mom stayed home with us until that became impossible. They made it work. They gave the three us of everything we needed. Love, kindness, morals. But money was tight. Always.

nikâwiy – my mother
nôhkom – my grandmother
kôhkom – your grandmother

> *nikâwîs* – *my mother aunt*
> *nimosôm* – *my grandfather*

Nôhkom and nimosôm moved into the city of St. Albert in 1975. They bought their first house. It had that stucco made with recycled glass. I remembered how the embedded glass would glint in the sun and still have the audacity cut up your arms or face or legs if you were so unlucky as to fall upon it. They also bought furniture to fill the house. New things to place in this new place. No longer on reserve, but part of this other world.

I could tell you an entire chapter about Nôhkom and her traumas, but hopefully you understand and don't need me to. Much like my mother would come to feel later in life, Nôhkom struggled to see herself in this white world. My mother was always an Indian in her own mind. Always something less desirable, less meant to fit in.

> *Notice*
> *these all start with "ni" meaning my*
> *Which is why "kohkum" is complicated*
> *It has become slang but it actually means "your grandmother"*
> *Ki means ""your*
> *So when we say, "this is my kookum"*
> *we are actually saying "this is my your grandmother"*
> *It's because when someone handed us to our grandmother*
> *they would say, "go see kookum" which makes sense*

In Nôhkom's house, the kitchen was always full. Mostly the women. This is where I learned to peel potatoes, where I learned to sit quietly and listen while the women spoke and cooked. Out from the cupboard would come the old pot. Old enough to have its own stories. The cupboards themselves were not much more the pressboard. But the handles . . . . the handles were bronze and large and concave and made the doors easier to open with a delightful "pop." That silver pot would be placed on the formica table surrounded by old vinyl chairs, and the potato peeling would begin. Huge amounts of peels would begin to gather, the pile growing ever larger as more and more peeled potatoes were added to the pot. I would sit and marvel at mother's hands. There was no need for a modern-day potato peeler, just a simple knife and steady hands that seemed to waste not a single of ounce of potato to the peeling process. Hands that could console, peel and embroider a story being told, all within the same moment.

> *You can see*

The word for "aunt" has its roots in the word for "mother"
You can think of your mother's sisters as mothers
Not birth mothers, but mothers
This also applies to my father's brother's wives
Complicated, but the kinship terms let you know the embedded relationship

Ecological Disaster and Frozen Futurisms I
Jodi Latremouille

Our current system divorces us from our hearts and bodies and neighbours, from humanity and animality and embeddedness in the world we inhabit, from decency and even from the most rudimentary intelligence. (How smart is it to destroy your own habitat? Who was the genius who came up with the idea of poisoning our own food, water, and air?) The truth is hat it is only through the most outrageous violations of our hearts and minds and bodies that we are inculcated into a system where it can be made to make sense to some part of our twisted and torn psyches to perpetuate a way of being based on the exploitation, immiseration, and elimination of everyone and everything we can get our hands on. (Derrick Jensen, 2004, p. 42)

The dire predictions of these "ecologically sorrowful times" (David Jardine, 2015a, p. xv) weigh heavily on my heart-mind; it is understandable, in knowing "both too little and too much" (Donna Haraway, 2016, p. 4) that I will continuously fall prey to many out-of-proportion responses. The metaphorical separation between the natural world from humans, the head from the heart, and the future from my actions in the present, then my various responses are ill-suited to the places and circumstances in which we find ourselves. One manifestation of this illusory separation is "ecological romance" (David Jardine, 2015a, p. xix) in which I objectify and idealize beautiful, "wild" natural places untouched by humans. I place inordinate hope in misguided and unrealistic anti-human conservation efforts, while also exaggerating nature's innate ability to heal itself from human destruction.

This separation alternatively allows me to make the conceptual pendulum swing from nature as wild and free, to nature as a machine to be controlled. The result is an unfounded ecological optimism, characterized by a "comic faith in technofixes" (Donna Haraway, 2016, p. 3; see also Moacir Gadotti, 2003) and the unquestioned logic of the endlessly innovative marketplace. I fall prey to industry "greenwashing" (Collins English Dictionary, 2012) practices, whereby large corporations download "eco-guilt" (Jodi Latremouille, 2018a, p. 6) onto consumers, brow-beating us into doing our small part to help the earth, save the environment, and save energy, through our "empowered, healthy, and guilt-free" consumer choices (Drea Knufken, 2010, p. 1). Large companies promote an "I am greener than thou" image through carbon offset credits, unregulated and misleading labels like "all natural," well-funded ad campaigns, and donations to respected charities, yet maintain their gross (*read: 1. shameless, 2. vulgar, 3. bloated, 4. obnoxious*) (Collins English Dictionary, 2012) profit margins by denying their rampant environmentally, economically and socially disastrous practices (Robert Nixon, 2011, p. 37; see also Ted Steinberg, 2013, p. 254)

American Dippers and Alberta Winter Strawberries III
David Jardine

> In the sixth month we eat wild
> plums and grapes,
>
> In the seventh month we cook
> sunflower and lentils.
>
> In the eighth month we strip leaves of their dates,
> In the tenth month we bring home the harvested rice,
> We make it into spring wine
> For the nourishment of the old.
> In the seventh month, we eat melons.
> (Wu-Chi Lui & Irving Yuchen Lo, 1990, p. 39)

Pulling strawberries into continuous presence, into continuous, indiscriminate availability is, in its own way, a sort of objectivism. These Alberta winter strawberries are only in the oddest of senses here in my hands, even though, clearly, here they are. Something about eating them is potentially dangerously distracting. They are no longer exactly Earth produce even though, of course, they are just that. But they are commodities lifted off the Earth and floating above it, taking me with them. As they begin to float up into detached, oil-soaked commodification, I, too, begin to float, detached, unEarthly.

Such odd, objective strawberries ripped out of the Earthy contexts of their arrival—no Earth to smell, no resignation to waiting fulfilled, no sunny warmth—can, however, also be alerting. This subtle disruption of a sense of seasonality (one that my own son was just barely raised up into) that transports and oils and technologies have brought us: odd pleasures, since, in the grip of cabin fevers, these strawberries have also saved my life.

I love them even though they are covered with oil this time of year. My love of them now, indiscriminately, is part of the "trouble in the Middle East." My pleasure is a reason for the war, just like the rainbow-stain gasoline that drove me out West to the edge of the Elbow River to see those Dippers in the first place.

Ecological Disaster and Frozen Futurisms II
Jodi Latremouille

I comb the news for some glimmer, sometimes even secretly hoping against all reasonable hope that the lies spread by Big Oil, Big Coal, and Big Tobacco's doubt-disseminating army (Robert Nixon, 2011, p. 39) of political consultants, pseudo-scientists, industry-sponsored university departments, might—just might—be . . . telling the truth.

But when I recognize that there is no solace to be found in the denials of the *Merchants of Doubt* (Naomi Oreskes & Erik Conway, 2011) and I attempt to face up honestly to our collective ecological "fix" (David Jardine, 2015a, p. xv), I often manifest the hubris of thinking I know enough to be able to predict that even a marginally livable and sustainable human future on earth is impossible (Donna Haraway, 2016, p. 4). In the grip of this "frozen futurism" (David G. Smith, 2014, p. 26) I find myself giving in to ecological despair, lamenting what I "already know" is lost forever. I wonder, "if the future is not open, why should I go on?" (p. 7). I begin to whip up "ecological panic," (David Jardine, 2015a, p. xix), flurrying around, feathers flying and eyes bulging, gobbling up each sensational news story in panic and horror, pointing and screaming uselessly at each new expulsion, evacuation, extraction, and extinction. I sometimes also manifest this despair in a strange kind of narcissistic ecological hopefulness.

"Improving our Schools"
David Jardine

The critical edge here is the crisis of a spirit dancing on the edge of the world coupled with a certain deadly playfulness, deadly because that is precisely what is at stake here: whether life itself has a chance. Many of us understand this crisis and the ways in which our children's lives, my child's life, my own life and the demons in the trees and Coyote howls in the wind are becoming co-opted by consumptive panic endemic to our so-called "postmodern era." As the fragments crack, the genuineness and spirit and address of [this] work are [often] only understandable as hopelessly naiveté. Let us all be naïve, then. Let us all give up hope. There, in that place of hopelessness, when the eschatological hallucinations of a "better world" are given up, genuine love and compassion are possible.

There, "life itself has a chance" (David G. Smith, 1999, p. 139) out from under the vicious, well-meant glare of "improving our schools." (David Jardine, 2016a, p. 94–5)

Ecological Disaster and Frozen Futurisms III
Jodi Latremouille

When faced with the startling and sobering realities of our ecological times, I suffer along my high school students' "game over" (Naomi Klein, 2014, p. 22) attitude: "Well, your generation screwed us over anyway, so why shouldn't we have some fun while it lasts?" (Joanna Macy, 2014, par. 33).

> . . . Or, as my (David's) son Eric said years ago, "Your generation failed to look. Now we're afraid to look."

And finally, having exhausted myself running the circuit of all other options, I sometimes settle into a soothing yet dangerous heart-mind split, an ecological "centrism" (Joanna Macy, 2014, par. 33) that would have me maintain an in-control, upbeat, becalmed attitude, at all costs and against all odds. Rather than true heart-mind-fullness, I practice a misplaced mind-lessness, making excuses to be listless, passive and numb. I rationalize that if I can just be quiet, focused, and centred enough, perhaps I can simply soothe myself through this mess, without actually having to *do* anything about it.

> In my heart-mind, I know
> this separation of the head from the heart is
>   an ecological disaster.

Nôhkom's Gloves: A Recollection of "Spirit" and our Family Belongings II
Lesley Tait

> A heightened sensitivity to object and stories is entangled within Indigenous methods; whether it is the love stitched into beadwork, bravery honored, or a wrenching story of trauma and loss. (Sherry Racette, 2017, p. 225)

It was in this house that my nikâwîs (aunt), Diane, bought Nôhkom her first piece of china. Not just any china, but china that was revered for its beauty. Royal

Albert Old Country Rose to be more precise. You remember this china from your own grandmother's china cabinets. It's the white china with those Victorian looking roses around the rim.

Diane had wanted to buy her something she otherwise could never have had. Something "royal," if you will.

Nôhkom now had enough china to fill this newly bought china cabinet in this newly bought house. That china sat there beautifully displayed. I can remember standing in front of it as a child, marveling at the sheer expanse of it all. The China cupboard sat just outside the kitchen, on the wall next to the dining table. Every nook and cranny of that cabinet was lined with china. Nôhkom had the teapot and teacups, the gravy boat, the serving platters and enough place settings to accommodate a large crowd. It held its place of importance in that house and watched over its people. It brought nôhkom joy. It would come out at times of importance, Christmas, Easter, maybe a birthday if you were lucky.

The last piece of china was something nôhkom really wanted. A two-handed sugar bowl. The last piece to complete her collection. Diane found it in England and had it shipped over for Christmas. Nôhkom opened it and cried.

Joyful Writing: Place-Stories for Troubled and Troubling Times I
Jodi Latremouille

> *Trouble:* from Old French *trubler*, "to stir up, to make cloudy, to disturb." (OED)

Joanna Macy encourages us "to make friends with our despair, to make friends with our pain for the world. And thereby to dignify it and honour it" (Joanna Macy, 2014, par. 33). I recognize that every possible reaction arises from *somewhere*, welling up from deeply entrenched myths, fears, insecurities, and disconnections from deeper ways of knowing and living in the world. An ecological pedagogy of joy does not deny or try to suppress these multifarious eco-social realities and my equally diverse, yet ill-measured reactions. The decolonizing practices of this place-conscious education begins with an "unstorying of these narratives" (David G. Smith, 2014, p. 7) in order to re-story and "re-inhabit" places in careful and conscious ways.

American Dippers and Alberta Winter Strawberries IV
David Jardine

I cannot stop remembering a tomato tossed out against the backyard fence in late Ontario fall and yielding the next spring, of itself, without me, beyond desire and necessity, a great green clump of bushes four feet across, with that unmistakable near-acrid smell of fat and furry vines. This Dipper-place is a harsh place, which will yield potatoes and peas and not much else.

Another walk, Moose cow, great Alert Being, chest deep in snow near the river. An odd coalescing point, a great gathering in what must be a large habitat. This moose body as a place of great intensity and great need. Seeing her munching on those small firtree tips seems near-ludicrous and courageous and near-impossible all at once. How large must the territory of tree tips be for there to be such a being? And me, in winter, here, sucking strawberries.

I am living in a place that a hunter should live or someone with animals to slaughter and offer and eat:

In the tenth month we clean the threshing ground
With a pair of goblets, we hold a village feast.
Let's slaughter sheep and lamb.
(Wu-Chi Lui & Irving Yuchen Lo, 1990, p. 11)

Out in the greenhouse, sheltered in part from the place, tomatoes. Great Alert Beings, here and yet not here.

An ecological grieving for that deeply imprinted place where I was raised and a joy over the potatoes, right here, burping up out of tilled soils, and the young Gray Jay just now flirting with the feeder.

Ecological grieving for the waiting that is no longer necessary.

Joyful Writing: Place-Stories for Troubled and Troubling Times II
Jodi Latremouille

Staying with the trouble is a way of remaining truly present to our experiences and interpretations, "not as a vanishing pivot between awful or Edenic pasts and apocalyptic or salvific futures, but as mortal creatures entwined in myriad unfinished configurations of places, times, matters, meanings" (Donna Haraway, 2016, p. 1) These ways of writing are an attempt to take up Donna Haraway's critical and creative challenge to make kin in lines of inventive connection as a practice of learning to live and die well with each other in a thick present. Our task is to make trouble, to stir up potent responses to devastating events, as well as to settle troubled waters and rebuild quiet places. (Donna Haraway, 2016, p. 1).

The standard academic language that has me so well-schooled is rooted in the history of economic exchange; it is a language governed by laws easily bent "in order that treaties might be broken, and wounded beyond healing" (Linda Hogan, 1995, p. 45). However, when I contemplate earthly, rough-textured living and dying questions, scarring and healing questions, my attempts to language them often come across as harsh, frozen, laid bare, highly abstract, out of proportion, when they are bound up by the technical restraints of this academic prose of commerce and domination (Laurel Richardson, 1994). I make a political choice to write in accessible and poetic language (bell hooks, 2003, p. 71), seeking to invite readers into "intercultural, synergistic, and unresolved" (Joe Kincheloe & Shirley Steinberg, 2012, p. 360) conversations that encourage individuals and communities to challenge, question, and "get to know one another again" (Dwayne Donald, personal communication, February 28, 2014).

Although this "worded world" constantly resists my attempts to capture it accurately and precisely, the place-stories of poetry and life writing (Cynthia Chambers, Erica Hasebe-Ludt, Carl Leggo, & Anita Sinner, 2012; see also Ann Fisher-Wirth & Laura-Gray Street, 2013), open possibilities for "a new way to speak" (Linda Hogan, 1995, p. 46) that may lend some necessary unknowing to these questions. These questions may thus retain their mystery: they may hint at harmony and dissonance of braided intimacies, and a renewal of relations amongst those who live together in "a soul-place" (Erika Hasebe-Ludt, Cynthia Chambers, & Carl Leggo, 2009, 14). I wonder how I might honestly participate in the languages of those places, learning to "think with everything" (Joe Sheridan & Dan "He Who Clears the Sky" Longboat, 2006, p. 369), that is, allowing the places' own languages to rise up in their own ways and forms, and to hold the language of clarity and precision at bay for a short time.

Nôhkom's Gloves: A Recollection of "Spirit" and our Family Belongings III
Lesley Tait

Nôhkom passed away in May 2000.

> *Spirit woven into the fabric*
> *Spirit woven into the being*
> *Imbued, if you will*
> *Even if you don't see it*
>
> *Hands that hold*
> *Hands that remember*
> *Remember who they are*

Calahoo funerals are not small events. As what happens at every family gathering, no matter the intent, crowds of relatives descended upon that house in St. Albert. Like every family funeral, no matter the intent, discussion turned to nôhkom's belongings. I would have asked for the china. Not because I particularly loved it, not because of the roses, not because nôhkom loved it, but because I understood the value assigned to things. I had learned the value of money. We never had it. Everyone else I knew did. It made me want it.

My mother did not want the china. She asked for nôhkom's black leather gloves. Gloves nôhkom had worn for the past 20 years. These were not special gloves only taken out for special occasions. These were her every day, driving to bingo, kind of gloves There might have even been a hole in the crease between the thumb and finger. These were gloves she would put on heading out the door and take off and place on the shelf as she came in the door. They smelled a little bit like cigarettes to be honest. My mother had to leave them outside for a few days when she got home. Give them a chance to breathe.

My mother also asked for the touch lamp from nôhkom's bedside table. The gold lamp with frosted glass inserts that you can turn on and off with a simple touch. It's the kind of lamp you mention to anyone and they can picture in in their mind. Hideous by today's standards but maybe the height of technology and convenience in the 80s.

The china went to Diane. I'm sure every meal served on it brings her joy. And memories.

> For Siksikáítapiiksi, these places (and belongings) and not simply piles of rocks ... they are places (belongings) imbued with meaning and history. These places

(belongings) are the equivalent of books, encyclopedias, libraries ... they are sources of knowledge and wisdom ... these places (belongings) are repositories for the knowledge left by the ancestors. (Cynthia Chambers & Narcisse Blood, 2009, p. 261)

Joyful Writing: Place-Stories for Troubled and Troubling Times III
Jodi Latremouille

Place-stories weave renewed biotic and intercultural relationships (Derrick Jensen & George Draffan, 2003; see also Kirkpatrick Sale, 2000; Gary Snyder, 1990) within places and times full of unjust and tragic endings but also the possibility for renewals "We—all of us on Terra—are living in disturbing times.... Mixed-up times are overflowing with both pain and joy—vastly unjust patterns of pain and joy, with unnecessary killing of ongoingness but also with necessary resurgence" (Donna Haraway, 2016, p. 1). A place-story allows us to experience the dyings and renewals of life taking place in all times at once. "Place stories connect—to other worlds and other places—and yet they are deeply local and embodied, participating in the materiality of local places" (Margaret Somerville, 2012, p. 68). Beginning at home highlights the possibilities of conversations between here and there—the local, particular, culturally, and naturally conditioned ways of knowing, and a global network of possibilities, located in their own particular times and places. Thus, a writer's work begins locally but must be oriented towards the well-being of everyone (Cynthia Chambers, 1999, p. 148).

American Dippers and Alberta Winter Strawberries V
David Jardine

In the fifth month the locust stirs its legs

In the sixth month the grasshopper

vibrates its wings.

In the seventh month, out in the fields

In the eighth month, about the doors.

In the tenth month the crickets

Get under our beds.

(Wu-Chi Lui & Irving Yuchen Lo, 1990, p. 10)

Winter has cracked, or at least blinked. I, too, am a Great Alert Being, surprised to find that some of that alertness, as well as some grieving, is carried here, to Alberta, from the place I grew up.

It took me years to even begin to actually experience this place and its beauties. Too much of my thinking, too much of my experience is placeless. And yet here, summer, finally, heartbreaking blue against the yellow green of pines.

Hale-Bopp's nightly bristle, Mars between Leo's legs, Orion set already set, the great hunter that I am not.

And "Liu-huo ('cascading fire')" (Wu-Chi Lui & Irving Yuchen Lo, 1990, p. 8), Antares, Great Red Giant in Scorpius, soon to rise.

Time to tend the tomatoes.

Because, in the seventh month, the cascading fire of the Scorpion descends, and winter begins its miraculous return.

Joyful Writing: Place-Stories for Troubled and Troubling Times IV (Jodi Latremouille)

I seek "a language that heals" (Linda Hogan, 1995, p. 59) the relationship between humans and the natural order; in poetic forms of inquiry and representation, I search for "a tongue that speaks with reverence for life" (Linda Hogan, 1995, p. 60). I take up the work of life writing and poetic forms of inquiry as an ecological and critical "subversive praxis" (Erika Hasebe-Ludt, Cynthia Chambers, & Carl Leggo, 2009, p. 9), as one possible way for "writer-activists" (Robert Nixon, 2011, p. 23) to unsettle-interject-smooth-subvert our dominant narratives, to challenge "conventional registers of value" (David G. Smith, 2012, p. xv) and limiting categorizations of what "counts" as knowing, both in schools and beyond the classroom. I dream that it may be possible to live well in our particular times and places, in reciprocity with all our relation (Erika Hasebe-Ludt, Cynthia Chambers, & Carl Leggo, 2009, p. 9; see also Thomas King, 1990). I engage life writing and poetic inquiry, "a sensuous-intellectual activity—centring, decoding, reframing, discovering and discoursing ourselves in ways that shows us something of what we are, literally, as embodied participants and observers" (Ivan Brady, 2009, p. xiii).

Nôhkom's Gloves: A Recollection of "Spirit" and our Family Belongings IV
Lesley Tait

My mother understood something it would take me many more years to even begin to learn.

> Walking on the bones and blood of our ancestors
> Literal and figurative
> I am only here because of the sacrifices my mother made
> Both good and bad
> I help to carry her load and my load through life
> The people I meet help to lighten the load I carry
> I can share the weight

Her mother lived in those objects. Her spirit had left its mark. Touching her lamp every night would allow her to say goodnight. Touching it in the morning would allow her to say good morning. Putting on those gloves would allow her to hold her mother's hand. It would allow her to visit, to talk, to share.

> "In Aboriginal philosophy, existence consists of energy. All things are animate, imbued with spirit, and constant motion" (Little Bear, 2000, p. 77).

Some say it's the hands that hold what is sacred, the hands that remember. It is your hands that teach you about the four stages of life and that how each stage is guided by spirit. Look at your left hand with palm facing you. Your pinky is when you were a baby. Your next finger teaches you about adolescence. Your middle finger is when you are an adult. Then your pointer finger is when you are old—you shrink a little bit. But it is the thumb that is the spirit that guides you through those four stages of your life. It the spirit that connects those four stages touches each one. This is one of the reasons why using your hands to make things is considered so important and sacred.

> *Teach a story*
> *Teach it alongside the thing itself*
> *Or teach it while making*
> *A skirt*
> *A scarf*
> *Beading*
> *Bead the story in*
> *Sew it into the skirt*
>
> *Remember it every time you make it again*
> *Remember it when you see that plant again*
> *When you see that place again*
> *Now tell it anew*

Some Small-Town Stories: A Setting for A Record Year
Jodi Latremouille

I am the descendant of French, English, and Syrian immigrants, with some Indigenous ancestry on my father's side. My grandparents were butchers, cowboys, bakers, homemakers, and foresters. My parents were born and raised in the interior of British Columbia and had set down roots in Merritt B.C. by the time I was born. I was raised on a five-acre mountainside hobby farm, in a log house that my father built, with a concrete-walled garden to keep the deer out, a homemade chicken coop and a log-rail pig pen. I helped to slaughter pigs, I built tree forts, I learned to chop kindling (well, my chopping skills are debatable: my dad still doesn't think I am safe with an axe), and I raised orphan kittens when their mothers got eaten by the coyotes that lurked on the perimeter of our property. I learned how to hunt grouse and pick huckleberries, to raise chickens and help slaughter them, to tend a garden and to can jams, fruit, and salmon for winter storage in the root cellar, to make a crockpot moose stew, to climb trees and to peel logs for a cabin.

I was raised in Merritt, British Columbia, a small Canadian city of approximately 8,000 residents and a "trade area population" of 15,000. Merritt's industries are logging, ranching, mining and tourism. It is a sleepy-industrious, easily forgotten small town, trying to be a city, trying so earnestly to jump to the other side of the fabled urban/rural divide, and yet also aware that "the city is utterly dependent on the hinterland" (Derrick Jensen, 2002, p. 139).

Merritt sits in the Nicola Valley, at the confluence of the Nicola and Coldwater rivers, which eventually flow into the Fraser River. It is the hub of the B.C. Interior highway network, triangulated between the three major Southern B.C. city centres of Kamloops, Kelowna, and Vancouver. The Nicola Valley is within an hour's drive of 156 lakes that offer camping, fishing, and hiking. The high-water shorelines of 10,000-year-old glacial lakes are visible on the mountainsides surrounding grasslands where cattle graze peacefully.

Merritt promotes a cowboy culture and history: Douglas Lake Ranch is the most famous of a multitude of ranches in the area. Distinguished as "Canada's Largest Working Cattle Ranch," it is home to 11 private fishing lakes. Merritt is the Country Music Capital of Canada and hosts the Canadian Country Music Hall of Fame. The Merritt Mountain Music Festival hosted big names in country music and brought in hundreds of thousands of festival-goers each year from 1995–2011. Its new successor, the Rockin' River Music Festival, promises a down-home-country experience every July (City of Merritt, 2016).

And yet, the Coldwater river, downstream from the Merritt Mountain Country Music Festival, used to flow for days, weeks, after the party, with discarded glow necklaces, spilled beer, and hamburger wrappers. It would run slick with oily sunscreen applied to thousands of music festival sunbathers who had set up their lawn chairs right in the middle of the shallow river to escape the blazing mid-July heat.

The organizers of the Merritt Mountain Country Music Festival have smartened up since the early days, declaring the river off limits to partygoers, a salmon refuge, a protected river, and have begun to patrol the massive tent cities where women in bikini tops and jean shorts used to tiptoe past rowdy parties, hoping to slip by unnoticed; where men in cowboy hats and tassel shirts would walk on eggshells, afraid to spark an unintentional brawl. Swarms of children used to play barefoot in the river at the cool and shallow Claybanks park near the edge of town. Now, years later, we remain wary of this Musicfest legacy, reminded by the occasional shards of glass that still make their way down to us, skip-creeping along the valley bottom at glacial speed.

Seven First Nations bands live in the valley, including the Upper Nicola Indian Band, the Shackan Indian Band, the Nooaitch Indian Band, the Coldwater Indian Band, the Siska Indian band, the Nicomen Indian Band, the Cook's Ferry Indian Band, and the Lower Nicola Indian Band, with a combined total of nearly 4,000 members (Daybreak Kamloops, 2015, November 15). One local artist, comedian, and Elder, Opie Oppenheim likes to say, "Look out, Merritt, we've got you surrounded!" (personal communication, 2013).

In recent years, Merritt residents, led by members of several of these First Nations bands, have begun to protest the import of toxic biosolids into our communities. Loads of processed human feces are being trucked in from large cities around B.C. and spread on ranchers' fields at private composting facilities in the Sunshine Valley near my hometown. Local residents have only recently learned of this practice, which has been going on for years in our valley.

Now, in 2017, the sense of urgency has subsided. And yet, residents of the valley continue to share stories and news articles, raising awareness and challenging the accepted practices around dispersing biosolids in small communities in rural British Columbia. The scientific evidence is conflicting.

Merritt is a resource town. We extract and export trees, minerals, fish, cattle, salmon, hay, our young, processed elsewhere and exported to urban consumers around the world: to Kelowna, China, Alberta, the United States. We also import human biosolids, homeless human beings, toxic products, cheap produce: from Vancouver, California, China, Bangladesh. A perfect feedback loop.

And yet, my home, the Nicola Valley, is not only a town of resources and tourism and pristine lakes and music festivals. It is also a place of mourning and waste and disease. It is a place of struggle and courage and danger and miracles. The inhabitants of this place make intergenerational commitments to this earthly place that sustains us, living consciously with forests, overturned soil, industries, and swampy marshes as they flourish and fade, celebrate and decay once again. Whether we properly honour our commitments to this place or not, the land yet remains: beautiful, scarred, telling its stories through those that stay behind—in gravesites, on reserves, in stands of aspen trees, and in the plots of forgotten land that continue to yield to each new generation of living and dying.

2017 was **A Record Year** for extreme weather in our region. This summer, the smoke from all of our 1,000 British Columbia fires mingled with the smoke from Alberta fires, Washington fires, Russian fires . . .

> (A colleague) and I have been working also on a piece on fire. I noticed as I read your parts how different it was from ours, as we were here and you were there . . . different fires . . . maybe some of the same smoke . . . all scary and all requiring some kind of hermeneutic interpretive work to understand what they mean

for our pedagogical work. So I thought that was really fascinating to notice the difference … not only place based but so dependent on the person doing the experiencing, the time, where we are, who we are with, what we are doing. (Jackie Seidel, Personal Communication, October 29, 2017)

Pain and Apathy
from Joanna Macy

Given our culture's fear of pain and the high value it sets on optimism, feelings of despair are repressed. Hidden like a secret sore, they breed a sense of isolation. But when one's pain for the world is redefined as compassion, it serves as a trigger or gateway to a more encompassing sense of identity. It is seen as part of the connective tissue that binds us to all beings. This self is experienced as inseparable from the web to life in which we are as intricately interconnected as cells in a larger body (Joanna Macy, 1989, p. 204).

It is good to look at what apathy is, to understand it with respect and compassion. *Apatheia* means, literally, non-suffering. Apathy is the inability or refusal to feel pain. What is the pain we feel—and desperately try not to feel—in this planet time? It is pain for the world. It is the pain of the world itself, experienced in each of us. That pain in the price of consciousness in a threatened and suffering world (Joanna Macy, 2007, p. 93)

A Record Year
Jodi Latremouille

Winter 2017: Record Snowfalls
Last year, in the Nicola Valley

where I was born and raised
and now live once again
last year, we had
the most snow we'd seen in 20 years
the old-timers told the stories
and I remembered too
(but, between you and me,
there was just not quite as much snow
as there used to be . . .)

highways closed
again, and again
"always carry tire chains"
they said
remote mountain passes were so slick, one night
I stepped outside my
highway-traffic-jam-parked car
and fell on the ice
slept overnight across the backseat
on the side of the road
until a helpful trucker honked me awake
at 5:00 in the morning

"good for the snow pack
the water table
should be nice and high this year"
they said
should keep the rivers running
in our semi-arid desert land
thank goodness: we were so weary
of worrying about the groundwater levels
year after year.
Spring 2017: Record Floods
And just like that
the snowpack melted
and flowed away to the Pacific Ocean
mid-May, yay,
summer's early! high temperatures
suddenly melted the high mountain snow
and combined
with rain

after rain after rain
and despite a dam installed years earlier
to mitigate floods and manage irrigation
our Nicola Lake swelled
to levels not seen
in a century, maybe two:
1.3 metres
and counting (CTV News Vancouver, 2019, May 9)

the Nicola River
flooded the valley
basement pumps bravely pumping
pulling the water up and out
pouring it into the street
as it flowed right back down
into our foundations
neighbour-kids paddling a dinghy
out to the chicken house
life paused to fill sandbags
once again

Evacuate: Cherry Creek

Evacuate: two lives lost

Evacuate: Upper Nicola Band

Evacuate: the seniors' care residence
wheelchair-bound grandmothers packed
through knee-deep water
to a waiting ambulance

State of Emergency (Lauren Pullen, 2017, May 18)
Summer 2017: Record Wildfires
Early July, our family travelled North
to a long-awaited family reunion
Little Fort, B.C.
We set up camp in the RV park
across the highway from the community hall
and the playground that bore our family name
the highway was treacherous

that weekend
so much traffic flowing
re-routed away from a wildfire
threatening the other highway just one valley over

late into Friday night
we laughed and chatted, visited
or avoided
long-missed/prickly/forgotten/jovial
relatives
Fire Ban
our faces lit only by the hot-red glow
of that brand-new wildfire
on top of that hill to the north
black stalks of charred trees spiking up
against the red rim of that fire
licking its way over that hilltop
just to the north

Suspected Cause: Person

at midnight, the RCMP came knocking
on campers and tent doors
Evacuation Notice: Little Fort
we packed up our tents and went across the river
to safer terrain

A family ceremony delayed
we wanted to bury my grandmother's ashes
alongside her beloved husband
of 60 years

some of us returned the next day
to complete the ceremony
against official orders
we, the stubborn ones, returned
we smelled the fire before our vehicles swam
into the smoke and the ash

we buried her in a tiny, ancient
mossy cemetery

nestled in a grove of spruce and fir trees
the daisies were blooming
this time of year
littering the cemetery
with their sparkly-crisp
white-nodding heads
we were the lucky ones
only our stories and ashes
were from that place anymore
Evacuation Notice: Rural Quesnel
helicopters landed
in the middle of remote hayfields
along the North Thompson River
a helicopter landed
in my best friend's hayfield

They raced along the highway
with a van full of humans and lucky animals
windshield wiping away the ashes and sparks
floating across the road
and onto their moving vehicle
they were the lucky ones
they only had to return to hungry,
traumatized but still-living pasture animals
and a fridge full of rotten food
they thanked their stars that the wind didn't shift

Evacuation Notice: 100 Mile House

Evacuation Notice: Williams Lake

Evacuation Notice: all their rural parts

that's 10,000 people just *here*
2–8 weeks
and counting . . .

hustled away from their
beds/photos/kitchens/barns/tractors/ greenhouses/trampolines
homes
cattle/sheep/horses/chickens/pigs/ducks/ladybugs/worms
neighbourhoods

fishing/sawing/mining/harvesting/butchering
livelihoods
bees/ravens/clover/black bears
friends

Structures Lost: 300 (News 1130, 2017, August 1)

the ones who weren't so lucky
returned
to the hollowed-out crematoriums
of their homelife-memories
framed in soot
by a few charred and tenacious steel posts and beams
burned-out-matchstick-trees poking up
out of the rubble
like war-blackened sentries

In my valley
we were the lucky ones
we received evacuees
from the wildfire regions
we called it
The Summer of the Red Sun
weeks and weeks
of heavy, murky blue-brown skies
and a blurred red-orange orb
angrily trying to shine through

Health Warning:
seek medical attention for
wheezing/burning eyes/cough/chest pain/shortness of breath
Air Quality Health Index:
scale of 1 to 10: 14
Extreme Risk: avoid strenuous activities outdoors (Air Quality Health Index, 2017, November)

don't breathe
muscles/grapes/throats/spirits/gardens/lungs
withered on the vine
that was the summer I got my first inhaler
it was only temporary

some of us escaped on holidays
to far-off clear skies
others had no option
birds living in town would sit very still
on their branches
panting, panting, panting
beaks wide open
dehydrated
we put bowls of water out
to keep the birds alive

Level 4 Drought
Extreme Fire Risk

water only on Mondays
and only if essential
reduce consumption voluntarily
because, you know, in the future, they said
"water will be
a highly valued commodity"

even our drought-resistant lawns
recoiled
crispy-yellow in the hazy sun
and yet
the city-owned
RV park across the road
from the dried-up Coldwater river
was as ever-green as could be

No Fishing Season (Cole Wagner, 2016, November 17)

extended
until further notice
on the record-low river
tiny minnows boiling over
trapped in shallow pools
salmon couldn't get up to spawn
100 days without rain
and counting . . .

over 1,000 wildfires
burned up and down
our province
"it was just nature's cycle,
forests need to burn"
they said
and yet

Suspected Cause: Person
2 out of 5
that's 360 fires
Under Investigation (Amy Judd, 2017, August 9)
and counting . . .

Elephant Hill Fire:
Suspected Cause: Person

Knox Mountain Fire:
Suspected Cause: Person

Lake Country Fire:
30 homes burned: 8 charred to ashes
Suspected Cause: Person

"nature was certainly not
giving us any help" (Tristan Martin-Woodhouse, 2017, July 22)
they said
Gustafson Fire:
No rain

Princeton Fire:
Gusting winds

Hanceville Fire:
Searing sun

0% contained
State of Emergency

Fall 2017: Not Yet Recorded
rain, finally returning to our valley
the Coldwater river

flush with rainwater
gushing down from the mountains
once again
muddy, dangerous, beautiful, wild
(but between you and me, we fear
it's still not quite enough
to save us from next summer)

summer apocalypse times
easily forgotten
as tiny green-slivery grass shoots
incredibly
dust the lawns between the dead-brown stalks
trying to make another go of it
before snow times
they are a bit confused
oh, but winter is setting in
frost on the car
this late-October morning
we miss summer already
my well-fed honeybees settle
into their winter cluster

and yet
summer endures
100 fires still burn in our province
mostly burning on "empty land"
but also including

7 Wildfires of Note (Global News Okanagan, 2017, September 28):
wildfires which are
highly visible
or which pose
a potential threat
to public safety

summer is somewhat less easily forgotten,
at least for
those living on "empty land"
those we might call
the less lucky ones

Aesthetics, Anesthesia, and Neurasthenia
David Jardine

From a brilliant piece written by Kevin Aho (2018) entitled "Neurasthenia revisited: On medically unexplained syndromes and the value of hermeneutic medicine":

[George] Beard [in a book entitled *American Nervousness, its Causes and Consequences: A Supplement to Nervous Exhaustion (Neurasthenia)*, 1881] attributed the rise of neurasthenia both to a hereditary predisposition as well as the wrenching social upheavals of modernization in the United States at the end of the 19th century, as large swaths of the post-Civil War population migrated from slow-paced rural communities to chaotic and bustling cities in the Northeast. Beard also cited new technologies of industrialization such as the periodical press, the telegraph, telephone, and steam engine, as well as the ubiquity of mechanical clocks and watches that "compel us to be on time and excite the habit of looking to see the exact moment" (George Beard, 1881, p. 103). These factors, taken together, contributed the excessive strain on mental and physical life, and help explain Beard's claim that the "chief and primary cause" of neurasthenia is not the result of some new organic pathology, but of "modern civilization [itself]" (George Beard, 1881, p. vi). (Kevin Aho, 2018, p. 2).

I responded (David Jardine, 2019):

Here is the non-hermeneutic question: is neurasthenia "really" a medical condition, now even a brain-chemical, serotonin-related matter, or is its cause "really" "modern civilization?" Hermeneutics, frustrating to many, has no answer to this question. It asks a far more terrifying cluster of questions: what might be at stake, who might profit, what might be lost and gained in these alternatives? More pointedly is the current ecological nightmare that surrounds our "aliveness" — the conditions under which it might cease to be sustainable. Let me put it this way. Let's us practice a hermeneutic commonplace in its attempts to understand our circumstances. *Think, for a moment, just how very much would loom up if we let ourselves believe that* "modern civilization" *is the cause of our current woes*. What would this ask of us? What would we forfeit and gain? Can I bear it? It is little wonder George Beard's original speculation about "modern civilization" being the cause of neurasthenia was not able to stand as a summons to thinking and action. Think of the unbearable weight of current ecological insight into the effects of "modern civilization" and the near-neurasthenic that can repeatedly loom up when we hear of it. It had better not be that little wonder is all we are left with. (p. 52)

An odd circumstance, where panic and neurasthenia are the offered alternatives.

And, as cited above, re-consider Joanna Macy (2007, p. 93), and her meditations on apathy:

This anaesthesia [note, literally, no *aesthesis*, no feel for the beauty of things and therefore no desire to "keep things (as much as we are able) radiantly well" (James Hillman, 2006a, p. 192; see David Jardine, 2016a, p. 161–166)] is largely the modern human condition. And, it is supported and promoted by our economics, our entertainment, our modes of communication and transportation, and, of course our medications (James Hillman, 2006b, p. 144)

. . . to say nothing of our schools.

The Prospect of Measured Responses: Cultivating Joy in *Not* Knowing I
Jodi Latremouille

What am I, in the terrible and fragile?
. . . At one time, if our ancestors refused to respect
they would perish–remember that now

> It's all one time.
> It's all one place (Jodi Latremouille, 2015, p. 42)

The world continues to defy my misplaced hopes "for knowledge equal to (and capable of controlling) the world" (Wendell Berry, 1983, p. 56). And so now, I ask, what is an ecological pedagogy that can bear *A Record Year*? What is a pedagogy that can dwell in a year of omens, a year of demons, a year of swift floodings and burnings, with slow-moving hazes still arriving, and more consequences yet to come? How do I let this devastating year pass lightly and loosely through my splayed, soft fingers? How do I navigate the rush of eco-guilt-romance-hope-denial-panic that rolls over me in waves as I read and re-read this year that we had, together with each other?

> How do I find my footing? How do I open
> the space to breathe, when my heart is
> halting, gasping . . .?

The Prospect of Measured Responses: Cultivating Joy in *Not* Knowing II
Jodi Latremouille

> "Has it only just *begun*?"
>   "hush, child . . ." (Latremouille, 2014a, p. 31)

> Yes, it looks bleak. But you are still alive now. You are alive with all the others, in this present moment. And because the truth is speaking in the work, it unlocks the heart. And there's such a feeling and experience of adventure. It's like a trumpet call to a great adventure (Joanna Macy, 2014, par. 11).

What is an ecological pedagogy that responds to this trumpet call to dwell adventurously in our "planetary anguish"? (Joanna Macy, 2007, p. 151)

We may undertake this imperfect, uncertain journey, lingering heart-mindfully with children, not because we are instructed to do so, but because we *must*, "out of a sense of joy . . . that wells up from within . . . It needs to be something that wells up from within. By respecting the land, you walk softly on it" (Derrick Jensen, 2002, p. 10). As storytellers-activists-researchers-mentors, teachers may work towards humble, relational, respectful, and heart-mind-ful responses.

"The Open Breath"
Lesley Tait

>the disposability of time
>of time misused
>letting it go as the river streams
>it sits on my shoulders
>heavy and waiting
>
>an expectation of more, of wanting
>calling to me to give it a name
>
>the greeting of the two sides
>   meeting in happy remembrance and sorrow
>   of the expectation unfulfilled
>
>letting it go, staying there for a while
>awareness of more and of less
>as shoulders sag
>the open breath
>sending away all that sits in opposite grain
>recognition of what true names may join me.

The Prospect of Measured Responses: Cultivating Joy in *Not* Knowing III
Jodi Latremouille

We may find unknowing ways to re-inhabit places and times together.

When I "stop looking away" (Naomi Klein, 2014, p. 6) from our collective ecological troubles, I recognize that the world is much more than I can know, control, fix, or save. In allowing myself to be intimately and joyfully *implicated* (Jodi Latremouille, 2014a, p. 6) in our common ecological possibilities, I may work to identify and deconstruct the stories and practices through which people and places are exploited and destroyed (David Gruenewald, 2008, p. 318). As "I spend my life and breath to open our minds, and to change our heart-minds" (Joanna Macy, 2014, par. 7) I nurture an openness to the myriad possibilities—of repeated and stubborn learning-failures; of students not caring a whit about my latest tirade for socio-ecological justice; of suffering with the heartaches of little fingers trying to dig deep into the soil of our radiant earth—in joyful contemplation of the prospect of *not* knowing how things will turn out (Susan Murphy, 2014, p. 83):

> Each generation bears responsibility for upholding principles of justice, fairness, openness and hope in its own time, not for the past, nor for the future but for today, and the responsibility may fall in unique ways on the shoulders of educators. What will the enactment of such responsibility look like, and how shall it be cultivated? (David G. Smith, 2016, p. xviii)

I remember that our children *long* to step up to find their place in the order of things—*in the midst of everything*—and to be responsible for renewing life in some small piece of our earthly home.

Staying with the trouble

heavy and waiting

is "both more serious and more lively" (Donna Haraway, 2016, p. 4) than turning away in panic, despair, or denial;

it sits on my shoulders

It is a joyful becoming-with (Donna Haraway, 2016, p. 4) that endeavors to respond in *proper measure* (Hans-Georg Gadamer, 2004, p. 251) to the big and unanswerable ecological questions and challenges that face us, here.

calling to me
to give it a name

I see the classroom as "a place of passion and possibility, a place where spirit matters, where all that we learn and know leads us into greater connection, into greater understanding of life lived in community" (bell hooks, 2003, p. 183)

the open breath

These responses, of course, being human and "bumptious" (Donna Haraway, 2016, p. 1) are never perfect or complete; they always necessarily entail their own particular inconsistencies, violences, enablings, and denials. A teacher-education student once reminded me that our "Creator's love for us is unlike our own fragmented love. Creator's love is abundant, pure and generous. This is our strength in times of weakness" (Ahstanskiaki ManyFeathers, personal communication, March 2015).

call up to the creators;
we are here, we are here.

(Judson Innes, 2015, p. 107)

As educators, we are called to "stand up as examples" (David Jardine, personal communication, January 14, 2016) of imperfect love in our commitments to our places, allowing and responding to all of the tiny heartbreaks and incomplete answers, so that our children may possibly inherit renewed abilities to also step up into these free, populated, heavy, messy spaces of loving the world well, passionately and imperfectly.

And so, some wonderings for the time being . . .

I wonder about what it might mean
for teachers to
critically and creatively
engage in a joyful ecological
pedagogy, as we work
to stay with these difficult, messy, courageous,
relational, intimate, tentative,
troubling
places and times . . .

meeting in happy remembrance and sorrow

I wonder what it might mean for teachers to un-story
entrenchments and to re-open
alternative imaginings and future
possibilities,
recognition of what
true names may join me

so that we might "make schools not just livable and sustainable but beautiful and wise" (David Jardine, 2015a, p. xvii)

∞∞∞∞

And I remember:

The work of teachers is a task of coming to learn to live with this lot and still pursue beautiful things . . .
  which are "never assured" (David Jardine, 2014, p. 186, 189)

∞∞∞∞

And I think with my heart-mind:
    Whatajoyful *(difficult-heartbreaking-shifting-miraculous-raging-impermanent)* prospect.

∞∞∞

examples of imperfect love

WAYSTATION II
Logger
Vern Latremouille

Who's going to live? Who's going to die? I get to choose. I don't feel godlike as I strap on my $120 rubber corks as the young guy ties up his $400 leather Vibergs.

But I do feel the weight of responsibility to pass on to him what I have learned in my blip on earth. Mimic nature and what has gone before, I say. He rolls his eyes and says, you just pay attention to the OGMA's, The ECA's the UWR and WTP percentage old man. Oh and don't forget to keep it under 40 hectares unless it's Pine that is greater than 25% dead or down or affected with beetle. Root rot and Spruce budworm don't count for salvage, remember. And stay out of that small wood polygon unless the piece size is greater than .21.

Yeah yeah, I mumble, remembering the time I had to go back and adjust a boundary that was 10m inside an Old Growth management area, and another time when I had to begrudgingly adjust a boundary out of Ungulate winter range when it was NOT ever going to be used by a Deer Moose or Elk in the summer OR winter. Lines drawn on the map from the office based on bio geo zones and a best guess.

The Equivalent Clearcut areas, Wildlife tree patches, riparian management zones and the like are easier for me to buy into. I get a huge sense of satisfaction when I visit a logged block and see a deer bedded in one of the WTP's I have left out of the block. And when I take a drink out of a creek downstream of a fresh logged block and the water is clean and sweet.

The rules didn't help me in Lawless creek where I was allowed to take every Spruce tree to the edge of the creek, they were all dead from beetle but when I came back 10 years later the banks were ravaged and the creek was twice as wide as when we logged. I had taken the trees that would have fallen in over many years and controlled the channel. A fire would have left some of those trees and mitigated some of that impact until the new trees were big enough to stabilize the channel. I had neglected to mimic nature.

The Natural World, always teaching!

An Ecological Pedagogy of Joy | 71

    I was sparked to write again at 5:00 am this morning amongst the calling loons, mating/nesting twittering birds and barreling trucks at a campsite on Monte lake south of Kamloops B.C. Mind sharp on day 5 of an avocado only fast. I awoke reliving in my mind an incident during a recent day of layout on Thynne mountain.

    I was hanging ribbon for a skid crossing on a Non-Classified Drainage (NCD) when I heard the gentle persistent thunder of running feet. Very like the sound when the cougar charged me in Prospect cr! TOWARDS OR AWAY!!! *HERE IT COMES! I grab for my moose horn handled machete, its out with a SHOUT. A black bear barreling at me, swerving to pass eight paces from me in a blur of speed. Hair on end I holler, his bobbing black bum over the hill and out of sight.*

    So . . . he wasn't charging, *he was running for his life! Now I'M ALERT, watching his backtrail, chortling from the adrenaline rush.*

Nothing shows, my scent or voice has deterred the potential aggressor. Feeling energized but fragile I sit and muse. Once again the upright ones have proven dominance. If only they knew how relatively frail humans are, they could kill us at will one on one. Without our weapons and numbers we would be easy prey.

The large predatory animals generally seem to have an intrinsic repulsion of humans in my experience. Whether learned or inherited this trait is worth reflecting on as it may point to how I could better interact with them. My belief is that we are all interconnected, including the supposed inanimate objects, plants rocks, soil, water and air.

Ironically trees can energize me. When I come upon an old Veteran Douglas Fir and place my hands on the deeply furrowed bark it refreshes my body and mind. Existing on through fires, winds and winters. Presiding over generations of seedlings, squirrels, bears, cougars and bird nests. Sheltering ungulates and coyotes and whoever else rests under its canopy. Finally succumbing to a tiny beetle or root rot and either crashing down for bug food or breaking off to become a bird hotel. These stubs can house many birds once the woodpeckers have created holes in the rotten core in their quest for insects. It is very satisfying for me when I have the opportunity to preserve these "condos" with my boundary, however temporary or short lived they may be.

What is temporary?

We could say the earth, the sun, and the universe is temporary.

In that context I view the forest as a garden with an 80- to 500-year rotation, depending on the species involved and geological zone.

One of the logging contractors was upset with me for laying out a high elevation Spruce stand with a 300-year rotation. We had many thought-provoking discussions over this issue. In the end I felt that the lumber was enough of a benefit to society to justify the disruption as the stand was becoming decadent and nearing the end of its rotation. It would be back to the same state in 300 years if the earth remained compliant.

During that time, though the cycle is slower than in lower elevations, it would go through the meadow phase, the shrub phase and eventually to the closed canopy phase. As long as we protect the water and soils during logging to mitigate any short-term impacts, our actions would closely mimic the natural cycle of this stand.

As this same contractor used to say, "you have to break a few eggs to make an omelette," and he always broke fewer eggs than most.

The land has always been good to me, giving me huckleberries, meat and mushrooms. Logs to build with, sticks for stilts, willow for whistles, pitch wood for fires. The First Nations People who have lived on this land for thousands of years had a vast knowledge of the plants and animals and how to utilize or coexist with them for health and well-being. Much of this knowledge is gone since the European invasion. How long before we could regain that knowledge? First we have to make it a priority.

How do we tick, how do we teach, how do we learn? Many years ago I believed that teaching and learning was a vocal exercise of telling and listening. After a personal development course called the Pursuit of Excellence I came to believe teaching and learning was more about being the best we can be. My words and actions will define my knowledge which can be assimilated by those whose respect I have garnered. All tempered by a little plaque on Pop's trailer wall, "It's what you learn after you know it all that counts," as well as his response to my question put to him at the age of 89. Pop, any advice for me before you pass on? He thought a bit as we watched some Elk in the Otter Valley. A man of few words he finally said, "Do unto others."

Thanks Pop.

Who's going to live? Who's going to die?

The responsibility is weighty!

"Slower, More Miraculous Returns"[1] I David Jardine

> Some wishes cannot succeed; some victories cannot be won; some loneliness is incorrigible. but there is relief and freedom in knowing what is real; these givens come to us out of the perennial reality of the world, like the terrain we live on. one does not care for this ground to make it a different place, or to make it perfect, but to make it inhabitable and to make it better. To flee from its realities is only to arrive at them unprepared. (Wendell Berry, 1983, p. 92)

There is a joy hid in wanting to know what is real. It is a subtle one, full of commiseration and exultation, and not always in equal measure. Keeping good track of a record year is heartbreaking, but it also hones our attention when its writ and

---

1 Bronwen Wallace (1989). *The stubborn particulars of grace.* Toronto, ON: McClelland and Stewart, p. 13.

read and puts practice to not being distracted or exhausted. We might become disillusioned but losing our illusions can give relief and freedom.

Rightly understood, over the long-term disillusionment is good news.

. . .

By addressing the deeply human fear of disillusion, could it be possible to imagine a world on the other side of such disillusionment?

. . .

What is interesting in each of [its] definitions is the underlying virtue of disillusion; namely, freedom—from illusion, mistakenness, faulty perception. Moreover, the implication is that the freedom inspired by disillusion involves a restoration of the ludic quality of human life, the joy of true play.

. . .

An ability to face the necessary disillusionment points paradoxically to the source of our hope (David G. Smith, 2020, p. 280, 288, 289, 291)

We have seen how children, old and young, are drawn towards what is real, and how delves in to the study of the perennial realities of the world make time fold in on itself, make attention deepen and slow and while and all this despite the well-known woes of schools. And how it can be a delicious relief when this happens. "Elephants in the noontime sun in summer" (Kunzang Pelden, 2007, p. 255) caught sight of a gaudy-shimmer, cool lake. Drawn into places where memory extends, and work takes hold of us and we of it, and changes who we are.

An ecological pedagogy of joy therefore bodes of habitation and the terrains we live amidst (not just surrounded by but made of), airs we breath, more-than-human bee-consciousness and phototropic plant turnings towards the sun, and all the shared and contested knowledge that has been entrusted to us for safekeeping, inside and outside of schools. *Gaudium*—the Latinate root of "joy"—is a sensate uprising, feels and forms, and the quick in-breath of finding just that map, or just that formulation, or just the right words, just that solvent resolution to a mathematical knot or the meticulous pin-counts of rings treed in wooden rounds in a Kindergarten class—my birth year, my mother's and sometimes arcs and arcs before that, fat rings full of growth and skinny ones betraying, well, what in 1874 interior British Columbia? Troubled rainfall? Cold? Or perhaps skies purpled with smoke, lower sun levels, less growth, like the unripened economies and values and desires that are fantastical, a world in which millions of people have lost any idea of the materials, the disciplines, the restraints, and the work necessary to support human life, and have thus become dangerous to their own lives and to the possibility of life. The job now is to get back to that perennial and substantial world in which we really do live, in which the foundations of our life will become visible to us, and in which we can accept our responsibilities again within the conditions of necessity and mystery (Wendell Berry, 1983, p. 13)

An ecological pedagogy of joy thus has two interwoven gestures—one of unearthing unearthly, unsustainable, miserable turns that pedagogy has taken, hidden complicities in ecologically disastrous ways of thinking and being. The other, unearthing the earth-bound work of stepping away from such self-imposed, unearthly miseries and stepping towards the great and sweet suffering that is at hand in good, solid, worthwhile work, teachers and students alike, young and old alike, in great concerts with the more-than-human world which we always already *are* in our deepest countenance. Earth-lings only exist at all in relations of dependent co-arising with suns and soils and waters; and the knowledge we have inherited itself lives in precisely these sorts of relations of dependent co-arising—living *fields*. We only exist in this embrace, one way or the other, aware of it or not, working in its terrible grace or against it.

Finding Myself in the Measure of Things: Introduction to "A Modern Hunting Tradition" I
Jodi Latremouille

My inspiration for "A Modern Hunting Tradition" came in the form of a quote by David Smith who wrote that:

> Some things reveal themselves on their own terms, when they are ready, not simply under the duress of a formal curriculum requirement at 10:30 a.m. on Tuesday. This is now well understood in the realm of ecology, for example, and the study of so-called "wildlife." The best way to see animals in their natural habitat is simply to sit still; then the animals will come out of hiding and show themselves (David G. Smith, 2014, p. 82).

tomatoes at season's end here in Bragg Creek, summer of 2018, a record year next door.

There is love, hereby, and patience, affection, and a deepening desire for fierce accuracies. Joy. Delight.

And the great dignities of real work. And well-thought-out disillusion from the undignified scurryings of some schooling. Joy itself falls toward "delight," Latin *delectare*, to allure, hiding *delicere*, "to entice" (OED), and then, hah!

Delicious.

Joy names the draws of affection.

An old saw from Thomas Aquinas, paraphrasing the *Ad Herennium*: "It is necessary that a man should dwell with solicitude on, and cleave with affection to, the things which he wishes to remember" (cited in Francis Yates, 1974, p. 75):

> If one's sight is clear and if one stays on and works well, one's love gradually responses to the place as it really is, and one's visions gradually imagine possibilities that are really in it. Vision, possibility, work, and life—all have changed by mutual correction. (Wendell Berry, 1983, p. 70)

> "To know the world, we have to love it" (Wendell Berry, with Bill Moyers, 2013)

> To use the hermeneutic adage, the world has become open to interpretation [to *exactly* the extent that I am open to the interpretability of the world]. And here is the great, seemingly paradoxical situation: "keeping ourselves open" and "keeping the world open" (Mircea Eliade, 1968, p. 139) are the same thing. As we become experienced, having cleaved with affection and made ourselves "roomier," the world's roominess can be experienced (David Jardine, Michelle Bastock, Jennifer George, & Judy Martin, 2008, cited in David Jardine, 2016a, p. 81)

A perennial reality that comes 'round in rounds. We have seen this. Not all the time. Not every time. Not anywhere for very long. We have worked with students and teachers, inside and outside of schools, for whom trivial work will no longer suffice. Trivial work has no prospect of dignity and joy, only "pay off." An ecological pedagogy of joy: "what is here is to be treasured" (James Hillman, 2006a, p. 192).

Treasured relations (Jodi Latremouille, 2014b). An ecological pedagogy of joy therefore hides a critique in plain sight, one that is burgeoning on many fronts in these "ecologically sorrowful times" (David Jardine, 2015a, p. xv):

> What we call the modern world is not necessarily, and not often, the real world, and there is no virtue in being up-to-date in it. It is a false world, based upon

"Slower, More Miraculous Returns" II (David Jardine)

So here is the declaration: we proposed an ecological pedagogy of joy precisely and exactly and deliberately and purposefully right now, in these—say it again, like a murmured chant that starts to vibrate the chest—"ecologically sorrowful times" (David Jardine, 2015a, p. xv). Stepping towards untying knots that have "bound us without a rope" (David Loy, 2010, p. 42) and also stepping away, out into the open and up into the updrafts of perennial wild airs and mortal prospects.

This perennial and substantial world is the world that appears when we read curriculum guides as repositories from the world of its living fields of knowledge that the world itself has deemed we should not forget, should take good care of, and cultivate in the hearts of the young. Properly read and practiced carefully and with ecological grace, these texts are field guides to real, ancestor-laden, memory-laden, living locales wherein real work will yield up finds, and knowledge will summon up into the air that surrounds us like the smells of good, cared-after soils turned—histories, geometries, grammars, periodic tables, quadratic equations, reading, writing, listening, experimenting, measuring, studying, periodic tables, and long and variegated inheritances of beauty and accuracy. We have seen this firsthand in classrooms from Kindergarten to Grade 12, in undergraduate courses, graduate courses, at scholarly conferences, in walks with our children finding stones or in the breath-take of that great old Calvin and Hobbes cartoon where, happening upon some water running through some dirt, Calvin declares that the whole day is now booked.

We've been smaller and larger parts of these fields, these guidings and leadings and followings. Dozens of our colleagues have written and written and written about how this looks even in the confines of, goes the snide innuendo, "one of those schools," why it is true of our human being and well-being and of the well-being of the more-than-human world, and how to deal with the low- to high-level panics that predatorially stalk some school hallways. And to imagine that the Latin root of school, *schola* (itself from the Greek *skhole)* means "leisure." When those stalks stalk, we tend to recommend two further readings of this Latin root which declare, we suggest, part of our ecopedagogical responsibility as teachers: "a holding back, a keeping clear" (OED) of those things that would distraction attention and devotion to the matters at hand. Scholarship.

It is hard to imagine. Teachers and students and the common wealth of the world's wisdom relieved, just for a moment, from the real-but-illusory, skittery rush of schools. Teachers as field guides who have themselves found the joy in the real work that the places entrusted to us require. Right there, where it seems that "time is always running out" (Wendell Berry, 1983, p. 7f), up jumps "something we thought we'd lost to the work of simply getting by" (Bronwen Wallace, 1989, p. 111).

Finding Myself in the Measure of Things: Introduction to "A Modern Hunting Tradition" II
Jodi Latremouille

I wanted to be reminded of what it feels like to sit still, to notice, to remember the more-than-human world (David Abram, 1996). In conversations with colleagues, friends and students, I have come to notice that growing up "in the bush" is, for a growing number of humans, a story of foreign lands. Places like Rock Island Lake, the fishing camp that my parents operated where I spent my first five summers; Fox Farm Road, the log cabin on the mountainside; Paradise Lake; and Nicola Lake—these are my places, where I feel at home. Joe Sheridan and Dan "He Who Clears the Sky" Longboat (2006, p. 366) explain that "settler culture" (Western society) has not yet "naturalized" to the land, in that it has yet to create myths that respect the possibilities of this place. Finding myself at home in the bush, not the forest that "to most settlers remains a dark and evil spirits in need of exorcism or destruction" (Joe Sheridan, 2001, p. 196), but the stomping-hunting-fire-building-silent bush of bushmen and bushwomen, means finding myself in a place that requires something of me . . . . for my (earthly) survival.

"Slower, More Miraculous Returns" III
David Jardine

Imagine. "To find it here, where it seems impossible that one life even matters" (Bronwen Wallace, 1989, p. 111). We have seen it happen, again and again. We've seen it tried and failed, too, make no mistake. But there is something to be said for failing, too, in something that has some good to it, and to let students see that this, too, is our lot:

> What is the real work? I think that it is important, first of all, because it is good to work. And that all of us will come back again to hoe in the ground, or gather

wild potato bulbs with digging sticks, or skin a pole, or scrape a hive. We're never going to get away from that. We've been living in a dream that we're going to get away from it, that we won't have to do it again. Put that out of our minds. We'll always have to do that work. So that's real. The real work is what we really do. And what our lives are. And if we can live the work we have to do, knowing that we are real, and that it's real, and that the world is real, then it becomes right. And that's the *real work:* to make the world as real as it is, and to find ourselves as real as we are within it (Gary Snyder, 1980, p. 81–2)

There is a joy hid in thinking of pedagogy as precisely such a joy. Relief and freedom in it. And then, in practice, singing, repeating, documenting, pitching harmonies and solos and choruses of Ravens and startling and sudden Grouse scurries. Real work.

Schools are tough work no matter which way you slice it. To be simply exhausted over the relentless and accelerating trivializations, panics and distractions is unbecoming of teachers, of students and of coming-to-know itself.

To have, even momentarily, times of real, tough work, is a joy. And the weariness that comes from giving ourselves over to it is itself a joy.

Glimpses of cool lakes.

Finding Myself in the Measure of Things: Introduction to "A Modern Hunting Tradition" III
Jodi Latremouille

I am mindful that "forgetting the animals leads to the animals forgetting about us" (Joe Sheridan & Dan "He Who Clears the Sky" Longboat, 2006, p. 377). Similarly, when I think of traditions passed down from elders to youth, I consider how they are constantly renewed in the attention given to them by each new generation. As youth coming into traditions, I hope that we may try to challenge and question everything that has been handed down to us, while our elders may wait patiently for us to sort things out, sometimes pushing back, other times conceding, always listening. If a balance is achieved, we find our tradition constantly renewed in the measure of things. What possibilities arise when we learn to walk softly, to entice the animals out of hiding, to spot cougar tracks in the snow? What does it mean, pedagogically, for our actions to find their proper measure (Hans-Georg Gadamer, 2004, p. 251) and thus, their consequences (David Jardine, 2008, p. 4) in these wild places and elder traditions that story us? Our human isolation from the earthly landscape is a precarious ignorance. David Abram (1996, p. ix) says, "We still need that which is other than ourselves and our own creations ... ... we are human only in contact, and conviviality, with what is not human."

An earthly tradition.

"Slower, More Miraculous Returns" IV
David Jardine

Oh, this is a fablelike joy and, like fables, it astounds and frightens and delights in turns. The inevitable cool-ways and harms-way and commiserations and gathering we up, talking, listening, noting, writing, and rest. Treasured relations cared for. Bodies of knowledge exercise and tested and made hale with a "continuity of attention and devotion" (Wendell Berry, 1986, p. 33). Hunting traditions. Trails and the arts of tracking down. Sniffs and finds and starting all over. Panics. Bloods. Flesh. Unmarked gravities.

The great curved circles of hearing the story told:

> Caught, as I used to be, by that trick and aunt or uncle'd use of always stopping right at the best part to take a bite of pie, a sip of tea, their way of learning back to look around the table, let the story sink right in. As if they hoped to find that opening in each of us from which, long after we'd been told what happened next, they could begin their slower, more miraculous returns (Bronwen Wallace, 1989, p. 13).

Abode. And biding. Place as a spot of wait and rest and attentiveness and the work proper to that place. Of the elders clustered around to tell just the right tale to just the ear cupped just right.

> The ancestors, our *relations*, human and other-wise, are always already amongst us and we amongst them, in the most ordinary of objects or words or images, in the texts, in the trees, in the dreamstates, in the gestures, even in the flesh-ache of muscle-born dry wood for winter and the panicky bugs that scurry over it. Or in the distant, unwarranted and perhaps inevitable fear for one's child, care sometimes gone amuck, monkey-mind in the midst of impermanence. And this is just as true of ravens nearby and long since disappeared, of trees long gone to soils, of the outbreath of this forest, here, now, around me, inhaled under the sun's slow returning (David Jardine, 2019, p. 129).

A Modern Hunting Tradition
Jodi Latremouille

My father, Vern, is the hunter. My mother, Lorna is the cook
Traditional. Cozy. Comfortable
Predictable and grounded, stewed in the crock pot
Savoury, only slightly spicy, unless I get my hands on it
I like my stews the new-fashioned way,
Just a little more exotic

I am a strong, capable woman well-marinated in this tradition
People who know me well half expect me to be a hunter–
Even if only because it challenges my gender role

But I am not a hunter. Well, not anymore.

I learned how to shoot a '22 at the age of 12,

and I once killed a grouse by stoning it to death

Shameful stoning

It was a loud and grisly scene, with me leading a wild pack of elementary-aged children across the barnyard and into the pine trees, hooting and screaming as we tortured and murdered that grouse.
    The moment that cracked me was when it was lying on the ground, unable to move, yet still breathing, eyes half-closed. I knew that as the instigator, I had to take responsibility for what I had done. I killed it with the final stone. We left that grouse in the woods and we never told my parents.
    We never spoke of that day again.
    We knew that we had dishonored the two codes that our hunting family lived by:

1. Do not cause unnecessary suffering.
2. Do not waste one ounce of a life given for your sustenance.

I can walk quietly in the woods. I can identify edible berries and see the signs of danger and promise in the earth. I can smell a campfire a kilometer away, tell time by the sun, and mark a path to return by. I know how to remove a tick embedded in my scalp, and I can build a shelter to keep the night away.

I know how to tie a fly and catch a fish. I can gut a fish and help skin a deer. I know how to pluck a chicken and use every last piece of its flesh and bones for a week of meals.

But I usually leave the killing to others.

Unless I was truly starving, of course, then I would do what I had to do.

I respect it. The killing.

I can observe it. I can participate in the ritual with sadness and gratitude.

But holding a warm animal, a squirming fish, in my hand as the final afterbeat of life drains slowly from its body, is too much for me.

Yes, I am known as "the emotional one" in my family. What of it? Would you rather I be cold, dead-living? Let a gal cry!

So I participate in our family's modern-day hunting ritual. My husband, Jason, is not a hunter, either, but my young daughters are showing interest and I hope that their grandfather will take them 1 day. Grandpa Vern, achy-old and curling up at the fingers like his father did before him, but strong and bush-humping along, beautiful-functional, still has so many things to teach them and learn from them, us. Jason is the "professional venison transportation agent" (a.k.a. a healthy, young and strong body which happens to be willing and to live down the road from his father-in-law) and because he helps pack the kill, our freezer is stocked and re-stocked with moose, deer—and salmon, huckleberries and morel mushrooms—each fall.

Every fall, we wait for the call.

"Ya, I got a moose. He's a big old guy this time, should be good eating though, not too tough. No, he's not too far into the bush, only a couple hundred meters over a little ridge." In Vern-speak, that is about 3 kilometers scrambling over rocky shale, wading through a creek and climbing rope-assisted up a small mountainside.

Vern is no road hunter. To the authentic bushmen of the Nicola Valley, that's almost like cheating. Unless, of course, you were truly starving, then you would take what you could get where it stood.

So, we plan the picnic. These days, we ask, "Is this a kid-friendly moose-packing trip?" And we pack up the snowsuits, hot chocolate, toilet paper, extra socks, snacks, the until-the-next-snack snacks, sleds, campfire kettle, and a full change of clothes for each child, "just in case." It is a little more complicated than it used to be when you'd grab a sandwich and an apple and march off into the bush with your matches, knife and packboard. The bush has taught me what it means to be prepared—if you have the room in your truck, bring it because you never know when you might need it. If you don't have the room, hope for good weather.

The men march out. Vern loves his grandchildren and would sit for hours with them on an anthill talking about ants and clouds and how to braid wild grasses into a wreath to wrap around their curly-top heads, but, "Son, we are wasting daylight. You women can see the trail, it starts right here. We'll meet you there in a few." Usually our fit, happy, childlike-wise mom-grandmother Lorna wants to stay at the truck and build a fire. She likes to sit and visit and drink tea, then go for a little exercise-walk. But she knows me better than that—sigh, she knows—I need action, I need to help with the man–woman work, and without uttering a word, she starts to pack up the lunch and the little ones for our snow-trek in the man-tracks out over the hills to the hanging moose. There are some cougar pawprints right there, but they are not fresh, so we keep the dogs close and walk tall and loud. We wonder if the cougar got any of the meat, but Vern knows to hang it high in the trees out of reach, so we expect that it will be waiting there for us. We haul our babies in the sled to the kill tree, and this time it is only about a half-hour hike. Grandpa Vern wasn't exaggerating for once. When we arrive, the ritual has just begun. The skinning knife is scritch-scratch, scritch-scratching against the steel, and the tiny wisps of new campfire smoke are trailing up into the fir boughs above. Gloves off, jackets put aside. We scatter to find larger pieces of wood as the little ones crouch over Jason's fire-building shoulder, helping.

The skinning. The anatomy lesson. The hide falling away. The familiarity of a human–moose body unveiled of its coat. The tendons, joints, muscles, hair. Bled, cold. Tongue, eyes, guts, heart.

Vern takes his hunkering place at the fire. "Wanna bite of moose heart?" As he slaps his stick-roasted slice into the middle of his cheese sandwich. Vern does the roasting for the little ones. They watch, eyes flame-shiny, as it browns and sizzles. He pulls it off the roasting stick and gently breaks it in two and hands it over. They sit on their kid-log in quiet reverence as the first mouthful satisfies their well-earned gnawing autumn hiking-hunger.

Sometimes I prefer not to be there, because I'd rather after-hear my home-safe, sweaty husband tell the laughing-horror tale of how he almost slipped and fell off a cliff under the weight of a 100-lb moose head. Yes, a moose's head alone can weigh 100 pounds. Imagine the rest of it. Five, sometimes six pieces if he is a big old Mr. Moose, sawed apart and sheathed in their white cheesecloth bag to keep them from getting dirty. Sometimes if you get a good hill, you can be a little bit crazy impractical and hop on to the moose-laden packboard, but be careful of hidden stumps and flailing hooves. When the terrain is right, and he can avoid strapping himself into the packboard under a 150 pounds of moose, Jason will do it the new-fashioned way—winding through the scrawny birch trees, dashing ahead of an out-of-control hindquarter as it plummets down the snowy mountainside. Vern shakes his head and keeps plodding under his burden. We walk ahead and wait for him at the truck. When Grandpa bursts out of the trees a few minutes later, screaming, "Look out! Moose meat on the loose!" we laugh as we dive into the snowbanks. You can, in fact, teach an old dog new tricks. The question is, do you want to?

My daughter saw her first dead animal hanging in my father's shed when she was 2 years old.

She called it "deer parts."

And it bothered her much less than the disembodied deer head trophy that my dad displays in his office.

That says something, now doesn't it?

Mostly, it says to never to put dead animal heads on display in my house (They scare the kids—c'mon, grandpa!) But the kids, too, will learn

I witness the trophy tradition
desecrated by sport hunters who have never eaten their kill
and maligned by activists who have never killed their food

But for my dad it is not a trophy
It is a single body of worship
Of participation in the world
A world that demands our respect

At one time, if our ancestors refused to respect
they would perish—remember that now
It's all one time
Our prey is watching over us

Every time I make a sandwich for a hike in the bush, or help haul a deer, or cook a moose roast, I remember that grouse

That grouse suffered, yes I regret

But it did not go to waste
A coyote dragged it off, cleaned it down to bones and remnants
Some birds picked at the remains, and others used its feathers for a nest
The worms fed off the tiny, dark stain
I, too, will be sustained by the grouse
It will remind me of what I am
What am I, in the terrible and fragile?
I will be as noble as the worm
I will not waste that grouse's life.

Part III

Entangled

Entangled Relations
Jodi Latremouille & Lesley Tait

Before We Begin: From Start to Close

In what follows, we tell the story of how Jodi came to invite Lesley, a close friend and colleague, to contribute to a formal research project as a citable source. Together, we consider what it means to relate ethically with others in this qualitative, interpretive, relational and ecological research. These relations can often (intentionally or not) become severed and misinterpreted by well-meaning institutional policies and procedures intended to predict in advance all possible outcomes so as to (impossibly) protect participants and institutions from all possible harm. We are interested in exploring the ethics of our own research. As is commonplace, we were repeatedly asked to withhold the names of other people, places or institutions. Part of the dilemma we faced in this process was that by withholding names, we deny the specificities and thus the responsibilities of a relationship. It thus becomes anonymous, erased, generalized; it is rendered bereft of accountability, the weight of thoughtful judgment and the intimacy of subjectivity. Our ethical considerations, between us two, Jodi and Lesley, are precisely about facing each other in good relationship.

In order to acknowledge those who contributed to the storyline, we sought permission to cite full names and accurate dates of our communications. When others asked or required that names of people, places or institutions be withheld, it was only ethical to respect that request, and we have done so in what follows, using the terms [Name Withheld] and [Anonymous Institution]. There is also an interesting turn—an important turn—where we see that Lesley is *required* to be anonymous, despite her preference to be fully named in the research. In any other verbatim communications, names of innocent bystanders have been removed, using the term [Unnamed]. In addition, in any case where permission has not been obtained to include the full name of all parties, all dates for verbatim email and text communications (written in italics) have been changed to protect innocent parties and conspirators alike.

In this account, we engage fiction as research practice (Patricia Leavy, 2013), to relate the story through a combination of writing forms: a truthful narrative account of the history of our friendship, a fictionalized email exchange with the ethics committee of an [Anonymous Institution], and some real-life possibilities for good relations in educational research. We intentionally mix up fact with fiction, weaving citable sources and verbatim, precisely dated emails with quiet, sometimes secret wonderings, layered footnote asides and resounding admonitions from on high. We layer and juxtapose figments and fragments of perhaps un/true conversations that have been extracted, extrapolated and sometimes absurdly exaggerated to the point of nonsense, to highlight the challenges and impossibilities of pursuing "truth" in a relational world that is made of only stories (Thomas King, 2003). As this research is ongoing, and our friendship will last (we hope) long into the future, we cannot tell you how the story ends.

"The truth about stories is that's all we are" (p. 2).

And my note, scrawled in the margin, from years ago: "how do we honour stories—judgment, care, non-violence."

Lesley: Jodi and I have a story to tell. The neat thing about stories is you start where they start and then follow them until they come to a close. Not a finish, not an end, but a close.

Jodi: My current research project considers teachers as eco-intellectuals, who engage in deep scholarly study, contemplation, and interdisciplinary thinking as they consider the deeper purposes of public education and their own role within it. As a non-Indigenous woman working in schools and in universities, I question the largely Eurocentric, linear and rational understanding of the intellect, bringing social and economic justice together with ecological and Indigenous sensibilities to inquire poetically and narratively into the possibilities for collaborative critical and creative thinking, rich teaching practices, and learning communities. Land-based knowledge, spiritual understandings, respectful relations, reciprocity, and rigorous academic inquiry are at the heart of the conversations with my participants, who bring their diversity of backgrounds, cultures, and life experiences into juxtaposition with my own. In my desire to "acknowledge and honour the significance of the relationships we have with others, how our histories and experiences position us in relation to one another, and how our futures as people in the world are similarly tied together" (Dwayne Donald, 2016, p. 11), I wonder what it might take for teachers as eco-intellectuals to restore the intimacy and responsibility of ethical relationships within an institutional setting. Deep "ethical relationality" (p. 11) cannot be contained by or properly described in a policies and procedures manual. In our collaborations, we must "write" this "manual" for and with each other, weaving and re-weaving our relations with each other in the best ways we know how.

Instead of conducting a formal recorded interview with Lesley, including all the permissions and paperwork that this would entail, in the end, as you will see, we decided to write instead about the experience of seeking permission from the institution to do so. There is a feeling of conspiracy to our work together, not as outlaws trying to break the rules simply for the sake of being rebellious, but rather as friends breaking out of tired logics and breathing new "bouquets" (Ivan Illich, 1998, p. 6) of possibilities into the free spaces. I ask, "What possibilities might emerge when these relations are well known, well entangled, and well cared for?"

Conspiracy: Fr. *conspirer*, common breath. Literally, to breathe together. (OED)

Lesley: I am happy living on the margins in the world of academia. My mother taught me how to live here. There is something about getting invited into the middle. You lose your outside perspective. By necessity. It has to happen. Can't be in two places at once.

To Begin. Tracing Back Through Relations: Scholarly Conspirators and a "Bouquet of Friendship"

Jodi: Lesley and I have been good friends and scholarly conspirators for several years now. We are currently co-authoring a book with David Jardine, our dear friend and mentor of many years. I originally intended to invite Lesley, as one of the most eco-intellectual teachers I know, to be a participant in this research study. But there is this: our entwined past–present–future relations might seem, from an institutional standpoint, just a bit too . . .

messy.

complicated.

contaminated.

fuzzy.

even inconceivable.

And there is this, from Ivan Illich (1998), regarding the spirit of friendship: "Only people who face one another in trust can allow its emergence. The bouquet of friendship varies with each breath, but when it is there it needs no name. [. . .]

spirit
[. . .]
soul
[. . .]
co-breathing
[. . .]
con-spiracy
[. . .]
a common atmosphere" (p. 7).

Conspiracy. Common breath.

"A Referendum"
David Jardine

Referendum. Literally, "a thing brought back" (OED) to mind, to memory, raised up as we speak back and forth, summoned, perhaps.

David Smith sent me a link to David Zvi Kalman's (2020) article, itself time-stamped March 11, 2020, 9:40 AM:

> In the early 1990s, some forgotten soul on the internet coined the term "meatspace" to refer to the offline area that most of us think of as "the real world." The term has always been only half a joke (David Zvi Kalman, 2020, n.p.).

David Zvi Kalman's meditations on religious gatherings contain great echoes even for those not so inclined:

Whereas offices are for working and schools are for learning, most of the purpose of going to synagogue is simply *to be present*: to be present with others, and to be present for the performance of ritual. For offices and schools, physical presence is a means; for religious spaces, presence is the goal. Whether that goal is reached with a virtual substitute is emphatically not just a question of resources and convenience; it is, instead, a referendum on the limits of virtual presence itself (David Zvi Kalman, 2020, n.p.).

I immediately thought, yes, I don't wander out in the woods as a means to something else, but to be present there. I don't puzzle over these very words this very morning in order to be finally done with these matters and rid of these thoughts, but in order to cultivate their ever-presence so I won't forget this entangle that we're in. I fret over the Fibonacci series and marvel at sunflower seed spiral arrangements, not to replace experience with words, but so that when I am in their presence, their marvel and mine "increases in being" (Hans-Georg Gadamer, 2004, p. 40).

David Jardine, 9:52 AM, Sun Mar 15, 2020: I think [David Zvi Kalman] correctly characterizes schools at their worst, but not at their best. Presence to each other. A theory of the intimacy of reading, too, I'd say ... perhaps why reading was once done out loud with breath as its carriage. Why we stop over flowers as a practice.

Jodi Latremouille, 10:03 AM, Sun Mar 15, 2020: Yes. At their worst, exactly. We are proposing schools at their best, as spiritual places, yes? Just living, presence, being together. And the coronavirus is a terrible metaphor for neoliberalism at its worst—the very embodiment of fragmentation and individualization and virtual life usurping real life, also at its worst. The Italians singing from the balconies ... we won't stand for it. Now, all issues require that kind of solidarity and understanding that we are nothing without community.

We can hear echoes, here, of Ivan Illich's (1998, n.p.) thoughts on conspiracy and the hushed voices of those gathering, and it gives me a nice pause over Jodi's use of the word "spiritual." Breath-places:

The impending loss of spirit, of soul, of what I call atmosphere, could go unnoticed. Only persons who face one another in trust can allow its emergence. The bouquet of friendship varies with each breath but when it is there it needs no name. For a long time, I believed that there was no one noun for it, and no verb for its creation. Each time I tried one, I was discouraged. Discreet silence about the issue I am raising seemed preferable to creating a misunderstanding. Then I suddenly realized that there is indeed a very simple word that says what I cherished and tried to nourish, and that word is peace. But to embrace this, one has to come to understand the origin of this peace in the conspiratio, a curious ritual behavior almost forgotten today (Ivan Illich, 1998, n.p.).

And we need to come to understand how "conspiracy" has come to mean precisely the opposite of peace had or sought. As happens so often in this terrain, old lessons teach new lessons to what we are currently enduring and suffering.

To re-cite: "Cultivate love for those who have gathered to listen" (Tsong-Kha-Pa, 2000, p. 64) or for those cuddled and huddled together around words carried on the breath about peace, about breath and Ravens breathing in air.

The Earth is all one body, all one breath. Entangled relations. Now I can begin to properly figure my own aging against the proper measure.

This cultivation of love and affection and kinship and kindness is no superordinate act. Why? Because it is love that has gathered us together in the first place, in amongst the birds and maps and commiserations over e-mail.

Peace and love are, daresay of course, both cause and effect. Don't let panic shorten your air. We are here. We are here.

Jodi: Our friendship traces a long way back to Jackie Seidel and David Jardine, through our participation in a Master of Education certificate program at the University of Calgary[1]. Hosted off-campus, each certificate ran over an entire year,

---

1 Drs. Jackie Seidel and David Jardine offered a series of Interdisciplinary cohort-based, year-long, four-course Master of Education certificates through the Werklund School of Education at the University of Calgary. The first certificate, entitled *Roots of Classroom Inquiry* (2012–2013 and 2013–2014), explored: *two interrelated roots of scholarly work* that have a supportive and elaborative affinity to authentic and engaging classroom inquiry: interpretive inquiry or "hermeneutics" and ecological consciousness. Although these two roots originate and extend far beyond most educational literature, each of them provides a rigorous theory of how knowledge operates and is cultivated in the lives of students and teachers. Understanding them can be of immense practical importance to the conduct of rich, rigorous, practicable, and adventurous classroom work for students and teachers alike. (Jackie Seidel & David Jardine, 2012). This second certificate, entitled *Storytelling in the Ecological Heart of Curriculum* (2013–2014 and 2014–2015), explored:the relationships between ecological consciousness in a vibrant, heartening understanding of curriculum. In contrast to some versions of "environmental education," we use the term "ecological consciousness" to point to a way of experiencing all and any aspects of the living disciplines entrusted to teachers and students in schools as constituted by living relations of dependent co-arising and narrative patterns of interdependence, of gatherings, places, plots and ancestries. Parallels between ecological consciousness and both hermeneutics and threads of Buddhist epistemology/ontology will be explored in order to broaden their applicability to sustainable classroom practices. (Jackie Seidel & David Jardine, 2016, pp. 249–250)

and was based on a cohort model. Although the certificates were independently offered, many students who finished the first year (Roots of Classroom Inquiry) immediately enrolled in the second year of the program (Storytelling as the Ecological Heart of Curriculum). In their time together, the graduate students—mostly practicing teachers—had the opportunity, to linger, to dwell, to discuss and ponder readings and curriculum questions through the sensibilities of ecological pedagogy, Indigenous ways of knowing, Buddhist pedagogy, hermeneutics. The class was a refuge, a place to breathe together, a place for whispering our common shared secrets and wonderings and suspicions. We oriented ourselves to place, to storytelling, to our own histories and classrooms and ancestries. Our conversations were heartbreaking, controversial, challenging, hopeful, tired, loving.

Our teachers were everywhere.

When I first joined partway through the second year-long certificate, "Storytelling as the Ecological Heart of Curriculum," I was a stranger entering a cohort of close-knit friends already deep into the work. When I entered on my first day, September 10, 2013, my professor, Jackie, pointed out Lesley across the room, and said, "That's Lesley. You two need to meet." Jackie intentionally paired us up in a reading group that year.

Lesley: I hate to evoke an allusion to Anne of Green Gables and the kindred spirits, but you must when you must. There were over twenty of us in the class, fewer still who took up Abram together. Elder Saa'kokoto speaks often of the spirit of things, in museums, in our homes and the honoring and recognition of these when we greet them again. Our spirits recognize each other. I don't love this yet, but maybe work with it a bit? Help!! I am trying to say that you and I spin well within each other's orbit because we have the same pull. There were so many people I connected with over the course of those 2 years, but very few who have stuck. Especially stuck in this way. Is that a spirit thing? Maybe. Using spirit here makes it sound like cheerleaders. Maybe that's part of it!

I sensed there was a whole lot going on here that I could not get my head around. "Like a stranger, they will not sit down and tell you everything immediately," Leroy Little Bear says. "Only when the rocks begin to know you will they tell you their story." (Don Hill, 2008, p. 42)

And So ...

Jodi: Over the next ten months, our class read David Abram together. Then we read Wendell Berry. And Cynthia Chambers. Lesley and I launched a collaborative writing project with our group, that never really turned into much of anything. Then we read Maxine Greene. And David Smith. And then we all went on a road trip together to Banff, where we met Dwayne Donald. Then Lesley and I went on another road trip together, up to Maskekosihk Enoch Cree Nation, for a holistic education course with Kehte-aya Bob Cardinal and Dwayne Donald. I stayed with Lesley at her in-laws' house, every second weekend for an entire semester. I was a little afraid in that dark basement bedroom, to tell the truth, with the dusty, creaking furnace and elusive light switches, but it was a cozy and comfortable bed. We had Korean food together. We got lost in the woods together, sat in sweat together, and once, we almost got stuck in the mud together driving off-road in my little VW Golf. We recorded a métissage together. Then we presented at conferences together. And then we vacationed together. And now we can be comfortable in silence together, too. Except there's not much silence between us—there's always just too much to talk about!

Lesley: Time not measured in kilometer signs,
but in conversation
It is thoughts that move through the hourglass
when we get together, not sand

We started eating Korean food together
Kimchi, rice, bee bim bap
Some relationships fade
Others stay

People get caught going to the sign to learn about the rock instead of going to the rock itself. In fact, there are pictographs on the rock that I don't think many people notice or even see because they don't spend time with the rock. They spend more time with the sign. (Ryan Heavy Head, 2015)

These are messy, complicated relationships
It's not about feigning perfection

Jodi: Lesley pollinates my thinking with her stories, her love for language and the land and life and rocks in pockets. She is a busy woman, often too busy to write more than a couple of pages at a time. But when she speaks and writes, her words, too, release me, and layer over the extraneous chatter. I am reminded of what is most important. We sometimes attempt to record chats in her car while driving up to Edmonton for visits with Kehte-aya Bob, or we sometimes plunk down in the middle of a bustling restaurant, with too-loud music blaring over Lesley's shoulder, an over-attentive server interrupting us every few minutes to fill our drinks, and busy inner-city highway traffic whipping by outside the window. No matter. We both understand that our conversation hasn't started just now, nor will it end here. In our conversation, we have no illusions or desires for "objectivity" (aka severing the heart from the mind). We like to talk about river walks, and being good neighbors, and ceremonies and homes and families, and taking folks out onto the land, and growing things that become our teachers. We sometimes visit places together. We smudge together. We sit by the lake and watch our kids play together. She points out the wolf willow along the highway.

Lesley: she takes care of me
not in the motherly sense
but in the spiritual sense
A mutual support system
born from necessity
now fed with love and time
and writing

Jodi: When I asked Lesley if she would be willing to contribute her thoughts to my research project on teachers as eco-intellectuals as a citable source, she had already said yes before I could finish my invitation.

Lesley: "Anything for you, nitotem (Cree: my friend)."

Jodi: Likewise, my friend.

Manifesting Real Possibilities for Permissions and Consent: "Leaning In, Head to Head, Chatting and Laughing"

> "If it actually exists, it *must* be possible" (Patricia Clifford, as cited in David Jardine & Jackie Seidel, 2014, p. 2).

Jodi: When I began my research project, I had originally intended for Lesley to be interviewed as a formal participant. I had reflected on the process of gaining "consent" (aka permission), in good ways.

Lesley: Starting in the formal way we are supposed to
Get formal clearance
Get the papers signed
Not in the friend way . . .?
Not in the tobacco way . . .?

Not in the wine way . . .?
darn

Jodi: I imagined that I would invite Lesley by saying something like, "Would you like to participate in my research?" (Which I did).

Lesley: And I would say, "Anything for you, friend!" (Which I did).

Jodi: And then, I would ask, "Who should I talk to for 'formal consent' (aka support) to do this research with you?" (Which I did).

Lesley: And I would tell you, "Just ask [my Unnamed Director]." (And that is exactly what happened).

And so, there's this real-possibility glimpse of a small, early email exchange with Lesley's [Unnamed Director] . . .

On Wed 2020-01-03 3:44 PM,[2] Jodi Latremouille wrote:[3]

Dear [Unnamed Director], (see Ursula le Guin, 1985)[4] I am contacting you today to seek your approval to conduct a research interview and an optional focus group with a colleague and close friend, Lesley Tait. I have secured [Anonymous Institution]'s approval.
I am conducting a qualitative interpretive study that inquires into the meaning of teachers as "eco-intellectuals," that is, teachers who approach their work with an orientation towards interwoven social justice and environmental sensibilities. This research

---

2   In any case where the author is named in emails and text conversations, the communications have been reproduced with permission.
3   In this section, the emails and text conversations (written in italics) are verbatim, except in some cases where they have been edited for length. No additions have been made, except where indicated using square brackets. All authors have been named, and dates are accurate. See footnote # for the exception regarding the emails from the [Anonymous Institution].
4   Ursula Le Guin (1985) writes about a reversal of the Biblical story of Adam naming "woman" as well as the animals. In this story Eve "Unnames" the animals as a freeing gesture, to hand back the names that were arbitrarily imposed upon them by humans without the animals' consent. In the context of research, the stripping of one's name (in whole or in part) from the "data" is intended as protection against abuses; we must not use others' names without their consent. However, this power to strip away names, when applied indiscriminately and without attention to proper relations, can result in an erasure of one's ancestries, histories, place-stories. It can be a move to power, a move to control all possible outcomes, which actually makes good relations impossible. My named ancestries and roles give me courage to rise up to the task of entering honestly into good relations with others.
    David Jardine: Take a moment, then, to consider all over again the removal of First Nations names in residential schools and the unmarked residential school graves.

is informed by critical, ecological and Indigenous ways of knowing, with land-based knowledge, spiritual understandings, responsible relations and reciprocity at the heart of the work.
I am attaching the formal request letter to the [Unnamed Director]1.
I think of these interviews more like conversations, and I hope that they will provide an opportunity for professionals to share their experiences around this form of pedagogy and study, as well as celebrate exemplary practices in education. I look forward to hearing from you.
Best wishes,
Jodi Latremouille

>Thu 2019-01-06 8:42 AM, [Unnamed Director] replied:
>*Hi Jodi,*
>*Your research looks really interesting.*
>*I support Lesley participating.*
>*I really think this is important work, and I hope it goes well.*
>*All the best,*
>*[Unnamed Director].*

Jodi: Simple and straightforward, just as I hoped. Of course, if we were to imagine all of the procedures and protocols of the mythical institutional domain on this "research participation" (aka conversation), all possibilities would of necessity be foreclosed, controlled, known in advance (David Smith, 1991, p. 187), nailed down—just for safety's sake, of course. There would be the small matter of the [Anonymous Institution]'s Ethics Committee Approval. The institutional ethics paperwork that I would complete in preparation for this project would clearly state that Lesley would be "free to withdraw at any time" (aka, if you change your mind, your secrets are safe with me). She would sign a "consent form" (aka anything for you, nitotem) to participate in a "1–1.5 hours maximum" (aka the length of a nice dinner together) "semi-structured interview" (aka a good chat over tea and muffins). To be honest, it would take a 100-page contract to properly nail down all of the "possible positive and negative psychological impacts" (aka the obligations, the excitements, the hurts and heartbreaks, the challenges and the admirations) or our entangled relations. Finally, she would be required to sign a separate form stating that she would have her [Name Withheld] (aka erased)[5] as per the established policy and procedure of the [Anonymous Institution]. She would be given permission to use her first name only. For safety's sake.

---

5   Note this turn: Lesley's [Name Withheld] was not at her own request.

Lesley.
Just
Lesley.

"isn't that . . . no, not ironic. tragic" (David Jardine, personal email communication, March 10, 2019, 8:44 AM).

"Through the Recess, the Chalk and Numbers" I
David Jardine

A person who wants to understand must question what lies behind what is said. He must understand it as an answer to a question. If we go back behind what is said, then we inevitably ask questions beyond what is said. We understand the sense of a text only by acquiring the horizon of the question—a horizon that, as such, necessarily includes other possible answers. The meaning of a sentence . . . . necessarily exceeds what is said in it. (Hans-Georg Gadamer, 2004, p. 370)

Because he is pointing to something, he has to exaggerate, whether he likes it or not . . . . to leave out and to heighten. (p. 113)

All interpretation is highlighting. (p. 400)

What happens when the interpretive urge meets coincidence? What happens when that urge outruns its pale, just like Hermes asks us to do? Jumps the fence, shall we say? Breaches the gate, the held, tucks itself down in through secrets, through safety's sake, and me, here, old enough to take that picture at a glance and arc back in memory, 1966, me 15 at the time, "through the recess, the chalk and numbers" (Van Dyke Parks, 1966). These uprisings demand that current circumstances share common breath and air-appearance.

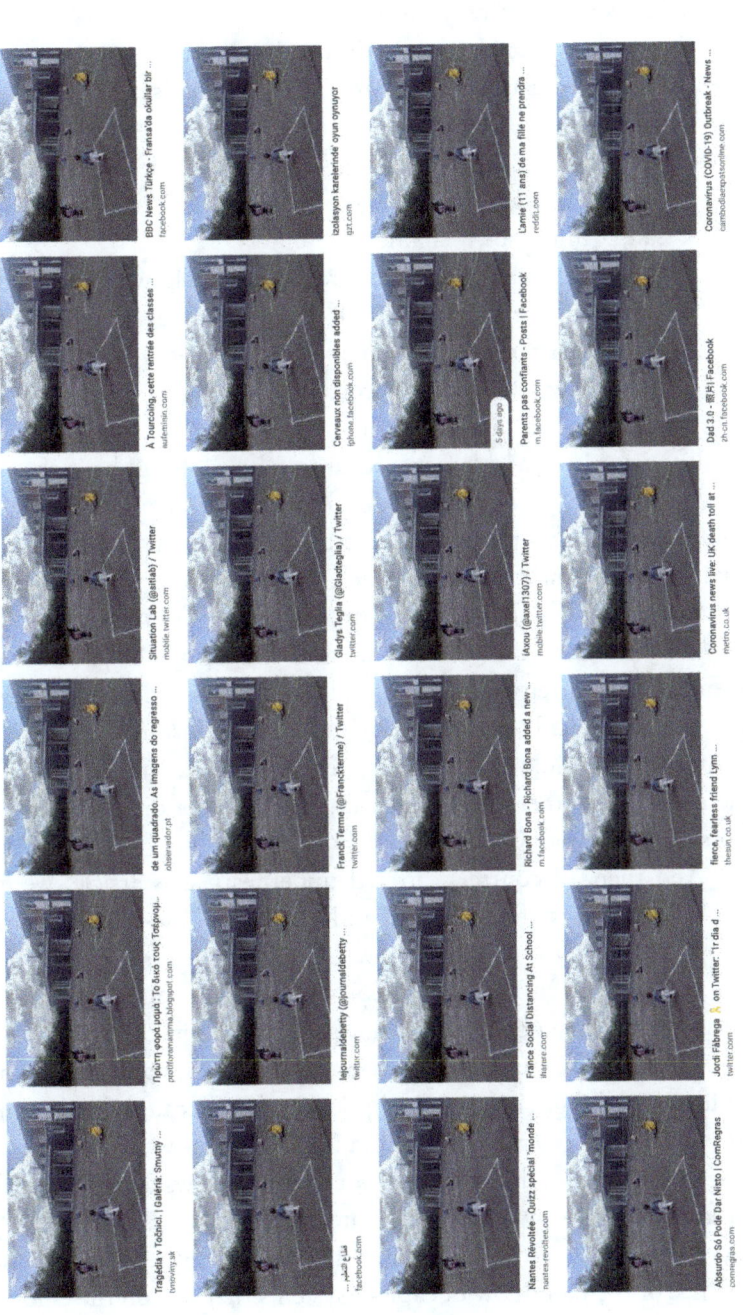

"Possible positive and negative psychological impacts" that outrun you before you can catch your breath.

You can't expect Hermes to do much more than grin when we trip over ourselves over this picture and allow the moist sentimentalities of our human being to drip and drool.

Coyote becomes the hidden giggle of our knee-jerks.

"Heart-breaking," "forced," "shock," "outrage" "like out of a horror film," "sad," "inhuman," "shameful," "outcry."

" 'I can't get over this,' said Laurence De Cock, who posted the picture on Twitter." (Peter Allen, 2020). Yes you can. Study.

And all these terms in one small online article from the online version of the Daily Mail found effortlessly, shared flirtingly over g-mail chat between father and son over morning coffee and reminiscences over small-town raising and laments regarding how "things have changed."

And, make no mistake, I deeply feel each one of these things in meditating on this playground picture, right down to skin and bone, having been an intimate part of such locales for so very, very many years.

And I deeply understand the urge to step right into this emotionally fraught mess and commiserate, suggest alternatives or provide encouragement to children and teachers alike in these weird, weird times.

It is so tragic. It is not right, not right. But this, in and of itself, does not free me to think, to consider, in responding like this. I'm just stuck in the muck with other flailers, each urging the other on. Conspiracy at its worst. Look at that! Oh dear!

And then, of course, scattered underneath this article, we get the bright-light blares of its real kith and kin, its real life-blood, its real life:

Chrissy Metz is so skinny now and looks like a model.

After 13 years of working at CNN, this is Don Lemon's annual salary.

Netflix just canceled these shows—was your favorite axed?

. . . .. alongside flashing side-bar ads that bounce and skitter and flirt with eye-catching, click-baiting opticality only because I had to turn off ad-blocker to get to the "news" item itself. That so-easily-forgotten adage that the purpose of this website is not to deliver news to me, but to deliver me to advertisers by means of whatever "news" baits clicks. The photo and the laments are nothing more that delivery systems of the real sustenance of the bloodflow of capital, systems that rely on the emotionally over-wrought dull-mindedness of reader's reactions and commiserations.

The children in the playground are simply a contagious virus that keeps the flow coming back and back again for another tsk-tsking look-see. Welcome back. Here's an ad for hand sanitizer. We—I—are all caught in a whole other contagious virus.

And then all of this is at work precisely because I sit here, squat in my own chalked-off, "in touch," keyboarded isolation. Cell-blocked. A referendum. And how much, after all, is enough of these silly, teasing puns and ironies and over-egged sentimental and heartfelt responses?

How about this for a knee-slapper?

France's schools open today as parents are still on the fence (www.euroweeklynews.com).

Get it? Funny how using language around to bait each other, to make a gag out of chalk-marked fences on school playgrounds is so easy and so commonplace these days. It is, in part, triggered by, I expect, an unconscious desire to find some sort of linguistic interconnection and relief to something that is occurring, some "meaning" of any sort at all that will open up the sense of isolation and cold containment, reveal the entanglements, the affections, the love.

Perhaps even simply some momentary distraction. It could also just be bad writing. Puns as surface-level "profundities" where no depth is sought or especially wanted or especially available. These, along with mewling like "oh my goodness" are signs of interpretation gone wrong.

There is no methodological mediator, here, to adjudicate these matters or to curtail them in advance of the venturing of them out into the open and then seeing if you can live with the consequences.

A Serious Conversation About Real Possibilities . . .

On Wed, Mar 6, 2019 at 2:26 PM Jodi Latremouille is writing to Lesley Tait and David Jardine:

Jodi: *[I just met] with some brilliant woman [Name Withheld].*

David (to Lesley and Jodi): *'She' can be quoted anonymously [in our upcoming book],*

yes . ?.if you get 'her' permission to quote 'her' at length in a context different than your original research ethics 'cover story' [meant in a nice way] . . . well. we/you/I/ Lesley could quote this conversation at length . . .! wouldn't THAT be interesting, eh, to have a voice left anonymous by us on purpose? I'm serious!

Jodi: *Tell me more . . . The cover story is exactly that. What can we uncover in making* these relations well known, well entangled, and well taken care of? I am already wondering how the hell anyone gets anyone done when these relations are supposed to be severed before we can do any "legitimate" research.

David: *this is getting weirder all the time!*

i know! Fictionalize both names, yours and hers. and we can put it in the book without explanation! two dream figures murmuring together.

Jodi: *Haha! Yes, the fictional and magical, mystical L and J! Isn't this weird?!?*

David: *maybe two animal names would work. it is weird, alright.*

Entangled Relations: "And Then I'll Hold It for You, While You Braid, Too"

Under these circumstances, the idea of submitting an ethics application for a project that is focused on ethical relationality, to strangers, for an "unbiased review" *(aka an erasure of relations)* in order to speak with my friend and record her words seemed ... unethical, actually. In contemplating having Lesley as a participant, I struggled with many questions. Were our relations so entangled that we shouldn't be speaking to one another about important topics? Or we could speak but we couldn't write it down for anyone else to see? Or we could write it down but not speak one another's names out loud? Would the data be ... "contaminated"? *(aka pollinated*—sounds kind of exciting!). How would I properly credit [Name Withheld] for her insights? How would it change our relationship if we signed a contract? I wondered about all of this.

Lesley : I didn't wonder. Blind faith. I wish I had a better word for belief, faith, trust. I always find myself hampered by language but here we are at faith nonetheless. Faith in Jodi. Faith that the kimchi and bee bim bap could not be overwritten by safety and the concerns of others. 40 hours in a car (gosh, I should really calculate this. I bet it's higher than we think). That's called putting in your time.

> We approach our lives on different trajectories, each of us spinning in our own separate, shining orbits. What gives this life its resonance is when those trajectories cross and we become engaged with each other, for as long or as fleetingly as we do. There's a shared energy then, and it can feel as though the whole

universe is in the process of coming together. I live for those times. No one is truly ever "just passing through." Every encounter has within it the power of enchantment, if we're willing to look for it. (Richard Wagamese, 2016, p. 38)

Jodi: I also remembered the story of another good friend and brilliant [Name Withheld], who once participated willingly and full-heartedly in a research interview, and felt later that her deep thinking, her scholarly work, her ideas, had been ... "aggregated" and "shared anonymously" (aka stolen). She vowed that she would never participate in a research interview unless her full name could be published, and that she would be given credit for her work. I listened to her story. I heard this story, and I wanted to do better. Our teachers, human and more-than-human alike, should be properly credited for the gifts that they give us so freely and humbly. And so, in my original research ethics application, I had listed the option for participants to include their "full name and institutional affiliation" (aka who you are and where you are and who your relations are and why that matters) when I shared their stories. And I explained that I would be recruiting through my professional networks, to connect with people who might be known to me prior to the research. For one [Anonymous Institution], though, this was—and from a certain point of view, understandably—a big problem. A big problem that lasted several months of back-and-forth questions, repeated explanations and pointed reminders. As we shall see, in the fictional email exchange that follows.

WAYSTATION III
Medicines Heal Your Heart
Emilia Tait

We pick sage for smudging. It smells good.

Smudge is when you light a match and light the sage and then you take the smoke and bring it to your eyes, ears, heart and everywhere.
So you can see good.
So you talk pretty good.
So you can hear what you need to hear.
You put it on your heart so you are loving.

You give the sage tobacco so the earth can grow it again. It smells good.
You can call it medicine.
Medicines heal us. Rest is medicine. Rest is a medicine cause your body doesn't have to fight and can relax and heal.

Ceremonies are medicine. They are medicine because the heal your heart. Healing your heart is when you calm down and make yourself feel better.

Kehte-aya Bob Cardinal from Maskekosihk Enoch Cree Nation reminds us to ask, "What is missing here?" I have to say that in an institution dedicated to building relationships between and among children, teachers, families, communities, cultures, and the world, one important thing that is often denied is . . . well . . . relations. In the interest of controlling and safeguarding any possible contact that a teacher might have with a researcher, the very possibility of good relations is being erased. From an institutional point of view, it might be nearly impossible to see through to the careful intent of a research project dedicated to building good relations. Given the circumstances, all they could see was threat. Because in a world where everything and everyone must be compartmentalized and controlled, that is what he is trained to see. And we see what we expect to see. With all of the best intentions in the world, of course. And thus, to the institution, in an interview without a rigid set of pre-determined questions, anything could happen, and if they didn't guard against every possible threat, well then, anything would happen. So, the result? An extensive list of questions was procured, with the exact context and situation for each question listed in bullet points. Within this context, what might be possible? How might I conduct an intimate, conspiratorial, relational research project premised on connecting with participants through my "professional networks" (aka my friends)?

"Through the Recess, the Chalk and Numbers" II
David Jardine

With interpretive work, its efficacy, its usefulness is most often only glimpsed, if at all, after the fact of its imaginative ventures and after the fact of its being read and read back by readers who must themselves take their own risk of taking seriously the reading they've read. "It would not deserve the interest we take in it if it did not have something to teach us that we could not know by ourselves" (Hans-Georg Gadamer, 2004,

p. xxxv), and this is not simply and straightforwardly a property of what is written, but a living relationship that must be cultivated between what is written and who is reading it, and when, and why. "The true locus of hermeneutics is this in-between" (Hans-Georg Gadamer, 2004, p. 295). Without the pursuit of that living relationship, we get the blankness of bad schooling, where the worthwhileness of, say, Shakespeare, or Pythagoras, is treated as a given, rather than as something that needs to be accomplished, again and again and again.

The difference between worked and overworked, between breaths of fresh air and gulps of wet-hot, dark breaths of conspiracy theorizing is not only razor thin. These cutting edges shift and move as I shift and move.

So, then, that playground picture of chalk recesses. Many years ago, I flirted with an idea that has since proved more acute than I could have then (originally, in David Jardine, 1992b) imagined:

> The increasing specialization of technical knowledge seems to bring with it the perception that one does not really understand the world, oneself, or others without such knowledge. Because an overwhelming technical knowledge of every conceivable phenomenon is possible, this possibility begins to harbor the perception that one is increasingly out of control if one does not pursue this possibility. One is increasingly in danger of no longer understanding. And this perception of being out of control without technical knowledge, of being "left behind," leads precisely to the anxiety that drives us to relentlessly pursue it, since it is precisely technical knowledge that offers us the promise of relative control. In this way, the mere existence of technical knowledge as a possibility creates the need for that possibility by engendering the anxiety for which it sets itself up as the remedy, not the cause. Technical-scientific discourse offers itself up as a remedy to the difficulties of life. Th[is] . . . . raises the question as to whether technical-scientific discourse, rather than simply being a remedy to life's difficulties, has rather come to recast the nature of life's difficulties into precisely the sort of thing for which a technical solution is appropriate; that is, life's difficulties are technical problems requiring a "technical fix." (Jardine, 2000c, p. 117)

So, take a leisurely deep breath. There have been many reports of how the manner of human living is causing the Earth to manifest responses. And don't forget, every single one of these is most probably no longer accessible online. I've left the URLs here on purpose as a sort of unmarked reminder of the pace of memory loss, of disinterest. The text in each case was a news-item title:

Spreads of lions laying on warm paved roads in South Africa (https://www.cnn.com/travel/article/lions-kruger-lockdown-scli-intl/index.html).

Sea turtles thriving on empty Florida beaches (https://www.cnn.com/2020/04/18/us/thriving-sea-turtles-lockdown-florida-beaches-trnd/index.html).

Wild goats taking over Welsh towns (https://www.theguardian.com/uk-news/video/2020/mar/31/goats-take-over-empty-welsh-streets-llandudno-coronavirus-lockdown-video).

Squirrels taking over Santa Monica parks (https://patch.com/california/santamonica/watch-squirrels-take-over-santa-monica-park-amid-coronavirus).

Sheep wandering golf courses in England (https://www.reporter.am/sheep-take-over-golf-course-in-england-act-as-greenskeepers/).

Wild boars on the streets of Barcelona. (https://twitter.com/CarolineLawrenc?ref_src=twsrc%5Etfw%7Ctwcamp%5Etweetembed&ref_url=https%3A%2F%2Ftheconversation.com%2Fcoronavirus-what-the-lockdown-could-mean-for-urban-wildlife-134918).

Shoals of fish back in bluer and clearer canals of Venice (https://www.theguardian.com/environment/2020/mar/20/nature-is-taking-back-venice-wildlife-returns-to-tourist-free-city).

Europe breathing fresher air (https://www.euronews.com/2020/03/30/europe-breathes-fresher-air-under-lockdown-as-coronoavirus-measures-ease-pollution).

Nitrogen Dioxide levels plunging in northern China (https://earthobservatory.nasa.gov/images/146362/airborne-nitrogen-dioxide-plummets-over-china).

A Cryptic Imaginary of (Im)possibilities: "One Holding Steadily While the Other Shifts"

"Don't you love cryptic stories? I do" (Thomas King, 2003, p. 11).
On Thursday 2019-01-20 12:50 PM, Jodi Latremouille wrote to Jackie Seidel:
Hi Jackie, [I finished my] ethics application to the [Anonymous Institution].

I submitted it just now!
Thank you!
Jodi
On Thursday 2019-01-20 1:27 PM, Jackie Seidel replied:
Wonderful! I hope it sails through easily. . .
Jackie

What Never Happened: An Extended and Fictionalized Email Thread
Subject: Research application: Teachers as eco-intellectuals

On [an Imaginary Day], [Name Withheld] would write:

Good afternoon Jodi,
Application received for the [Anonymous Institution]
Approval process . . .
Long time. Long, long time.
An unspecified period of time.
Stay in touch.
(. . . but actually, don't
get
too close.
That would be inappropriate.)

Signed,
[Name Withheld]

PS: The contents of this email and any attachment(s) are confidential and intended for the named recipient only. If you have received this email in error, please notify the sender immediately, delete this email and do not copy, use or disclose it.[6]

---

6   Exception to the previous rule: All emails sent from the [Anonymous Institution] are written in bold italicized font, and fictionalized and only slightly (or more likely very, very) exaggerated, to protect innocent parties. Please imagine that the disclaimer at the bottom of every email from this Institution would read as follows: "The contents of this email and any attachment(s) are confidential and intended for the named recipient only. If you have received this email in error, please notify the sender immediately, delete this email and do not copy, use or disclose it" (Oh no, now I am even more turned around. Can I even reproduce *those* words here? I had better watch my step). All emails from the [Anonymous Institution] have been fictionalized. All names, dates and times, places, the colour of underwear worn, what was eaten for breakfast, the songs that were listened to on the commute to work, the names of all unborn children, and all other identifying features are fictionalized. I repeat, they are fictionalized. Do not believe anything that is written here.

Jodi would reply:

Dear [Name Withheld], thank you for your reply. [.].I will address your questions in the copy/pasted email below.[7]

[Name Withheld] would write:

Hi Jodi:
Please visit our "How to Do Research"[8] **website.**

Director must approve.

    serious protocol to recruit and collect [Anonymous] data.

First Contact: Director.
No touching until
Approved. Director is always touched first, of course.
Also . . .

interview questions
many questions
list any possible questions
always and forever anywhere anywho anywhy questions.
No Surprises: I recommend-command-commend-amend you.

Jodi would reply:
Thank you, I will amend this. I will employ the [Anonymous Institution] Form to inform the Director and get their permission that way.

The list of questions provided for the initial interview encompasses all possible predetermined questions for the possible follow-up interviews as well. As these are all semi-structured interviews, the follow-up questions may be different.

Would you like me to provide anything further for this? I can re-word if needed.

[Name Withheld] would send the following:
Warning: the [Anonymous Institution]
Must Not be Named.

---

7   Exception to the previous rule: All of Jodi's emails in this section (written in italics) are verbatim. Word for word. They are really real, except for the date. They are almost too real, I am afraid. Believe those . . . Or not, it's up to you. But don't tell me years from now you haven't heard this story. You've heard it now (see Thomas King, 2003, p. 61).

8   Since the [Anonymous Institution] cannot be identified, we have not provided the URL for this website. This is to protect innocent parties, of course.

Delete. Delete. Delete.
Not an option.
This is for everyone's safety, I assure you.
Many happy returns,
[Name Withheld]

Jodi would reply:
On the permission form for the participants, it clearly indicates that their level of anonymity must be approved by their Institution.
I would like to be able to include participants' full names, or first names only at the very least, at their choice. I would generalize their location, in order to remove any institutional affiliation or chance that this may be inferred. It does sound like your Institution would approve this level of anonymity, is this correct?

[Name Withheld] would reply:
I must remind you. Please give a Warning: Participants must be Professional. Conduct themselves by the Code.
                                    (hint: this message is written in code.
Check your anonymous decoder ring for further instructions).

You must make them sign. And initial. And pinky swear.

Take great care,

[Name Withheld]

Jodi would reply:

I take the Code of Conduct and the creation and protection of good relations within an institution very seriously. My research is based in ecological and Indigenous principles, and I see it as my deep responsibility to honour and respect the participants, their professional relationships with others, and the important work that they do in schools. I am attaching the revised application and relevant attachments.

Jodi: What I would not anticipate in this imaginary scenario would be the sheer heartbreak of having a research project—devoted to good relations, responsibility, trust, and love for the world—be so deeply misunderstood, mistrusted and questioned. I imagined that I would, on a certain level, understand that an Institution has a legal obligation to protect their members, but often more pertinently, their own Institutional Image. I imagined that I would understand that there may have been abuses committed by researchers with misplaced intentions and incriminating evidence.

Entangled | 111

Lesley: Careful
Wheel alignment is critical
Helps to avoid going off the road
Once you are in bushes
Saving you can be tough
Please stayed on the marked trails

[Name Withheld] would send the following:
Attention. We have been alerted:
You suffer from Premature Activation of your Network.
Please note: You may not touch our Members, as you are contaminated.
Do not approach any Members
of the [Anonymous Institution]
(even those in your Prematurely Activated Network)
without prior permission.
Stay away from our Members.
They have not been released yet.

Jodi would reply:
Thank you. Yes, I am aware of the policy and respect the intent. I did not recruit a participant, however as I must employ my professional networks for this type of research, a small number of teachers from your District and elsewhere may already know about my work through prior professional relationships. I fully intend to communicate through supervisors and get their approval first before asking any participants. I look forward to hearing from you soon.
Best wishes,
Jodi

Jodi: Through a back and forth Q & A email chain, it will be revealed that that the reviewer will find out that I have known the "unnamed participant" (Lesley Tait) for an unspecified amount of time already, (aka I had "prematurely activated my network") and that under no circumstances will I be allowed to communicate with her before I will receive the imaginary formal approval from the institution and from her Director.

[Name Withheld] would write:

Hi Jodi. I repeat:
The policy prohibits
premature activation of your network.
Approval. Paperwork. Pre-Approval. Pre-Paperwork

hitherto-wherefore-furthermore-whenceforth- ...
You are bypassing-evading-sidestepping-skirting-circumnavigating-eluding-outwitting-cheating
Procedures.
Only. Ever. Touch the Director first.
Stay away from our Members.
Politely,
[Name Withheld].

Jodi would reply:
Understood, thank you [Name Withheld]. This was not intentional, and I recognize that now. Thank you for clarifying.
Jodi

      Jodi: But what if I have a bad day and I need her support?
          What if we want to plan a coffee date?
         What if she wants to share her latest poem?
        Will I have "permission" to talk to her then,
             at that future date?
    And how will I even find out who her [Unnamed Director] is,
        if I am not able to talk to my friend?
           Weirder and weirder ...
   Lesley: What if we go to a sweat at Bob's and accidentally touch?
         What if our toes cross the line?
      I didn't know that there is such a distinct line
          Between research and living
     Kind of thought they were supposed to exist together
            Maybe not
      Research brings us closer to the thing we study
         Which in turns makes it sacred
         Not the other way around
       We can't get close to sacred things
    (Need to maybe reference Shawn Wilson here.
       Found it! *Research is Ceremony* [2008])

(I will need be careful. Watch my step.)

"Through the Recess, the Chalk and Numbers" III
David Jardine

Only. Ever. Touch. The. Director. First. Watch your step. There's a suncurved Coyote half-squint and warm, so warm.

So yes, "getting back to normal." It is easy to imagine that, as with any living body, responses to threat just might include forcing the marginalization, isolation, and abating of those threatening actions. But the full range is here: viruses and the sense of feeling threatened brings out the guns, of course, of course, of the childish men who cannot stand the thought of their Earth-Mother chiding them.

And, through this recess into the bilge-murks of dark threat-water, full of all our inherited and invented and real and imagined psycho-pathologies of real and perceived threats: viruses, wild animals, women, dark skin, breached borders and boundaries. And even this, a trickster sun hot near an empty bench, ears back just in case:

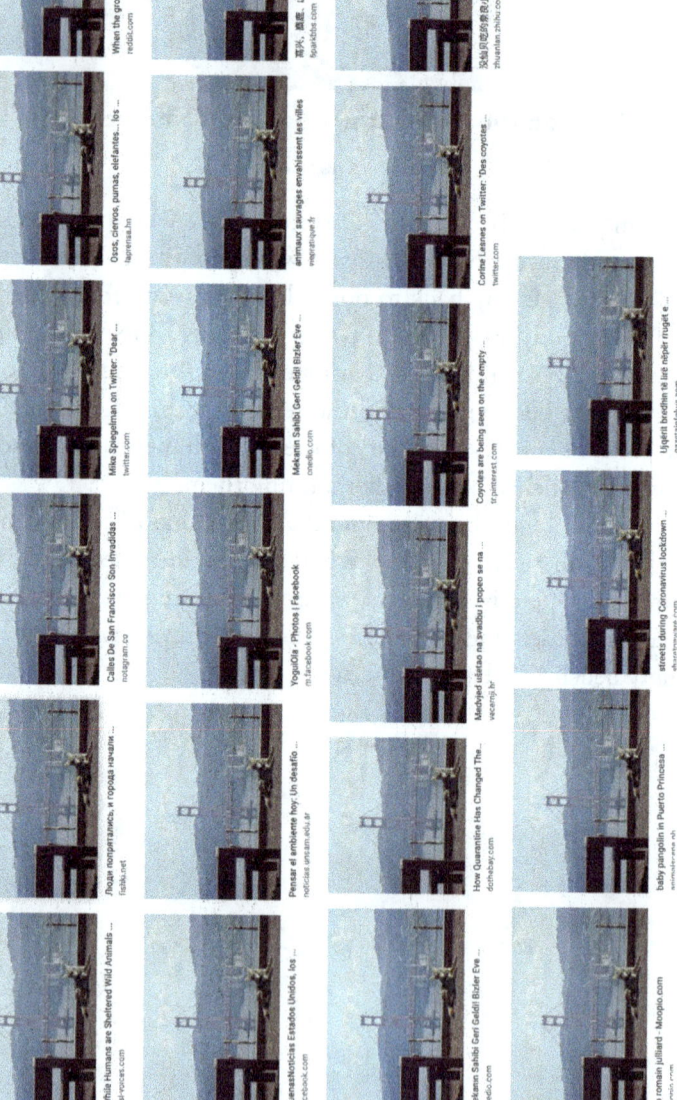

This is how an immune system works.

The satellite pictures of clearing skies during the recent pandemic are ripe for such animistic speculations, that the Earth has pushed us to cure itself of our human excesses and has given us ruddy and simple proof of these matters.

And part of the proof of these matters is not just Coyotes basking in the sun, but also the gone-viral photos of armed and confederate-flag masked two-footeds with their weapons on the steps of Michigan's legislature.

Blunt edge: all men with their unzipped weapons out, protesting, in Donald Trump's words, "that woman from Michigan" who he never otherwise names.

[Governor Gretchen Whitmer, by the way, put in brackets so as not to scare the locals].

Blunt edge: If I feel threatened, there must be an enemy that I can be brave and manly about, right? Hard, cold, steely dildos slung over shoulders, out on public display, as psycho-pathologically obvious as the day is long. As the barrels long.

Okay, got it. That woman!

Blunt edge: If a shot actually gets fired, we all know full well that "she made me do it" is just around the corner.

If I feel threatened, I have the freedom and the God-given right to shoot my mouth off and more, if need be.

Welcome back to a normal that never quite left.

Fears of an abnormal proposal are not just silly and reactionary. "For everyone's safety" is not just silly and institutionally punitive. There are real threats. Don't forget the "before" pictures in NASAs satellite photos of clearing skies over Italy and China as we human drew back away from our relentlessnesses.

There really is aliveness and however—much—entangled relations to protect.

A gentle reminder. So hard to summon love for the little boys and their guns and their well-cultivated and easily manipulated fears.

[Name Withheld] would send the following:

Hi Jodi
Thank you for your quick reply.
a bit different, this

abnormal research proposal
trying to understand
access
Who? When?
No, No. We must not have too much access.
You must limit access. Especially any possible access at any time in the future.
It could be very dangerous.
You must limit access. For everyone's safety
as noted in a previous email.
Just a gentle reminder.
Respectfully,
[Name Withheld].

Jodi: Through this process of lengthy descriptions and misunderstandings, and strict warnings to follow institutional procedures long since rendered insensate to what it might mean to live with others in the world, I will wonder, *how did we get here?* Under the circumstances, the well-meant intentions may, with some intense squinting and grimacing, perhaps, be glimpsed. Under the circumstances. But on a deeper level, I will wonder if it is really possible that the institution will be *unable to see the difference?* That *this* work will *not be that?* It certainly will be "a bit different," won't it?

Entangled relations.
Patience, Jackie will say.
Be pedagogical, Jackie will say.
Your research is relational.
Explain carefully. Explain to the Institution.

And then, a text from Lesley, (paraphrased):

Lesley: *Sorry, nitotem. You may be hearing from the [Anonymous Institution] soon.*

[Name Withheld] would send the following:
Hello Jodi
Delayed until further notice. Once again.
Thank you for your patience.
I would like to overlook-oversee-overstep-overview-overkill-overwatch your application. Again.

A bit different, this one.
tiny edits. a few small details.
Please make the following 3,047 tiny changes as requested.
(Oh, and just a quick reminder, in case you forgot: The Institution Shall Remain Anonymous).
Finally, clarify
some of your communication with staff
has come to our department.
With Lesley's permission, I am pasting [your] email communication.
Can you please clarify the following:

Jodi, in an email to Lesley:
"There could be some potential for future co-writing there too."

Please clarify:
what will you do? What about the raw data?
who has access? We prefer no access.
Please clarify.
We understand . . . her own words
Her own story
future learning . . .
and all that
We understand
But generally speaking . . .
You should only use the generalized-depersonalized-sanitized-numbered-aggregated
data.
You shouldn't use the personal-rare-intimate-touchy-feely-squishy-named-raw
data.
Thank you for your patience.
As you know, fragmenting and isolating and severing and chopping and erasing is demanding and time-consuming and important work.
Warm regards,
[Name Withheld]

Jodi would reply:
Dear [Name Withheld], Thank you for your email. I have amended the application based on your tiny edits.

My strong ethical preference is to write with co-authors whose contributions are publicly recognized in the writing.

As my research is based on in-depth conversations with a very small number of participants, I will not be basing the writing on aggregate data, but rather on the anonymized qualitative data.

I hope this answers all of your questions.

I understand that this ecologically based research project might be a bit different from the ones you are used to reviewing, and so I can understand.

I appreciate all of your efforts to ensure that all parties are treated with respect, confidentiality, and care.

Please find attached my [slightly] amended application.

Best wishes,

Jodi

And then . The End of Time Has Arrived

On [An Imaginary Day], [Name Withheld] would write:

Hello Jodi. Congratulations! We have approved your research project. The end of time has arrived.

Please try not to do anything we wouldn't do.

Sincerely,

[Name Withheld].

Jodi would reply:

Much appreciated, [Name Withheld]. I am looking forward to it.

Best wishes,

Jodi

"Through the Recess, the Chalk and Numbers" IV

David Jardine

Take a breath if you're able. Stop.

Look back at that playground photograph, because there is yet another, more pernicious layer lurks behind and beyond this one. I'm going to end abruptly, here, and leave this in your hands. Think back to the "meat space." Think back to the "conspiracies of breath."

Via this weird gone-viral pandemic, we have not only pulled back from our overly enthusiastic ravages of waters and skies and seen the clear evidence of its clearings, clear lessons taught by Coyote teachers, even lessons about our frailties and panicky, unresolved child/animal impotence glinted in guns. But there is something else here.

Look again at that school yard chalked-off, and the tough and wise efforts of teachers to make it a strange game, one hopes, of hope and connection and the entangled relations that remain.

Look again and allow me some interpretive over-reach in an effort to see what comes of it. Those children have become the perfect manifestation of the social isolation for which the technologies of social "interaction" are the solution. It is as if Facebook, in cahoots with the happenstance of a virus, has turned us into precisely what it needs: chalked-off isolates for which it provides precisely the purchasable, surveillable, technological solution. And let me be blunt. My citing of Facebook in this instance will go out of fashion before you know it, because that, too, is how the "cure" maintains that for which it is a cure just enough to make us ripe for the next promise, the next ameliorating purchase.

It is just a coincidence. There are no cahoots afoot here, even though Coyotes at rest in the sun remind us all that tricksters come in many guises. That a virus would, by coincidence, bring about precisely the conditions under which a human technology becomes the cure but that this is precisely because human technological over-reach has precipitated the very conditions under which viruses have become more virulent. . . . . yes, okay, coincidence, then.

Let's invert it, though, and then slip out the back door. It is as if social media technologies were a cure looking for a disease, creating that disease (what? Being out of touch?—a perfect pandemic phrase!). As if all the technological over-reaches of human life in recent decades that have led to pandemic viral distortions feedbacking into our living and distorting the very conditions of our living are now summon precisely that very technological over-reach as the cure for the disease it has caused. There it is, that "heart-breaking photo of nursery children forced to play in isolation chalk squares sparks outcry." It looks, too, just like a recent mosey of mine on the University of Calgary campus, where I, with no cellphone to hand, old, out of touch, seemed like the only one "there," surrounded by dozens and dozens of other beings urgently staying "in touch" at the beep-y urging of their "devices" (etymologically ironic, meaning "the means by which something is divided" [OED]).

Now all of that is "normal." It makes perfect sense and it a tale older than the hills.

We are being remade in the image of the gods we worship, like the white dog and the black dog and which one we feed.

Speaking of Coyotes and dogs we feed, the terrible trial of interpretive work is that we have to take that picture as our teacher, not just a chance to commiserate and emote, but to learn. Interpretive work is inherently pedagogical. Its lesson, in this time of ever-immanent emergency, is a terrible trial and this trial, too, is as old as the hills.

Tracing Back Through Ethical Relations: A Real-Life Conversation over Tea and Muffins *(said in a conspiratorial tone)*

Lesley Tait. She is the daughter of a Cree mother who wrote a poem once. She lives and works as a guest on Blackfoot territory, and when she takes teachers to the land, she acknowledges the people who belong to this place.

Jodi: When I listen to Lesley speak, I have trouble catching my breath, sometimes. She tells stories about her grandmother, and teacups, wolf willow and ceremony, and we debate "authenticity," and we wonder what it means to be a teacher in these times. I love how she will roll her eyes and almost growl when making an ironic, funny point, and how her smile will creep up on one side of her face, as she leans forward, and I will lean forward too. "We talked about this before, Jo, you remember!" Sometimes I do remember, and I will smile back, loudly. Other times I don't remember, and I will ask for her to tell it again, just as good as the first time.

> In grad studies,
> I was a witness to everything.
> Everything.
> A coming into her own . . . a return.
> Culture, language,
> authority, love,
>   ancestors,
> embodiment of a life.

Lesley: Jodi has taught me to think. How to think about things in new ways, how to connect my thoughts to thoughts I had last year, how to layer in my thoughts, how to weave them together to made new thoughts. I write like her now. Not intentionally, but it's there. I can hear her voice in my head when my fingers touch the keys. I like this bit about the hands, but I think it needs to be brought back a few more times. See this bit here . . . .it could move down with this other bit. She taught me how to be a scholar. In every sense of the word. Jodi is my teacher. I am in awe of her.

Jodi: I tell stories like you now. Or at least I try.

Lesley: Oki/ Tan'si. nitsikāson ochi niya Michel First Nation mēkwac niwikin otiskwanīk. (Lesley). My name is Lesley and I am a member of Michel first Nation and the Calahoo family. My grandparents were Roderick Calahoo and Alice Calahoo. Roderick was chief of Michel first nation. His parents were Johnny and Sophie Calahoo. Johnny Calahoo was the founder and first president of the Indian Association of Alberta. My great great-grandfather is Michel Calahoo for whom our nation was named.

My family is beautiful. We are wide spread and rarely does a large interjurisdictional meeting occur where I do not meet a new cousin. We are doing great work in many ways. We also have our traumas, our struggles and our stories that have not yet found their way. These dualistic realities are not uncommon and result in the handing down of many legacies. The Calahoo legacy of strong leaders is my favorite story. The legacy of shame is my least favorite story. This legacy of shame is a legacy handed to us and placed upon us. It comes from a deep understanding that society feels you unworthy. It is a lesson my mother learned better than most.

My mother and her siblings attended an off-reserve school with non-Indigenous children. There, she quickly learned that being native or "Indian" was never going to be good enough. She encountered systemic and subtle racism at every step. Generation upon generation of my family experienced economic, social and political marginalization. It is in this way that my mother was handed down a sense of shame and learned a very honest truth of the time: don't be an Indian.

I would like to share a poem with you. A poem written by my mother:

I have a long history
But do not know from
Where I come

I could not ask
But knew wrong had occurred

Perhaps I was to blame

I must be clean
I must behave
I have to achieve but yet be last
Mistakes are made
But I can only sense

We do not talk
Only answer quietly
With heads down when asked
(Sheila Ewasiuk)

I am only able to do the work I do today because of my mother. Her strength, her resiliency and her deep unconditional love have shaped me, and I am grateful. (Lesley Tait, personal communication, March 19, 2020)

Braiding Sweetgrass: Something *is* Possible . . .

. . . There it is! The perfect introduction for my friend:

> A sheaf of sweetgrass, bound at the end and divided into thirds, is ready to braid. In braiding sweetgrass—so that it is smooth, glossy, and worthy of the gift—a certain amount of tension is needed. As any little girls with tight braids will tell you, you have to pull a bit. Of course you can do it yourself—by tying one end to a chair, or by holding it in your teeth and braiding backward away from yourself—but the sweetest way is to have someone else hold the ends so that you pull gently against each other, all the while leaning in, head to head, chatting and laughing, watching each other's hands, one holding steadily while the other shifts the slim bundles over one another, each in its turn. Linked by sweetgrass, there is reciprocity between you, linked by sweetgrass, the holder as vital as the braider. The braid becomes finer and thinner as you near the end, until you're braiding individual blades of grass, and then you tie it off. Will you hold the end of the bundle while I braid? Hands joined by grass, can we bend our heads together and make a braid to honor the earth? And then I'll hold it for you, while you braid, too. (Robin Wall Kimmerer, 2013, p. ix)

March 1, 2019, 2:50 pm. Text exchange:

Jodi: *Lesley, there is a word in Cree you have called me before. I wonder, do you remember?*

Lesley: *nitotem?*

Jodi: *YES! That means friend, right?*

Lesley: *Yes. ni. Meaning my. kitotem meaning your friend. But t's sounds like a mix between d and t.*

March 10, 2019, 5:32 pm. Text exchange:

Jodi: *Lesley, mulling over some things.*

Jodi: *Do you see the email thread with David? Lol. feeling all tangled! overwhelmed by the limits/possibilities.*

Lesley: *No stress. We will figure it all out.*

Jodi: *I'm not stressing, it's just very interesting. Lol. [.].Using your first name doesn't give you proper credit, but it doesn't "protect" you adequately either . . . and from what? From publishing a book together?*

. . . whose story?

And then, from Thomas King (2013), read so long ago together:

Take [this] story, for instance. Do with it what you will. Tell it to friends. Turn it into a television movie. Forget it. But don't say in the years to come that you would have lived your life differently if only you had heard this story. You've heard it now. (p. 61)

And my own note, scrawled in the margin, years ago:

ethical responsibility towards the research
        No stress, nitotem. We'll figure it all out.

                      Jodi: Sometimes the sweat takes my breath away.
                            Lesley: Heat, darkness, sacredness

        Jodi: Sometimes my voice wavers. I just can't finish what I started.

                Lesley: Don't worry, nitotem, you were perfect.

                Jodi: My breath returns. My body breathes for me.

To begin a story, someone in some way must break a particular silence.
(Ruby Wiebe & Yvonne Johnson, 1999, p. 4)

On Thursday 2019-03-07 2:39 PM, Jodi Latremouille wrote:

Hi Jackie, I have written a (very draftish, messy) introduction about Lesley, and what I am starting to think is that . . I had a beautiful, wise conversation with her . . .

Well, in writing about the journey with ethics . . .
What I want to do . . .
[is that I want to] put this chapter in the [research], with her full name and permission [to cite nitotem],
[but] not as a [research] participant.
What do you think?
Jodi

Yes . . . "tragic" (David Jardine, personal email communication, March 10, 2019, 8:44 AM)

But . . .

Yes. Something is possible.

On Thursday 2019-03-07 2:59 PM, Jackie Seidel is writing:

LOL!
I just read your whole document. I literally laughed out loud several times in my office just now. It's funny/not funny! I've been wondering about this all along, and I remember we had conversations about it. Yes, I think [she should not be a] participant for all the reasons you say.
[.] AND . . .
. . . actually, this is important . . . what you are trying to articulate matters for many people if we (people like you and me) are hoping to describe and live more ecological ways of being in this beautiful, messy, ethical world in a way that actually sustains life. Think about it. [.].It would actually be a thrilling narrative to many people, I think . . . it reminds me of those pieces on writing as a research method . . . think how important those are to so many researchers! How much power and courage and strength they have gifted. When I read your piece, I thought "yes!" This is like those. I really believe that . . . a piece like this is like nothing I have ever seen regarding research ethics and methodologies.

So, yes, really think about [that].

Geez . . .your project is stretching my heart wide open . . . it makes the world seem more POSSIBLE.

Jackie

Part IV
"To Re-teach a Thing its Loveliness"

Environment I
Jodi Latremouille

> Environmentalism, in its deepest sense, is not about environment. It is not about things but relationships, not about beings but Being, not about world but the inseparability of self and circumstance (Neil Evernden, 1999, p. 142)

The word "environment" refers to a wide-ranging aspect of human participation in life on earth. It has long been associated with equally broad concepts, such as nature, habitat, ecology: that which surrounds us. Most North Americans continue to see ourselves as self-enclosed human entities at the centre of the "surrounding" two-dimensional environment. In this perception of an encircled environment, vast tracts of wilderness or urban grasslands are easily designated as "empty" lands waiting for our development, and deep oceans seen as "bottomless" reservoirs for our effluent.

In North American society, our relationship with the natural environment is most commonly characterized by a denial of relationship, which allows the Enlightenment dichotomy of romance and control to dominate.

Birding Lessons and the Teachings of Cicadas | David Jardine

I went birding last summer with some old friends through the Southern Ontario summer forests where I was raised, crackling full of song-birds and head-high ferns and steamy heat. It was, as always, a great relief to return to this place from the clear airs of Alberta where I have lived for 11 years—academic, Faculty of Education, curriculum courses, practicum supervision in the often stuffy, unearthly confines of some elementary schools.

As with every time I return here, it was once again a surprise to find how familiar it was, and to find how deeply I experience my new home in the foothills of the Rocky Mountains through these deeply buried bodily templates of my raising. It is as if I bear a sort of hidden ecological memory of the sensuous spells (David Abram, 1996) of the place on Earth into which I was born. How things smell, the racket of leaves turning on their stems, how my breath pulls this humid air, how birds songs combine, the familiar directions of sudden thundery winds, the rising insect drills of cicada tree buzzes that I remember so intimately, so immediately, that when they sound, it feels as if this place itself has remembered what I have forgotten, as if my own memory, my own raising, some of my own life, is stored up in these trees for safekeeping.

WAYSTATION IV
A Conversation with David Geoffrey Smith on the Prevenient Givenness of Life
David G. Smith & David Jardine

David Smith, 11:13 PM, Friday, March 22, 2019

Is it actually ridiculous to say or think or do anything at all in these nutso times? I look around my living room with books piled everywhere many of which I have read at least 2/3 of the way through. History of capitalism; internet theory; 9/11 research; the Jewish study Bible; critical biblical studies; primer on political theory; A Short History of African Philosophy: stack of London Review of Books; Surveillance Capitalism; The Letters of Marshall McLuhan; a Dogen reader; etc.

What's it all for? What purpose? Am I just another victim of knowledge accumulation addiction? Google addiction is just another version of book reading addiction surely. Gk. *pleonexia*, bad infinity

I used to think I was working on some kind of post Western Civ[ilization] synthesis but now realize that's all vanity. I used to think it was possible to see through all the screens of propaganda to some version of real truth about what's really going on in the world. Now clearly that's a delusional vanity too. So, what's left for an old fart like me? Maybe just time to shut up and sit in silent meditation? The very act of studying seems pointless now.

But maybe all this is part of a cosmic invitation, not just to me but the culture generally to begin a new form of mind-work, to think of thinking differently, to apply one's human energies in a different way. Particularly the question of how to be sane when insanity is deepening all around one, to say which is not in itself just another delusion, or is it? No, no, no, we deeply know intuitively that a better way is possible. The birds tell us this, the trees in their stately wisdom waiting in silence for us to wake up to the Life beyond words, beyond ratiocination, waiting to welcome us into the Great Fold of Being.

I've actually started to have real conversations with three families of magpies who visit from neighboring spruce trees each morning for their dawn treat of last night's fat trimmings. We actually have a good laugh together as they find my efforts to speak magpie hilarious and tell me so in no uncertain terms.

The deep fellowship of Life that is always already there right in front of us in its full potentiality if only we can be present to it, enter it gracefully, gratefully.

Oh my goodness how far as a species we have become removed from this essential condition by our vanity, our narcissism, our relentless tail chasing.
David Jardine, 6:31 AM, Saturday March 23, 2019

    What a great email, David. Really. Because if I read it tail-chasingly, read to the end and THEN read the beginning, the question and the answer collide. Those honey bees, those magpies ... there is no great synthesis to be invented, only the pointing out of honey bees and magpies which shows that great synthesis, if you know how to look. Galway Kinnell [2002]: "Sometimes we have to reteach a thing its loveliness." And then, learning how to look is the practice of silent meditation. [Chogyam] Trungpa [2004, p. 58]: "the purpose of meditation is not to get higher but to be present." Once present to those magpies, the whole world of their relations becomes part of the visit, just as the whole world of yours becomes theirs. That is the remedy to the nutso, and That need to be studied, written about, in ways that demonstrate exactly how it unwinds the anxieties and binds that bind us without a rope (to quote David Loy). That isn't just groggy, withdrawn silence but a vivacious summons to speak beautifully and clearly and with love and full attention. I'm recalling Carl's advice to Jackie that I heard about years ago, re: all the smothering crap of graduate work—just turn away. It can harm you if you don't step out into the wild. You'll end up with a critical-theory induced crone's hunch that is built from thinking you can undo samsara single-handedly with just one more thing, just one more thing. George Harrison:

> It can hit you
> It can hurt you
> Make you sore and what is more
> That is not what you are here for.
>
>   from Beware of Darkness [George Harrison, 1970]

I think your email glances a bit on why my own work is getting, what? Wilder? Because the purpose of writing is, I'm finding, to be an inducement to something beyond belief, beyond mine and my own. Magpies. I want to effect something in a reader [because, of course, I'm looking to concentrate on and practice that effect in myself underneath the roil of my own woes and ear-buzzings], not just give them information about their bondage but give them a glimpse of their already-won freedom (Confucius "Everything has its beauty, but not everyone sees it."). Real freedom, not fake Americano-Christian Lord's-work otherworldly hallucination freedom, but real, fleshy death-freedom lived out with those bees seeking sweetness, needing pollen protein. This is earth-bound true: without bees, I cannot write. Everything has synthesis already, but not everyone sees it. It is not in the eye of the beholder.

So, you're right. A new kind of mind-work which is profoundly and eminently practical and practicable. This is the relief that many students have found in your writing and in mine, because it steps away from the Trump [just the latest avatar, penny-ante distraction]-driven-narration-sickness.

David Smith, 8:41AM, March 23, 2019

Yes. Life beyond words can be another delusion. Instead "In the beginning was the Word" i.e., the world actually speaks before I do, a speech that finds articulation in all those forms of beckoning calling us out of ourselves into our personal and collective Original Face, our true freedom. It's in good art, and in the magpies who reveal a side of my humanness I intuitively know I need to deal with somehow, the solitary magpies who reveal gluttony by secretly hoarding pieces of meat under Fall leaves then quickly returning to gorge the rest of the offerings before any other birds arrive. I know that impulse exactly and I know it's wrong for me as a human being, bad for my health producing obesity, bad geopolitically because it produces envy and wrath in others through its lack of generosity and potential unfairness.

The various polemics against religion cause me to reflect on my own deep sense of faith which I simply cannot deny since it has been very real all my life guiding me through many trials and difficult times. Has nothing to do with sky gods but with this deep sense of the prevenience of Truth, that the truth of life is always out there in front of us beckoning us to be true to it, to be true to the deep-down Truth of things. I think this is what is revealed in the lives of the saints like St. Francis and what Jesus bore witness to, obedience not so much to a father (a time bound metaphor surely) but to this prevenient givenness of life, the giftedness of its primary primordial nature that we are called to tune into very fundamentally if we are to live well, called in fact to be.

Accepting the prevenient truth of things and its call means that to be human is fundamentally to be a follower, lit. a disciple and all the full-throated discipline that such a condition entails. As a species we are not creators but creatures called to investigate and discover the world in which we always and already find ourselves. Key word is discipline, learning the conditions under which the world will reveal itself to us. If we are too presumptuous, about our intelligence, our meaning-making, our plans and creative intentions, everything goes into hiding. This may be precisely the condition of our time; not a time of post-truth but a time of truth's hiddenness because we refuse to face ourselves in the face of it.

Recently a major league baseball player who happens to be very handsome but whose name l forget, was asked "If you were stranded on a desert island what's the one thing you couldn't be without?" Answer: "A mirror."

Point is, if what we produce (create) is only a product of our own limited imagination, limited by being conditioned only by historical precedent, then what is produced is only a mirror we hold up to review for ourselves our own excellence. But if what we produce is a response to the call of life from beyond ourselves then there is no longer any mirror since we simply, difficultly become what we have seen, what we have learned. We become Real human beings without objectification, free at last from the chains of desire to be something other than what we are, what we have always been in our deepest latency.

Last night l had a weird dream. Julie and l went to a lecture by Derrida.

> To find nobody else came.
> Before his talk he bowed.
> After his talk l went
> up to him and asked if he knew
> Kierkegaard's Prayer
> "Lord deliver me from my disciples."
> He smiled and mumbled something
> l couldn't decipher.

David Smith, 6:59PM, July 3, 2019
Any chance you could note at the poem at the end that originally the text was not a poem, but you thought it read like one, so rendered it as such?

If difficult to do at this stage, no problem.

I really like the exchange. Quite beautiful and poignant actually.

Environment II
Jodi Latremouille

Our approach to environmentalism oscillates between the romantic naturalist and conservation philosophies and the rational management ethos of problem-solving and natural resource development (Sean Blenkinsop, 2012, p. 354). The National Geographic Magazine (2016) "Environment" webpage, for example, on one hand encourages us to fall in love with full-colour images of adorable baby orangutans so that we will be more inspired to protect them, while on the other, educates us on the connections between climate change, development, and the plight of refugees in hopes that we will find ways to resolve and "fix" these problems (Robert Nixon, 2011, p. 152) Across the social studies curricula and resources in North America, the environment is consistently represented as a singular, abstract, external entity, framed in Enlightenment terms either as the object of a child's romantic and emotive care and concern, or as a problem that needs to be rationally managed and balanced against the advancement of human interests.

Based on the premise that "all education is environmental education," David Orr (1991, p. 54) asserts that we teach students about their place within our environment not only by what and how we teach, but also through our collective denial, that is, by what we do not teach.

And by How We Imagine and Teach *Whatever* we Teach
David Jardine

The term "environmental education" can give us pause to consider how ecological awareness, ecological attunement, might be more than simply a particular topic among others in the classroom. It might help us glimpse how it is that *education itself*, in its attention to *all the disciplines that make up schooling*, can be conceived as a deeply ecological in character and mood. Ecology can provide us with images that help us re-conceive the traditions and disciplines of education as themselves deeply ecological communities of relations, full of long, convoluted histories, full of life and lives, traditions and wisdoms that require our "continuity of attention and devotion" (Wendell Berry,1986, p. 34) if they are to remain generous, sustainable and true, if they are to remain *livable*. For example, mathematics can become conceived as a rich, imaginative place, full of topographies and histories and tales to tell, full of relations of kin and kind, full of deep patterns and powers. Mathematics might become conceived as itself a deeply interconnected, Earthly phenomenon, linked to patterns of breath and bone, bearing kinships to patterns of language and song, linked, too, to symmetries etched in stone, to the spiral doings of leaves and to the sun downarching towards *sol stasis* and return.

(David Jardine, 2016b, p. 63)

I propose that our relationships with our *environment* may be much more dynamic than the dual Enlightenment mythologies of romance and control, if we embrace a deep cultural shift towards an *honest participation* in Being (Leroy Little Bear, 2000, p. 80). Interpreted through Kehte-aya Bob Cardinal's Cree principles of security, love and discipline, this honest participation is an interactive and intersecting relationships with/in and through human beings, the more-than-human, and the earth.

Birding Lessons and the Teachings of Cicadas II David Jardine

Cicadas become archaic storytellers telling me, like all good storytellers, of the life I'd forgotten I'd lived, of deep, fleshy, familial relations that worm their ways out of my belly and breath into these soils, these smells, this air.

And I'm left shocked that they know so much, that they remember so well, and that they can be so perfectly articulate.

I became enamored, during our walk, with listening to my friends' conversations about the different birds that they had been spotting. They spoke of their previous ventures here, of what had been gathered and lost, of moments of surprise and relief, of expectation and frustration. Their conversations were full of a type of discipline, attention and rich interpretive joy, a pleasure taken in a way of knowing that cultivated and deepened our being just here, in this marsh, up beside these hot, late-afternoon sun-yellowy limestone cliffs.

Updraughts had pulled a hawk high up above our heads. We spotted a redwinged blackbird circling him, pestering, diving.

Sudden blackbird disappearance.

Hawk remained, over a hundred feet overhead, backlit shadowy wing penumbras making it hard to accurately spot.

Where had that blackbird gone?

"There. Coming down the cliff face."

Sudden distinctive complaint around our heads. He had spotted us as worse and more proximate dangers to this marsh than the hawk that'd been chased far enough away for comfort.

Environment III
Jodi Latremouille

Love Story I: Project Engage

Stephanie Bartlett from Calgary, Alberta, works with 6-year-olds to inspire entire schools and communities to action. She and her kindergarten class created *Project Engage: Living our Lives for a Sustainable Future*.[1] It is described as a school-wide project whose vision is to increase environmental stewardship within the community through authentic task design and partnerships outside the school. It includes a metal collection station, a Christmas light collection and recycling campaign, a sweater day to raise awareness around energy use, and a partnership with a local community centre re-design (Chinook Park, 2016, pp. 1–2). This year, the class worked on a sound sculpture from recycled metals, highlighting resource use and the relationship between art and the environment.

Stephanie has felt called to interpret curriculum, teaching and the world through the lenses of environmental sustainability, economic justice and community. When a teacher such as Stephanie sees herself as integral to the life of a community, she may find ways to "live and breathe moments of deep engagement and connection within the institutional contours" (S. Bartlett, personal communication, April 2016). She is asking critical questions with her kindergarten students: "what is needed here, now, in this time and place, under these particular circumstances?" Along with other teachers who take up environmental work in a deeper way at all levels in the field of social studies, Stephanie is "broadening the spectrum of what counts as environmentalism" (Robert Nixon, 2011,

---

[1] I am grateful to Stephanie Bartlett for her permission to share the story of Project Engage. Details of the ongoing project can be found at https://twitter.com/cbeengage and https://www.facebook.com/Project-EngageLiving-our-Lives-for-a-Sustainable-Future-924246637631395/

p. 5), invoking place-based environmental education, inquiry and community involvement.

"Greenwashing Pedagogies" *of Romance and Control.*

In reviewing definitions for *environment* in Merriam-Webster's dictionary, I found the following definitions the most relevant for the social studies:

1. "the circumstances, objects, or conditions by which one is surrounded."
2a. "the complex of physical, chemical, and biotic factors (such as climate, soil, and living things) that act upon an organism or an ecological community and ultimately determine its form and survival."
  b. "the aggregate of social and cultural conditions that influence the life of an individual or community" (Merriam-Webster, 2016).

The root metaphors of romance and control originated in Descartes' Enlightenment dichotomy, which denied relationships and created a chasm "between the mind and the whole of the material world" (David Abram, 2010, p. 108). Western dualistic mythologies of mind/body, culture/nature, and so on, assert that humans are discrete beings who remain "cleanly divided from the surrounding world of persons and places" (Catherine Keller, 1988, p. 1), completely separate from the life cycles of the earth.

Birding Lessons and the Teachings of Cicadas III
David Jardine

My friends' conversations were, in an ecologically important sense, of a kind with the abundance of bird songs and flights that surrounded us—careful, measured, like speaking to like, up out of the hot and heady, mosquitoed air. And, standing alongside them there, sometimes silent, certainly unpracticed in this art, involved a type of learning that I had once known but, like cicadas, long-since forgotten.

I had forgotten the pleasure to be had in simply standing in the presence of people who are practiced in what they know and listening, feeling, watching them work.

I had forgotten the learning to be had from standing alongside and imitating, practicing, repeating, refining the bodily gestures of knowing.

I had forgotten how they could show me things, not just about this place, but about how you might carry yourself, what might become of you, when you know this place well.

Part of such carrying, such bearing, is to realize how the creatures of this place can become like great teachers with great patience. Such a realization makes it possible to be at a certain ease with what you know. It is no longer necessary to contain or hoard or become overly consumptive in knowing. One can take confidence and comfort in the fact that this place itself will patiently hold some of the remembrances required: like the cicadas, patiently repeating the calls to attention required to know well of this place and its ways.

So we stood together in the bodily presence of this place. Listening, watching, waiting for knowing to be formed through happenstance arrivals and chance noticings. Seeking out expectant, near-secret places that they knew from having been here before, often evoking slow words of fondness, remembrance and familiarity— intimate little tales of other times. Repeating to each other, with low and measured tones, what is seen or suspected. Reciting tales from well-thumbed-through books that showed their age and importance. Belly-laughing over the wonderful, silly, sometimes near-perfect verbal descriptions of bird songs: "a liquid gurgling konk-la-ree or o-ka- lay" for Roger Tory Peterson's (1980, p. 252) version of the red-winged blackbird.

Then settling, slowing, returning, listening and looking anew. Meticulousness: "at the edge, below the canopy of the oak, there, no, left, there, yes!"

Environment IV
Jodi Latremouille

When we interpret the environment as merely a "surrounding," external to ourselves and our narrow human interests, North Americans may become vulnerable to the romance/control inspired "greenwashing"[2] of large corporations and industries: airlines sell carbon offset credits, grocery stores stock "all natural," yet

---

2   Greenwash. (noun). "A superficial or insincere display of concern for the environment that is shown by an organization, often to deflect attention from an organization's environmentally unfriendly or less savory activities" (Collins English Dictionary, 2012)

still factory-farmed meats, and fuel stations tout hip-sounding "biofuels" such as government-subsidized, GMO corn-based ethanol. Large companies also make highly public donations to popular earth charities in order to promote an "I am greener than thou" image, while refusing to disclose or change their own large-scale environmentally destructive practices, for fear that this may cut into their profit margins (Ted Steinberg, 2013, p. 254):

> Gargantuan transnational corporations like BP, ExxonMobil, Shell, Freeport McMoran, and Walmart have wised up to the kudos they can gain from greenwashing in the countries of the rich, through high-minded advertising campaigns, through strategic donations to NGOs and universities, by buying out or intimidating scientists who might testify against the slow violence of their practices, and through rarified talk about being fine stewards of our delicate planet. (Robert Nixon, 2011, p. 37)

They skirt responsibility and download eco-guilt onto consumers, playing off the Lorax's dire warning that "unless someone like you cares a whole awful lot, nothing is going to get better. It's not" (Theodore Seuss, 1971).

3 Rs

David Jardine

Speaking of guilt free consumer choices:

> There has been a disturbing loss in the area of ecological awareness. Currently, in Canada at least, there are three 'R's' to environmentalism: reduce, re-use and recycle (some have introduced a fourth 'r': recover). Several years ago, there was another, different fourth 'R' which has since gone missing: refuse. It is vital to not misread this missing fourth 'R.' It is not simply 'refuse' in the sense of 'garbage'. It also suggests refusal. The most potent form of ecological action is

> simply saying 'no' to those elements of our lives and our ways that are unsustainable, that befoul our nest. *Refusing.* The loss of this fourth 'R'—the loss of the power and potency and responsibility involved in the act of refusal—is, unfortunately, not very mysterious. It leaves us with a vision of ecology which does not demand that we take responsibility for our own consumptive desires except *after* they are fully satiated. We can consume anything we want as long as we deal with the garbage *after*. In a horrible twist of logic, the relinquishing of the power of refusal leads to precisely that sense of rootlessness and powerlessness and futility that makes one susceptible to becoming a relentless consumer who is unable to refuse. (David Jardine, 2000b, p. 62–3)

By admonishing individuals "to do our small part," to "reduce, reuse, and recycle," (Drea Knufken, 2010, p. 1) to "save the environment," to "go green," and to compete to see who can make the most "empowered, healthy, and guilt-free" consumer choices (Martin Lukacs, 2017) these companies are encouraging us to ignore the more central ethical inconsistencies propping up the "bottom line" of consumer culture and environmental extortion:

> People whose governing habit is the relinquishment of power, competence and responsibility, and whose characteristic suffering is the anxiety of futility, make excellent spenders. They are the ideal consumers. By inducing in them little panics of boredom, powerlessness, sexual failure, mortality, paranoia, they can be made to buy virtually anything that is 'attractively packaged'. (Wendell Berry, 1986, p. 24)

And meanwhile . . . a mere one hundred global corporations go on "torching the planet," emitting 71% of total carbon emissions since 1988 (We Movement, 2017). These greenwashing practices are widely encouraged in schools across North America, with recycling programs, "save the polar bears" campaigns, and quick-and-easy litter clean-up initiatives. Teachers can select from a wide range of charities, pre-planned events, educational resources and corporate-model programs, in the quest to "empower and enable youth to be agents of change," and asks the familiar question, "if we don't take action, who will" (Leanne Betasamosake Simpson, 2014, p. 9)?

Educational Philosophy I
Lesley Tait

> Indigenous education is not Indigenous or education from within our intellectual traditions unless it comes through the land, unless it occurs in an Indigenous context using Indigenous processes. (Leanne Betasamosake Simpson, 2014, p. 9)

My educational philosophy has been gifted to me by my Elders. These are not my thoughts but the teachings of the many who have come before me and have honored me with their time and their teachings. I learn from them. I watch how they teach me and how they teach others. It is this watching, patience, trust, that informs how I have moved forward in my understandings of what it might mean to lift this work.

Environment V
Jodi Latremouille

Teacher professional development workshops and curriculum support materials often uphold this model, providing practical lesson plans and printable worksheets for teachers to replicate and deliver "controlled activism" in their classrooms (see, for example, Calgary Board of Education, 2015; Calgary Catholic School District, 2015). These programs allay students' eco-guilt and offer a certain sense of satisfaction, without asking them to question the root metaphors and social narratives at the heart of environmental issues, the deeper impact of their actions in their own communities, or the complexities of the environmental challenges that we face today.

WAYSTATION V
"Out of Control" Activism
Sydney Tait

I think animals are a non-renewable resource. I disagreed with my Grade 4 teacher about that. And my friends. They are non-renewable. You can't just make more. There might new types of sheep, but never the same sheep. Therefore, animals are non-renewable. We argued about this in class. I don't think she ever agreed with me.

If we think about the rhinos, we humans hunted them for their horns and their skin to make stupid leather pouches and we have made them almost extinct. So.

A resource is something you would use to survive or something makes your life easier or something we make. Not always things we need. Like plastic bags. Resources are things we take from the earth to make things. The word "resources" is an odd word. Resources means "go ahead and use it" or that we think that we have the right to take things.

People think we can just take the rhinos horns because we want them. We have to believe that rhino can be killed off, just for our sake. We have to believe humans are better than animals to call animals a resource. So if you follow all of that, then we can't think of "renewable resources" as "resources." Wouldn't those just be life? So resources shouldn't really be a word.

Birding Lessons and the Teachings of Cicadas IV
David Jardine

These are, in part, great fading arts of taxonomic attention, and the deep childly pleasures to be had in sorting and gathering and collecting (see Paul Shepard, 1998). There is something about such gathering that is deeply personal, deeply formative, deeply pedagogical. As I slowly gathered something of this place, it became clear that I was also somehow "gathering myself." And as I gathered something of the compositions of this place, I, too, had to become composed in and by such gathering. And, with the help of cicadas, I did not simply remember this place. Of necessity, I remembered, too, something of what has become of me.

A birding lesson: I become someone through what I know.

This little lesson may be the great gift that environmental education can offer to education as a whole. Coming to know, whatever the discipline, whatever the topic or topography, is never just a matter of learning the ways of a place but learning about how to carry oneself in such a way that the ways of this place might show themselves. Education, perhaps, involves the invitation of children into such living ways.

This idea of a knowledge of the "ways" (Wendell Berry, 1983) of things and the immediacy, patience, repetition, persistence and intimacy—the "attention and devotion" (Wendell Berry, 1986, p. 34)—that such knowledge requires, is ecologically, pedagogically and spiritually vital. It suggests that a knowledge of the ways of red-winged blackbirds is not found nestled in the detailed and careful descriptions of birding guides. Rather, such knowledge lives in the living, ongoing work of coming to a place, learning its ways and living with the unforeseeable consequence that you inevitably become someone in such efforts, someone full of tales to tell, tales of intimacy, full of proper names, particular ventures, bodily memories that are entangled in and indebted to the very flesh of the Earth they want to tell.

It was clear that my friends loved what they had come to know and what such knowing had required them to become. They took great pleasure in working (Wendell Berry, 1988), in showing, in listening, in responding to the simplest, most obvious of questions. There is a telling, disturbing, ecopedagogical insight buried here. Because a knowledge of the ways of a place is, of necessity, a knowledge webbed into the living character of a place and webbed into the life of the one who bears such knowledge, such knowledge is inevitably fragile, participating in the mortality and passing of the places it knows. A knowledge of ways, then, must, of necessity, include the passing on of what is known as an essential, not accidental part of its knowing. It is always and already deeply pedagogical, concerned, not only with the living character of places, but with what is required of us if that living and our living there is to go on.

Environment VI: Historical Roots of Romance and Control in the [American] Conservation Movement
Jodi Latremouille

[American] conservation efforts in the second half of the 19th century were generally concerned with generating appropriate techniques and programs to maintain and utilize the natural environments in practical and beneficial way. As the

20th century approached, several prominent political figures committed to preserving the country's wilderness against over-exploitation. Theodore Roosevelt, governor of New York (1898–1901), and U.S. president 1901–1909, used his political influence to protect the state's and the country's natural resources and watersheds, stating that "there can be no greater issue than that of conservation in this country" (Theodore Roosevelt, 1912, p. 29). The Theodore Roosevelt Conservation Partnership (2017) focuses on safeguarding public land for habitat preservation, maintaining access for sportsmen, and the outdoor recreation economy. Gifford Pinchot, the primary founder of the Society of American Foresters in 1900, argued that a practical conservation should yield "the greatest good, for the greatest number, for the longest run" (Steve Grant, 2017, par. 6). He fought for regulation of timber companies and electric utilities, and in his 1905–1910 term as chief of the US National Forest Service he was responsible for the increase from 60 forest reserve units (56 million acres) to 150 protected national forests (172 million acres). John Muir, founder of the Sierra Club in 1892, argued that Pinchot was "too pragmatic" in his willingness to sacrifice wilderness for the sake of development, most notably California's Hetchy Valley watershed in Yosemite National Park in order to provide water to San Francisco wilderness to sustainable development (Steve Grant, 2017, par. 6). John Muir, a more staunch protector of wilderness, helped establish Sequoia and Yosemite National Parks.

Educational Philosophy II: Learning is Relational
Lesley Tait

> I sensed there was a whole lot going on here that I could not get my head around. "Like a stranger, they will not sit down and tell you everything immediately," Little Bear says. "Only when the rocks begin to know you will they tell you their story." (Don Hill, 2008, p. 42)

What faces Indigenous education and the lifting of Indigenous worldviews in schools today, is not an informational problem (Dwayne Donald, 2010). It is a relational problem. While the content and the "information" certainly pose a new and unique challenge to educators facing the delivery of content, it is how they understand the relationship between Indigenous knowledges and its validity in the curriculum that is of greater impact to how Indigenous perspectives are taken up within the learning. This evokes a wahkohtowin sensibility. Seeing relationship as central to the teaching and learning of all, allows us to lift Indigenous ways of knowing, being and doing.

Environment VII
Jodi Latremouille

After World War I, Aldo Leopold espoused an ecological "land ethic," arguing that nature was the vast system with which all human activity—culture, philosophy, the arts, values—interacted, for better or worse. Any abuses of the environment could be attributed to improper social and cultural beliefs rather than inappropriate management techniques. In his influential book, A Sand County Almanac (1949), he wrote,

> "We abuse land because we regard it as a commodity belonging to us. When we see land as a community to which we belong, we may begin to use it with love and respect" (p. 7).

In the 20th century, however, wilderness preservation embraced a more romanticized view of nature and animals, focusing on preserving scenic parklands and "charismatic megavertebrates," while ignoring earthworms, fungi, and less spectacular but more diverse landscapes such as grasslands and river valleys (Derrick Jensen, 2004, p. 85). The romantic conservationist ethic was perpetuated by David Brower, first executive director of the Sierra Club, who "wanted to save as much as the planet as possible from humans," overseeing the exponential growth of the Sierra Club which began with 7,000 members when he joined in 1952 and expanded to over 77,000 members when he left in 1969 (Ted Steinberg, 2012 p. 246). His group significantly expanded the national park network, and successfully protected all national parks from damns, logging, and other forms of resource extraction, most notably protecting the Dinosaur National Monument by stopping the damming of the Colorado in Echo Park (p. 245). The Dinosaur National Monument, however, came under the stress of heavy tourism inspired by Brower's highly successful Sierra Club film and print publicity campaign, undermining the very wilderness he was trying to save (p. 246).

Educational Philosophy III: Learning Occurs in Place
Lesley Tait

> If curriculum can be understood as stories we tell about the world and our place in it, then we need to start telling different stories in order to renew balanced and sustainable relationships with the more-than-human entities that give life.

What can be the sources of inspiration for these stories of relationship renewal? Becoming wisely aware to the unique animacy of places is a very good place to start (Dwayne Donald, 2019, p. 160).

Learning is situational. We do what makes sense in this place, for these people and in this time. Blackfoot Elder Leonard Bastien has taught me, in many different ways, that all learning begins on the land. Learning is contextualized where and how we live. We need to invite everyone to experience place through learning and creating a collective biography of who we are, where we are from, how we came to be in this place together, and what we can do to move forward as relations. We need to listen to the language and story connections of the land and to uncover the stories of sky science, plant growth and math that live in that place. The curriculum is alive and well in place.

Environment VIII
Jodi Latremouille

In Canadian elementary provincial educational curricula, this 20th century romantic ethic of "care, concern and protection" often dominates, in the hopes that if young children spend more time in nature, they will somehow naturally learn to love it and take better care of it (Alberta Education, 2006a; Ontario Ministry of Education, 2011) while failing to address the complexities of natural relationships or the consequences of heavy eco-tourism. In the United States, many supplementary curriculum resources promote environmental education that brings awareness to over-consumption without challenging the popular belief that "the world is our oyster." The Think Earth Online Curriculum Project is an American non-profit, public–private partnership providing free curriculum resources from Grades 1–9 which help teachers educate students to conserve natural resources, reduce waste, and minimize pollution. This site focuses on content delivery and individual lifestyle choices, encouraging students to use less paper, water, and electricity, to carpool, and to recycle and put litter in the trash. Not surprisingly, Think Earth is sponsored by companies such as Toyota Motor Sales, U.S.A., and Edison International, a public utilities holdings company (Think Earth Environmental Education Foundation, 2016a).

Rachel Carson's pivotal book, *Silent Spring* (1962), helped hasten the shift from a "humans vs. nature" conservationist ideology to the more ecological "socioenvironmental" outlook that served as a powerful model for environmental justice movements in the later years of the 20th century (Robert Nixon, 2011, p. xi). The growing environmental movement served to expose the consequences of consumer capitalism, with 75% of Americans considering themselves "environmentalists" in 1990 (Ted Steinberg, 2012, p. 241). Today, however, despite increasing widespread awareness of environmental issues, both the conservationist and socioenvironmental outlooks have given way to increasingly competitive resource exploitation. The natural environment—while still romanticized for its exotic beauty—is simultaneously gravely exploited for its seeming endless wealth in order to promote human economic activities such as resource extraction, tourism, and technological replacements for natural processes, based on the unquestioned myths of progress, growth and development. Ever-advancing technology promises not only management but mastery of nature, which from this perspective becomes "a standing reserve" for human consumption and wealth-creation (Derrick Jensen, 2004, p. 208). With this "environment vs. economy" mindset, the inherent conservatism of ecology is seen as a barrier to food production and resource extraction even while economic disparity increases at an alarming rate.

Educational Philosophy IV: "Go to the Rock"
Lesley Tait

> People get caught going to the sign to learn about the rock instead of going to the rock itself. In fact, there are pictographs on the rock that I don't think many people notice or even see because they don't spend time with the rock. They spend more time with the sign. (Ryan Heavy Head, 2015, February 15)

There are two words that cycle and recycle through my teaching. One is Cree, the other is Blackfoot. One was taught to me by Kehte-aya Bob Cardinal on Maskekosihk Enoch First Nation, the other by Dwayne Donald.

> miyowashkowowin.
> Walk in a good way
> Pay attention
> Tread lightly
> Immerse yourself
>
> aokakio'siit.
> Pay attention
> Be wisely aware
> Look around you

See what is happening
Acknowledge it

To learn about the rock, we go to the rock. To learn about what students know, we go to the students. Not the text book and not the test. In practice, we walk alongside those who have much to teach us. We notice the spring crocus has decided to show itself this morning. We stop and circle around the crocus. One of us tells the story of how the crocus came to be purple, how it came to have the heart of the sun and how it came to stay warm in the early spring. Another of us says the word in Blackfoot. That word is related to the word for "old women," I wonder why. Another of us answers that thought. We move forward from this place knowing how to greet the crocus should it say hello to us again.

From Matsuo Basho (1644–1694)

From the pine tree
learn of the pine tree,
And from the bamboo
of the bamboo.

(see http://www.ahapoetry.com/haiku.htm)

Environment IX
Jodi Latremouille

In junior high and high school, the social studies curricula shift to a more rationalistic stance that views the environment as a passive object to be studied and manipulated by humans. It is a "contemporary issue" listed alongside—and often in competition with—trade, war, poverty, debt, disease, and human rights.

High school students are expected to learn about human-environment relationships order to control them more effectively (Alberta Education, 2006b; British Columbia Ministry of Education, 2016).

Aborigines in Australia have dubbed European colonizers the "future eaters," those who consume without thought to replacing the resources used (Robert Nixon, 2011, p. 96). Now, in the early 21st century, as participants in a closed earth ecosystem, human beings in many locales around the world are being forced to face the hard limits of our environment. These limits are not borne equally by all. Paul Shepard, a key American conservation activist, teacher and author, argues that we have long been in the midst of a slow disintegration of natural systems—evidenced by such wide-ranging symptoms as recessions, poverty, mental-health epidemics, suicide, disastrous weather, political conflicts, famine, social upheaval—that is nothing short of a creeping "planetary ecological disaster" (as cited in Derrick Jensen, 2004, p. 256). Some endure a gradual, attritional destruction, a "slow violence" of environmental and social degradation that too often remains invisible, buried under more sensational tales of natural disaster, war, and discrete events (Robert Nixon, 2011, p. 2).

Although North Americans occupying privileged positions may be most responsible for these consequences, we often feel relatively disconnected from these larger issues (Sean Blenkinsop, 2012, p. 353–368) Teachers often agree that "we pay lip service to the environment in our curriculum" (Marie Matthew, personal communication, June 8, 2016). We feel challenged and overwhelmed by deeply troubling and complex environmental problems of our times yet distracted and paralyzed by the eco-guilt built up through greenwashing techniques and corporate environmentalist slogans. Wendell Berry (with Bill Moyers, 2013) responds to this trouble by reminding us that in proposing responses to large and overwhelming socioenvironmental problems, we do not ultimately have the right to ask if we will be successful or not. We are each challenged to respond in the best way that we know how, for the time and place that we find ourselves in, in all its local particularities and dynamic relations. The responses are necessarily multifarious. The David Suzuki Foundation's Blue Dot movement, based on the simple principle that "this blue dot is our only home" argues that it is a human right to live in a healthy environment, and that each community is charged with upholding this right by addressing the particular needs of their locale (David Suzuki Foundation, 2016). Sandra Steingraber's (2010) investigation of cancer and the environment connects chemical contamination by industry to cancer incidence in rural underprivileged populations, long denied in public health campaigns. Standing Rock protests against the Dakota Access Pipeline are being described as "a new civil rights movement where environmental and human rights meet" (Rebecca Solnit, 2016). These examples evoke deep ethical questions regarding what constitutes a proper relationship for humans with/in our environment, in their localized responses to the multiple and diverse challenges that we face in our time.

Birding Lessons and the Teachings of Cicadas VI
David Jardine

Another birding lesson: if this place is fouled by the (seeming) inevitabilities of "progress," the cost of that progress is always going to be part of my life that is lost.

Some days, it makes perfect sense to say that all knowledge, like all life, is suffering, undergoing, learning to bear and forbear. Because of this fearsome mortality that is part of a knowledge of ways, we are obliged, in such knowledge, to cultivate a good, rich, earthy understanding of "enough" (Wendell Berry, 1983, p. 79). We are obliged, too, to then suffering again the certain knowledge that in our schools, in our lives, in our hallucinations of progress and all the little panics these induce, there never seems to be enough.

Sometimes, in bearing such knowing, I feel my age. I feel my own passing.

Environment X: What is Not Taught? Reviving Relationships with Security, Discipline, and Love
Jodi Latremouille

In Indigenous philosophies and holistic ways of knowing, the divides between the mind and the body, culture and nature, humans and the earth, are false and disruptive to the "happenings" that characterize our multiple earthly relationships. Leroy Little Bear (2000, p. 78), an educator and scholar from the Blood Indian Tribe of the Blackfoot Confederacy, describes the relationship between humans and the environment as cyclical. It is in constant motion, yet characterized by regular, recurring patterns. The migration of the animals, the seasons of the year, the arising and disintegration of bones, bodies and landforms, require continual nourishment by humans, through "renewal ceremonies, songs and stories" (p. 78). As we gain more nuanced and lively understandings of our environment, this seemingly two-dimensional, self-enclosed earthly sphere becomes a textured, living, breathing "circle of kinship" (p. 78) in which humans participate fully and equitably. No longer do we operate from a discrete, singular and isolated centre, but rather from diverse points within a dynamic and lively "spider web of relations." Kehte-aya Bob Cardinal of the Maskekosihk Enoch Cree Nation in Alberta shares his philosophy of *security, discipline and love* in relationships (Kehte-aya Bob Cardinal, oral teachings, July 11, 2016). This philosophy unsettles the root metaphors of romance and control, as we deny and violate humanity's deep relationship with the environment.

Educational Philosophy V: Learning is Holistic
Lesley Tait

> I have watched my children lament over the loneliness of a solitary stone, create entire stone families, and stop mid-sentence to address the needs of a distant rock calling out to them. To them, these stones are precious. They have the ability to feel, be lonely, cold, and afraid. They can also be comforted and feel love (Lesley Tait, 2016a, p. 166)

Kehte-aya Bob Cardinal asks me, kiikway ot'e-ohpinaman? (what are you trying to lift?). It is this question that reminds me to live and teach from a holistic understanding.

In the East sits the bear who teaches us patience, compassion, and knowledge of the past. The bear reminds us to learn from what has come to before. To acknowledge our ancestors and to honor them with what we do today.

In the South sits the humble, loving Grandmother Mouse who teaches us about nurturing and giving. It is my teachings that I am never the holder of knowledge. It is not mine. It is ours. And it is what nourishes us.

In the West sits the Thunder Being who teaches us to communicate in respectful ways and honor the life journey of others. We are relational beings. We exist in relation to each other, to our past and to our future.

In the North Sits the Buffalo who teaches us to utilize all and not waste any gifts. We are all born full complete. We are all given gifts. We are leading the lives designed for us when we are able to share our gifts. (Kehte-aya Bob Cardinal, oral teachings, fall 2014)

Environment XI
Jodi Latremouille

Matthew Fox (in Derrick Jensen, 2004) argues that the persistent separation between humans and nature, and thus the need to control nature, is rooted in a false perception of the universe as unfriendly. The underlying assumption that "there is something profoundly unfriendly and threatening in nature" (David Orr, cited in Derrick Jensen, 2004, p. 25) motivates the human obsession with technology that monitors and controls our lives with ever-increasing accuracy. The underlying fear of nature brings about a need to control all aspects of one's environment and perpetuates the cycle of unnecessary destruction (p. 71). However, Kehte-aya Bob Cardinal's notion of security may "restory" our environment as an essentially benign and abundant place (p. 25), opening spaces for humans to move beyond our denial of relationships with the environment to deeper appreciation of our role in the grander cycles and seasons of life itself. These understandings of the dynamic world require our honest participation, that is, to "speak the truth" in the "the spider web of relations" (Leroy Little Bear, 2000, p. 80)

Birding Lessons and the Teachings of Cicadas VII
David Jardine

At one point we stood on a raised wooden platform in the middle of a marsh just as the sun was setting, and the vocal interplays of red-winged blackbirds' songs, the curves of their flights and the patterning of both of these around nests cupped in the yellow-and-black-garden-spidery bulrushes—audible but invisible sites bubbling full of the pink, wet warbling smallness of chicks—were clearly, in their own way, acts of spotting *us*.

"Ways" bespeaks a thread of kindredness with what one knows, a sense of deep relatedness and intimate, fleshy obligation. But it betrays another little birding lesson: that we are their relations as much as they are ours, that we are thus caught in whatever regard this place places on us:

> The whole ensemble of sentient life cannot be deployed except from the site of a being which is itself visible, audible, sensible. The visible world and the eye share a common flesh; the flesh is their common being and belonging together. (John Caputo, 1993, p. 201)

Or, if you like, a more drastic mosquito lesson about living relations: "flesh is .. .. .. a reversible, just insofar as what eats is always edible, what is carnivorous is always carnality" (p. 200). So just as these mosquitos eat up my sweet, sweaty blood skinslicked under the lures of CO_2 that drew them near, I get their lives in return, gobbled up into liquid gurgling konk-la-rees. This is the meaty, trembly level of mutuality and interdependence that crawls beneath all our tall tales of relations. This common flesh is the fearsome limit of our narrativity.

In a knowledge of ways, I do not simply know. I am also known. These cicadas and I turn around each other, each forming the other in kind, "both sensible and sensitive, reversible aspects of a common animate element" (David Abram, 1996, p. 66) Even more unsettling than this, as we know this place, so are we known by it (Parker Palmer, 1989). That is, the character of our knowing and how gracefully and generously we carry what we know reflects on our character.

Environment XII
Jodi Latremouille

> We cannot, for example, "save the rainforest" without listening to the people who live there. Speaking the truth requires a more grounded and disciplined recognition of our true selves, "co-extensive with other beings and the life of our planet" (Joanna Macy, 2007, p. 148).

As security grows, we may shift from a romance or control-based ethic to a deeper, more careful, more complex and loving relationship with the earth. David Jardine, following Wendell Berry (with Moyers, 2013), says that "the secret goal of education is to fall in love with the world. You can't fall in love with something if you don't know it. And you can't know it if you don't stay put" (Personal Communication, 2015). When educators make loving intergenerational commitments to the earthly places that sustain us, living consciously with forests, overturned soil, towns, resource industries and swampy marshes as they flourish and fade, celebrate and decay once again, we make careful judgments that require us to "say no as often as to say yes" (David Orr cited in Derrick Jensen, 2004, p. 25). Our decisions leave marks on the land: beautiful, scarred, telling its stories through those that stay behind—in gravesites, on reserves, in stands of aspen trees, and in the plots of forgotten land that continue to yield to each new generation of living and dying.

Vandana Shiva reminds us that we belong to an earth democracy, whereby the land is a sacred trust for human sustenance (Sarah Van Gelder, 2017). The committed love of staying put requires intimacy and affection, but unlike romanticism, recognizes limits and defines parameters for dynamic, mutually suffering and sustaining relationships with/in and through the environment (David Orr cited in Derrick Jensen, 2004, p. 25). These three principles lay embedded in a deeper environmental premise that humans must participate in this world truthfully and with discipline, so that we may responsibly love the environment with "open heart-minds" (Joanna Macy, 2014) in reciprocal, responsible relationships of security, discipline, and love.

Love Story II: What is a Biosolid, Anyway?

In my work as a high school teacher in British Columbia, Canada, I asked students to consider their community as they undertook socioenvironmental justice projects involving localized research and real community connections. One group learned that local First Nations groups were leading protests against the applications of biosolids on farms in the valley surrounding our small, rural community. These treated human wastes, or sewage sludge, are deemed "safe" by the companies that ship them in from larger cities in the province, but these claims and the research that they are based on are considered suspect by local activist groups and independent scientists alike.

In a work period early in the project, my students were discussing a plan of action for their small group project. They had spoken with members in the community, done in-depth research, and were contemplating how to bring the active phase of their project to fruition. As they were debating big plans, such as organizing a community rally, writing letters to government officials, and conducting various interviews, another student, eavesdropping on our conversation, asked, "So, what is a biosolid, anyway?" This query evoked Wendell Berry's (with Bill Moyers, 2013) critical ecological question, "what is needed here, now, in this time and place, under these particular circumstances?" Despite their extensive research and grand plans for change, the group needed to recognize and respect the relations at play in their environment. They realized that many members of the community were not even aware of this problem contaminating our very own backyards, and they wisely shifted their focus to building awareness in our community. They decided that an informational presentation was the most reasonable starting point for their project.

Later in the year, our class attended a public forum featuring local community groups, specialized scientists, government officials, and biosolid management companies. The students found the content of the talks highly technical, and very challenging to follow. When I asked them afterwards how they felt about the day, one student replied, "It was very boring, with so much information! When we went to our Me to We Day[3], they entertained us with famous guest speakers, cool music, and fun games for the crowd. They gave us lots of swag, and they really pumped us up!" Another student snapped back, "Well, this is not about entertainment, this is about our community!" This young woman had recognized the increasingly popular "greenwashing" activism that discourages young people from deeply contemplating their relations with other human beings, natural communities, and the land. As educators we are often encouraged to engage in these well-meaning, yet generalized, over-simplified, and entertainment-based forms of socioenvironmental "activism."

Shifts in Pedagogy: "The World is not our Oyster"

Socioenvironmental justice in schools and beyond, interpreted as a dynamic and active interrelationship, asks for the *honest participation* of all those involved. The social life of Social Studies:

> is meant to provide an articulation is actually lived out in locales of great intimacy, particularity and grace. Families, practices, languages, roles both inherited and resisted, times, places, heartbreaks and joys, geographies known through the body and breath and the labour of hands, and, too, great arcs of reminiscence, ancestry, old ways barely recollected or inscribed in practices learned hand over hand, face to face, full of forgotten-ness. (David Jardine, 2015b, p. 1)

The principles of security, discipline and love demand an intimate, lively, participation in the field of social studies. Kehte-aya Bob Cardinal shows me how to expand deeply outwards from learning *about* other ways of being, to learning *with and through* each other's traditions, cultures and ways of Being (Dwayne Donald, 2003) Human beings learning *with and through* our environment may perceive it not as an external, flattened sphere that we interact with and influence, but rather a dynamic, living, circle that demands our honest and perceptive participation. This participation may shift the "bottom line" from a self-referential notion of human happiness towards "peaceful interspecies and multispecies coexistence" (Derrick Jensen, 2004).

---

[3] ME to WE is an "innovative social enterprise that provides products that make an impact, empowering people to change the world with their everyday consumer choices" (We Movement, 2017).

Phonos

David Jardine

Here's a whispery secret. I *adore* these: *jeeah, jay, queedle, queedle, shaaaaaar, shek shek shek, whidoo* and I've often joked about how these make me want to teach phonics to young children. They also make me wonder about what an interesting job it is to be assigned to write these. Whorly ears. David (Jardine, 2019, p. 75)

Perhaps this irreplaceable, unavoidable intimacy is why our tales of the Earth always seem to include proper names ("obligations require proper names" [John Caputo, 1993, p. 201]) always seem to be full of love and heart, always seem to require narrations of particular times and places, particular faces, particular winds, always seem to invite facing and listening and remembering.

It is squarely here that a great deal of my own work has come to rest: how to carry these birding lessons home, back into the often stuffy confines of elementary schools, back into the often even stuffier confines, for example, of elementary school mathematics (David Jardine, 1990), back, too, into the archaic, often literal-minded narrows of academic work and the forms of speaking and writing and research it allow.

Just imagine: mathematics conceived as a living discipline, a living topography, a living place, full of ancestors and kin and living relations, full of tales told and tales to tell. And imagine, too, mathematics education conceived as an open, generous invitation of our children into the intimate ways of this old, mysterious, wondrous place.

As social studies educators entering into these open, dynamic and intimate relationships between and amongst species, landforms and ecosystems, recognizing the environment not as something to be romanticized, controlled, ignored, or even saved, but as a dynamic, participatory arc that is never complete, closed or settled, we may be better able to see what is needed in our particular times and places. Michael Derby suggests that we are living in a time that calls teachers to re-story our environment, to set "a new tone for sustainable and holistic ways of understanding in a world confronted by an escalating ecological crisis" (Michael Derby, 2015, p. 1). If "the world is not our oyster" what stories will we tell as social studies teachers (Max Oelshlaeger, in Derrick Jensen, 2002, p. 212)? How will these stories will be told, who will hear them, and how will we invite others to participate in them truthfully and lovingly? These questions must be deeply rooted in our own communities, as we endeavor to untangle the deeply intertwined threads of social, economic and ecological justice.

Birding Lessons and the Teachings of Cicadas VII
David Jardine

One final birding lesson for now. Catching a glimpse of a blue heron pair over past the edge of the marsh, tucked up under the willowy overhangs.

Shore edge log long deep bluey sunset shadow fingers.

Sudden rush of a type of recognition almost too intimate to bear, an event of birding never quite lodged in any birding guides:

"It's that pair!"

What a strange and incommensurate piece of knowledge (Jardine, 1997), p. 18–21). How profoundly, how deeply, how wonderfully *useless* it is, knowing that it is *them*, seemingly calling for names more intimate, more proper than "heron," descriptions richer and more giddy than "Voice: deep harsh croaks: frahnk, frahnk, frahnk" (Roger Tory Peterson, 1980, p. 100).

Such knowing doesn't lead anywhere. It is, by itself, already always full, already always enough.

WAYSTATION VI
The Joy of Learning: Upsetting What We Know
Gail McNicol-Jardine

I find any experience that deepens, widens, or refines my understandings to be the most joyful form of learning. It is exciting and it is fun to have my understandings turned upside down, to have them shattered into parts that swirl into a new constellation of insights. *Ah hah*!

Listening for the truth in what another is saying is an important way to do this. We learn this from Hans-Georg Gadamer who said at a July 9, 1989 Heidelberg Conference, "the possibility that the other person may be right is the soul of hermeneutics" (cited in Jean Grondin, 1995, p. 124).

The most salient experience I have had with this is when I was teaching in the Siksika/Intercultural Option of the University of Calgary's Master of Teaching program. Class members were all from the Siksika Nation. It was early in the school year and we were taking up case study that highlighted issues around the ways students are sometimes labelled. I thought of my Grandfather's family, where half of my 14 Great-Aunt and Great-Uncles are blue-eyed and half of them are brown-eyed. I also thought about an experiment a classroom teacher did in the 1950s when she wanted to teach the children why they should not discriminate or be prejudiced against people for any reason. She divided the class by eye colour because in her experience, one didn't sort people by this. The teacher set it up so that students of one eye-colour picked on students who had the opposite eye colour in prejudiced ways for 1 week. Then the groups of students switched. These two experiences formed how I thought about eye colour and I had decided that, unlike skin colour, it was never anything anyone took notice of when they were thinking of "them" and "us." After I happily explained this, one of the students said, "Gail, we do." It was only the second class of the 2-year program and I was nervous. I thought she had misunderstood something about how acts of labelling can represent arbitrary choices, with little meaning. So I launched into a slightly different explanation of it. The student again said, "Gail, we . . . do!"

Then I got it. I suddenly realized that not taking any particular notice of eye colour must have originated in Western Europe. The indigenous Celts of The United Kingdom, Ireland, and France were brown-eyed. But these countries experienced multiple invasions of blond, blue-eyed Vikings who settled on the land and intermarried with "the locals." Hence the mixture of eye colours in these nations, even within one family. I was helped to suddenly realize that this experience should not be universalized. In most places, people within one family, or even within one country, are either all brown-eyed or all blue-eyed; so a different eye colour stands out.

This is an example of experiencing the disruption of my pre-judgments. Gadamer describes it this way:

> Long before we understand ourselves through the process of self-examination, we understand ourselves in a self-evident way in the family, society and state in which we live ... That is why the prejudices of the individual, far more than his judgments, constitute the historical reality of his being. (Hans-Georg Gadamer, 2004, p. 356)

But Gadamer's writings are all about why and how we are not forced to stay with these "historical" ideas and expectations that we have inherited about "the way the world is." We can suspend what we have thought and listen in an open way to try to understand the truth in whatever they are saying, especially when what they are expressing is a new, contradictory, or strange idea. We live in "a truly hermeneutic universe" (p. xxiv). When we are alert to the strange, the different, the other, and we listen openly and let the new and the strange interweave with our previous understanding, we gain new insight. In Hans-Georg Gadamer's words:

> Every experience worthy of the name thwarts an expectation ... Insight is more than knowledge of this or that situation. It always involves an escape from something that had deceived us and held us captive ... Insight is something we come to. It too is ultimately part of the vocation of [human beings]. (p. 356)

Our vocations are those aspects of life that we are meant to be doing, almost that we are born to do. We passionately give our all to a vocation and it is fulfilling and joyful to do. To work to understand anew, to listen to the other and learn, to gain insight by seriously examining what we meet and letting it challenge our preconceptions, these things are a vocation for humans. This is why learning hermeneutically is joyous.

I was happy to understand that my previous ideas about the significance of eye colour needed to be limited and refined. It is exciting to learn that there are other ways of thinking in the world and to welcome encountering them. Our understandings of this world are all enriched by opening to this process, as more becomes known to us. In Gadamer's words, "the content of tradition in its constantly widening possibilities of significance and resonance, [is] extended by the different people receiving it" (p. 462).

But there is more to these encounters with the other, as we can learn from Michel Foucault. Systems of knowledge, the self-evident ways of thinking and acting that we were taught as children, before we could examine them for new possibilities for ourselves in relation to others, what he calls discourses and the circulation of multiple associated acts of power, can function as system exhortations laid out as true, that, thought by thought, and expectation by expectation, intend to, and often do succeed in, disciplining and controlling the thinking and actions of most members of a society, often for the exclusive benefit of those in power in that society. (Michel Foucault, 1980, p. 93)

Here it is also vital to question the appropriateness of the thoughts, expectations, practices and actions that constitute a regime of power hermeneutically, by opening to the other. In Foucault's analysis, interrupting a discourse, a regime of power, and opening to other, newer and stranger possibilities can come by examining how things were done and what was believed in other times and places or by listening to marginalized discourses. The marginalized are those understandings, expectations, practices and people who have been turned into "insignificant others" in a society. They live within other possibilities for what is true and appropriate to believe and do.

Through his analysis of how regimes of truth function through acts of power, Foucault presents a more sinister understanding received knowledge. The worry now becomes how we can establish discourses, expectations, and practices that are good for humanity—whether by innocently questioning what is true in the unexpected, or by purposely by taking seriously marginalized or historical insights and practices. How do we build understandings that are good for all? How do we tell? Is this an impossible task?

Michel Foucault (1990), says this about engaging in such critique:

> A critique is not a matter of saying that things are not right as they are. It is a matter of pointing out on what kinds of assumptions, what kinds of familiar, unchallenged, unconsidered modes of thought the practices that we accept rest.
>
> ...
>
> [Through criticism, we] see that what is accepted as self-evident will no longer be accepted as such. Practicing criticism is a matter of making facile gestures

difficult.... as soon as one can no longer think things as one formerly thought them, transformation becomes both very urgent, very difficult, and quite possible... I think the work of deep transformation can only be carried in a free atmosphere, one constantly agitated by permanent criticism. (p. 154, 155)

In our times, I believe we need to engage in an analysis of how our relationship to nature has come to us, and how we have been led to think and act as we do by the regime of truth and the acts of power we have inherited. We are coming to realize that we are an integral part of the natural world around us, neither separate from it nor controlling it. What if we start anew from the idea that we can closely observe natural cycles and learn to mimic them, as Jane Jacobs (2000) argues.

> Can we learn by mimicking ways that systems of life on Earth handle the creation of health? In A Sand County Almanac (1949) Aldo Leopold declared: "A thing is right when it tends to preserve the integrity, stability, and beauty of the biotic community. It is wrong when it tends otherwise" (p. 262).

Following this, dialogues are right when they tend to preserve and support the integrity, health and beauty of others and yourself. We can often see that another is thriving, or is harmed, by the power of our expectations, understandings, practices, and actions. And if we cannot see this, provided we are listening and others are speaking free from fear, and with integrity and honesty about what they feel and need from themselves and others, then we can come to see this, and we can create a healthy community for all.

Dialogue is an exchange of understandings with room for new understandings to appear and thrive. This is what we need now.

We cannot give up, even when manipulators of truth for their own power and financial gain appear to "have slipped one (or more) by us"—this written on the night that William Barr, benefitting Trump, went beyond the cautiousness of the Mueller Report and declared to the Nation, "No obstruction."

Part V
Relations, Aliveness, Love

And So. Relations, Aliveness, Love I
Jodi Latremouille, Lesley, Tait & David Jardine

>The fascination of water
>is the laughter of geometry
>Wind plunges down the hillside:
>   a longing to embrace.
>   Jan Zwicky (2013, p. 51), excerpt from Five Songs for Relinquishing the Earth

In what now follows, we explore three life-affirming and life-sustaining Cree ideas: wahkohtowin, wicihitowin, and sakihitowin. Practicing these ideas can help align work inside and outside of schools with the characteristic spirit (*ethos*) of our earthly being. wahkohtowin[1] means, briefly put, "all things are related/ all things are our relations" and wicihitowin refers to "the life-giving energy that is generated when people face each other as relatives and build trusting

---

1   Following the textual practices of Neal McLeod (2007), the Cree or Blackfoot words used herein are not capitalized regardless of where they appear in a sentence. This is an aesthetic choice intended to emphasize difference and make the point that indigenous language use need not conform to conventions of English language use. (See also Jodi Latremouillle, Antonella Bell, Zahra Kasamali, Mandy Krahn, Lesley Tait, & Dwayne Donald, 2016).

relationships by connecting with others in respectful ways" (Dwayne Donald, 2016, p. 10) sakihitowin means "love."

We explore how images and practices of relations, aliveness and love provide a way to reconcile knowledge and its schooled pursuit with the wisdom required in our current, ecologically desperate times. We heed the call of a curriculum in the spirit of the earth, and we endeavor to participate honestly in those intricate and intimate relations (Little Bear, 2000, p. 80). And as we do so, we try to tether (from 1570's: "A measure of one's limitations" [OED]) ourselves within the times, places, and worlds to which we properly belong, with a sense of earthly proportion and propriety.

"You Need Accuracy": An Appreciation of a Modern Hunting Tradition and a Grouse's Life Unwasted I

David Jardine

> What am I, in the terrible and fragile?
> Our prey is watching over us.
>
> from Jodi Latremouille, "A Modern Hunting Tradition"

Families, practices, languages, roles both inherited and resisted, times, places, heartbreaks and joys, geographies known through the body and breath and the labor of hands, and, too, great arcs of reminiscence, ancestry, old ways barely recollected or inscribed in practices learned hand over hand, face to face, full of forgotten-ness. To be properly understood and articulated, these locales of intimacy don't lend themselves to forms of research that demand generalities or methodological anonymity as is proper to various social sciences. They demand a form of research that is proper to the object of its concern—an old Aristotelian idea, that knowledge must "remain something adapted to the object, a mensuratio ad rem" (Hans-Georg Gadamer, 2004, p. 261)

And So. Relations, Aliveness, Love II
Jodi Latremouille, Lesley, Tait & David Jardine

Schooling-Stories Emptied of Relations, Aliveness, Love: "Need[ing] a Reminder of [our] Place."

Keith Basso writes about the tradition of the 'agodzaahi ("that which has happened") story (David Abram, 1996, p. 156). These stories are usually very brief, and they always begin and end with a place-name: for example, they will say that the story "happened at 'men stand above here and there'" (Keith Basso, 1996, p. 156). When a member of the community has behaved offensively or perhaps needs a reminder of their place in the tribe, and elder will wait for an appropriate moment, and "shoot" the person by recounting an 'agodzaahi. Although the offender is not identified or named aloud, they will feel the "arrow" story make them ill and weak as it penetrates their skin. The story will then work outwards from within, making them desire to "replace" themselves, "to live right." Their behavior changes, but the story stays with them, in their repeated physical or mental encounters with the place. "The place, it is said, will keep 'stalking' her" (Keith Basso, 1996, p. 158–9).

"The land is always stalking people. The land makes people live right. The land looks after us. The land looks after people" (Anne Peaches, age 77, in Keith Basso, 1996, p. 38).

'agodzaahi stories happened in the long ago. They have no beginning and no end. Earthy, life-layered stories.

They teach me, without telling, to act right in the future. Without knowing how it will turn out. Only stories.

They aim true: arrows for the meaty flesh of my heart-mind. I cannot afford to rush; the place is waiting for me if I arrive. If I rush, it turns me back, spins me, trips me, tosses me aside.

When I pass warily through a place, I am stalked again: they teach me, over and over again, to stand up right. They steal my delusions.

They watch me carefully over their reading glasses, waiting for the tell. This 'agodzaahi is custom-told for me, or so it would seem.

I am given a heart-wrenching gift: they know more about me than I can possibly know about myself. I vow to *look after* that place in return.

Empty stories happen in the nearest future. They have no past, and no long-term prospects. Single-use plastic stories.

They tell me, in no uncertain terms, what is missing. There is no room for ambiguity. Only wanting.

The target is clear and precise: that empty part of me that wonders why a 5-minute newscast now seems almost too long to bear. I often only read headlines these days. Woozy from *narration-sickness* (Paulo Freire, in David Smith, 1999, p. 135).

I have long ago learned my simple lesson. No need to tell me again, and yet I am told and re-told.

When I steal through my placeless places, the empty story renders them to pixilated dust: I should be somewhere else. This place is nothing. I know the next face cream/vacation/magic bra/recipe/ news story won't change my life. But *maybe* they will . . .
empty stories custom-made for me.

So I click. I am had. I am stalked, preyed upon: they know more about me than I can possibly know about myself. I vow to walk more warily next time. I vow to not be *had*.

These ideas of 'agodzaahi and the arrow's sting remind us of a similar experience of reading something about our very lives as teachers and parents and writers and readers, "something we thought we'd lost to the work of simply getting by" (Bronwen Wallace, 1989, p. 13). Strange, thought. It was lost from memory and speech but was still silently at work.

Reading about Fredrick Winslow Taylor for the first time, all of us long-since "in" education, and suddenly recognizing how his legacy of industrial efficiency formed part of the atmosphere of our work, our lives, our profession our thinking, our breathing. The shock was in recognizing the story we seemed to be *already living out,* already long-since at work, long-since silently, tacitly agreed to by our actions, our concessions.

Suddenly, the arrow. A reminder of the place we've forgotten that we made for ourselves, us, enamored of the regimes of management and control and colonial impulse that have shaped the West and that provides rich soils for the emergence of efficiency and its demands. This is the bed we (who is this "we?") made that we (who?) now sleep in so restlessly. A place precisely dedicated to the desecration of places and questions of sustenance, in favor of isolated, bits and pieces and their standardized, disinterested, manageable, profitable, assembly. No affection. No relations. None of the energies and aliveness of human living or the life of living disciplines.

'agodzaahi

This, in some small part, is "that which has happened," silently imbued into our hearts and minds and taken-for-granted practicalities and practices but fell-swooping up and overhead from behind our backs, out of sight of careful, pedagogically alert attention.

One of the most tragic over-extensions of the efficiency movement (see Robert Kanigel, 2005; Fredrick Taylor, 1911; Marie Battiste & Rita Bouvier, 2013; Sharon Friesen & David Jardine, 2009; David Jardine, 2013) was its application to the nature and pursuit of knowledge itself, and thereby, with its insinuation into our understanding of how the living disciplines of the world, our shared and contested ancestries of both practical knowledge and long-standing wisdom, live and breathe and survive in hale and healthy ways. Its insinuation into how we live with each other and learn and teach of this world and our dignity and work in and about it.

Knowledge becomes fragmenting in a re-capitulation of disassembling industrial objects, and the consequent sequencing and standardization of their assembly has had dire consequences (it is no coincidence that efficiency in industrial assembly and a behavioral theory of knowledge emerged in each other's embrace in the early 20th century in America). This shift changed our understanding of the living disciplines entrusted to teachers and students in schools. Living relations and topographies and places became disassembled bits. Pieces for us to stalk, to order and assemble and to dispensate on tests of our command of such bits. As it becomes disassembly industrial pieces, not only to we become mere assemblers. Our relations to each other—child to child, elder to child, teacher to student and student to student to world to Ravens and Grouse—become measured through our command of the standardized rules of assembly.

Any sidelong glance becomes suspect.

An ecological pedagogy of joy warns: "Watch out for humans to assume that *they* make all the patterns" (Wendell Berry, 1987, p. 5).

It reminds: we want to be truly tested and measured and try to measure up to the heartbreak of a grouse's life. It cries out for time unwasted over trivial school work.

Out, instead, in the wilds of coming to know with accuracy and affection, out "under the tough old stars" (Gary Snyder, nd.; see David Jardine, 2000a).

> Worn-out story emptied of its relations:
> "Why?
> Well, you need this in
> Grade K-1-2-3-4-5-6-7-8-9-10-11
> so that you will be ready for Grade 12.
> It's a very important year."
> *Click.*

This shift changed how we understand ourselves. Again, when knowledge becomes an assembled industrial object, we become anonymous, obedient, replaceable assemblers. As things lost their place, we lost our way.

This shift to efficiency and assembly even shifted our experience of time itself, as we experience so well, now, in the current rush and flickering twittering. Time becomes experienced as something that is like an empty sequence of slots. It is no longer tethered to any particular thing or place or life whose time it weighs. It needs to be simply "filled" (Hans-Georg Gadamer, 1970, p. 342–3; see Sheila Ross, 2006). This image of "empty time" perfectly replicates the fragmentation central to efficiency and is all-too-familiar to anyone working in a school—rush, acceleration, time running out (David Jardine, 2016a, p. 179–192). It perfectly parallels how a curriculum topic becomes, in this light, something to be "covered," a sequence of things to be gotten "through" in an allotted period of (empty) time. As the object we are considering becomes bits and pieces and loses its sense of place and relation and interdependence, so, too, does the very experience of the time needed, now, not for dwelling over it, but instead for its reassembly. Reassembly beckons for efficiency. It no longer beckons for the lingering time of contemplation, dwelling, kinship, obligation, love, cultivation, fascination.

Nothing calls for a practiced and studious "halt in the middle of the rush" (Hans-Georg Gadamer, 1977, p. 15).

Dwelling over some place memorable and soaking up the tales told and trying to measure up to its ways (the work of learning, in an ancient sense that you can feel in your bones) becomes replaced with speedy memorization of fragments emptied of their relations.

Once the regimes of efficiency take hold of our imaginations, an affectionate and lingering relation to some aspect of the world, becomes understandable only as *inefficiency*. From a June 4, 1906 lecture by Fredrick Taylor (cited in Robert Kanigel, 2005, p. 169):

> In our scheme we do not ask for the initiative of our men. We do not want any initiative. All we want of them is to obey the orders we give them, do what we say, and do it quick.

>   Worn-out story emptied of its resonance:
>   A poster prominently displayed in a high school physics class . . .
>   "Don't ask me why we are learning something,
>   Ask yourself how you can learn it!"
>   Click.

In its educational manifest, teachers and students alike are unspokenly subjected to this regime. It is more than tragic when we might then, out of such unknowing of what has been done to us, complain of lack of initiative in students. It is a horrible amnesia about "that which has happened." We are all required to do what they we are told, in the sequence we are told to do it, at the speed determined by the machinations of efficient production, and we are all assessed by those who will measure the efficiency of such work. "In 1903, William C. Bagley identified the ideal teacher as one who would rigidly 'hew to the line.' He repeatedly stressed in his writing a need for 'unquestioned obedience.'" (Charles Wrege & Ronald Greenwood, 1991)

'agodzaahi

This is why we study. To find out where we are and what has happened to us "over and above our wanting and doing" (Hans-Georg Gadamer, 2004, p. xxviii) and what we might now do with this new alertness. There are many things to do.

Under the penumbra of fragmentation and efficiency, knowledge is no longer something that surrounds and sustains us and to which we might add our living attention. Our attentive application is not needed in such a world. "To be glib, little [in a world of knowledge envisioned as industrial assembly] requires human application, so little cultivates it" (Sheila Ross, 2006, p. 111). Worse yet, attention, initiative, aliveness, application, become seen *as threats to efficiency that need to be eradicated*. Questions become problems to be fixed so there will be no more questions. The fear becomes that any sort of letting go of the rigidity of the rules might mean that all hell breaks loose in the halls of a school:

> a "continuity of [our] attention and devotion" (Wendell Berry, 1986, p. 32) to some classroom work is very often not simply *unnecessary* but *impossible* because the school-matters at hand have been stripped of the very memorability and relatedness . . . . . . that might require and sustain and reward such attention and devotion. (David Jardine, 2012, p. 175)

It is no longer surprising that the proffering of an ecological pedagogy of joy in such circumstances appears only as a swoony, unrealistic, naïve romance.

We have often heard this efficiency/breakdown-inheritance in schools referred to as simply "the way things are," "the real world." Such is its dominance that any alternative to it is understood in advance as marginal, fluffy, unnecessary, an empty succession of words.

But here is the rub. *It is not* "the real world." It is just how the world happens to have turned out according to causes and conditions (daresay shared and contested "relations") that can be understood and studied and untangled. Once untangled, what once seemed like the real world is finally able to be experience as *possible* but not *necessary*. Once experienced as possible, it loses its ontological grip (the grip of seeming to be [but only seeming] "this is simply what is" [Greek, *ontos*]).

Worn-out story emptied of its [onto]logic:
What's it gonna be . . .
Economy or Environment?
Make your choice.
Click.

And then another nauseating tragedy. How many teachers have said to us and to so many others that they would love to take time over some difficult, beautiful, engaging place of knowledge and experience, but they simply don't have the time? How many students have become so well-schooled that they have no patience for the rich patience of study and its affections? "Tell me exactly what it is you want in this assignment" (David Smith, 1999, p. 11) and I'll do it:

> "Education is suffering from narration-sickness," says Paulo Freire. It speaks out of a story which was once full of enthusiasm, but now shows itself incapable of a surprise ending. The nausea of narration-sickness comes from having heard enough, of hearing many variations on a theme but no new theme (p. 135–6)

This dominant narrative proves its dominance by being able to name alternatives to it. We become—what is it called these days?—"snowflakes"? caught in emotional reactiveness and overly personalized self-annunciations and ecological swooning. Fuzzy, personal, weak, feminine, undisciplined creativity, woozy, disorderly, telling your unique story, wild, wholeness, mush. Many well-intended attempts at resistance are storied as, and often even become, "simply a projection of what the dominant voice ... . allows alternatives to be" (David Jardine, 2012, p. 7). Such is the character of colonial dominance: the colonized can sometimes take on the language of the colonizers, struggling to break free within the same orbit as their chains, unable to imagine an alternative beyond and other than the simplified dichotomy of efficiency/inefficiency, unable to be exorbitant.

Worn-out story emptied of its ancestors:
Let's meditate!
Let's get back to nature!
Let's share our feelings!
Let's celebrate diversity!
Click.

"Resistance is futile because even resistance has been coded" (David Jardine, 2012, p. 8). Oppositional Defiance Disorder.
Enough!

"You Need Accuracy": An Appreciation of a Modern Hunting Tradition and a Grouse's Life Unwasted II
David Jardine

Vital to the power of this writing is, again, that it must find its proper measure in the things that are its subject. I have found this, myself, in pursuing such writing, that it is not flimsy or subjective or random, but needs a terrible accuracy. Otherwise the whole thing deflates and becomes nothing but a self-referential, overly personal reminiscence. It loses its beckoning. Here, in this writing, we have profoundly personal reminiscence, but it is cast out into the world and its ways. This is why it is so effective for me as a reader. It is careful in its heeding of the life-world in all its meticulous detail. Part of its power to address us is in this accuracy. Without it, it betrays its object and betrays its own weakness.

"But what to do, what to do?
The geese say only, 'study'" *(Robert Bly, 2008)*

"If It Actually Exists, It Must Be Possible" I
David W. Jardine, Jodi Latremouille, Lesley Tait

I don't know of any topic in any Canadian curriculum guide that is not worthy of love, devotion, and study. I've never seen any topography, treated with affection, that cannot become an open and rich and living field of good work, good questions, and thrilling, often humiliating and painful and worthwhile discoveries and lessons. Loved, such places begin to glow and shed their light on us. "Sometimes it is necessary to reteach a thing is loveliness". This is our central task as teachers, not just with students, but also with all the knowledge entrusted to us in[side and outside of] schools. (David Jardine, 2018a, p. 224)

So, no. We don't need urgent cures for urgency. Urgency changes landscapes and locales into bordered territories; it changes places into battlegrounds where love and studious affection have no chance. (p. 224)

What we are proposing instead is long-standing, rigorous, difficult, well-documented in and out of schools, in line with the well-trod auspices of the living disciplines entrusted to teachers and students in schools.

"You Need Accuracy": An Appreciation of a Modern Hunting Tradition and a Grouse's Life Unwasted III
David Jardine

I mention all this because Jodi shared with me an email she received from her father, Vern, after she sent him an early version of "A Modern Hunting Tradition," and it points to something vital to the power of this writing [and the nature of this sort of work, this ecology, this pedagogy, this joy]. Included in parentheses are Jodi's comments on how her writing was edited in response:

Enjoyed your writing, not sure if you need accuracy but if you do: I never skid anything in the Cheesecloth Game bags, they are only when we put them on the packboard. [I had originally written that my husband skids a piece of moose down the hill in the game bag. Edited as per this e-mail]. Small moose in five pieces, big one in six with the head attached to the neck making it a pretty good load as J. will attest. Ha Ha. [I had originally written 3 pieces, 5 if very large. Edited as per this e-mail].

"If It Actually Exists, It Must Be Possible" Part II
David W. Jardine, Jodi Latremouille, Lesley Tait

"Cultivating love and affection for the ways and runs and paths of things (Latin *currere*) is a 'terrible trial' (Wendell Berry, with Bill Moyers, 2013)" (David Jardine, 2018a, p. 224) and that trial is called *study*, and study must be pursued under the actual, living conditions in which we each find ourselves and find each other, our students, or elders, our children, trapped in the confines of school traffic jams, or out under the sun for just a moment. It can be no other way.

We are suggesting that cleaving *more closely* to what gives a living discipline its life in the traditions inherited by teachers and students inside and outside of schools, and that the moments of such joyfully tough allure are a secret that many already know, that many have secreted away and practice in huddles away from the glare. The classroom door can always be closed if need be. "When the relations of production are based on mutual respect, patience, generosity, authentic listening and speaking, and a certain kind of hope shining forth from nascent senses of empowerment" (David Smith, 2016, p. xvii) we may imagine "entrust[ing] ourselves to what we are investigating to guide us safely in the quest" (Hans-Georg Gadamer, 2004, p. 378).

We have had enough of "this is not possible" where what is perceived as possible remains spell-bound by circumstance and exhaustion:

> Up against the too often pronounced exhaustion and desperation and despair of "this sort of thing is not possible in my school/with my sort of students/in this part of town/at this grade level/with this school administration/in this school board/in this subject area/with these parents/under these economic conditions," and so, on and on, we offer an old and pointed response of our late colleague, teacher and friend, Patricia Clifford: "if it actually exists, it *must* be possible." (Jackie Seidel & David Jardine, 2014, p. 2)

We have seen this way of relations, aliveness and love at work in classrooms, with teachers seeing "something that needs to be done and starting to do it, without the government's permission, or official advice, or expert advice, or applying for grants or anything else. They just start doing it" (Wendell Berry, with Bill Moyers, 2013, n.p.).

In our ecologically sorrowful times, we say, just start doing it. The heartbreak often is witnessing those caught in the spell of "this is the real world," this world of my exhaustion and distraction and panic. And terror over one misstep. The heartbreak comes because, no matter how often we feel this uprising joy, the sullen gravity of our inherited woes adheres and smothers still, like a stuck second skin. There is no once and for all, here. There is no easy path except alertness, again, again, meeting, talking, taking refuge in the real work and refuge, just for a moment, out of the spell-bound and spell-binding frays of "the real world."

One small breath: Shashi Shergill, from Connect Charter School in Calgary Alberta, carried out an inquiry project entitled All My Relations. Her students studied the historical and contemporary relationship between Aboriginal and non-Aboriginal peoples in Canada. They reflected on the meanings of collective rights as they analyzed documents including the 1996 Royal Commission on Aboriginal Peoples, and shared their learning through artistic representations and discussions with pre-service teachers from local universities (Canada's History, 2015).

wahkohtowin

One small thread: Jodi: My high school students and I studied the effects of toxic biosolids and joined local efforts to resist dumping in our community. It was eye-opening, boring at times, empowering, depressing, energizing. Some fell asleep during the local scientific roundtables and longed for the excitement and "infotainment" of Me to We Days (We Movement, 2017) while others marched in protests on weekends and came into their own as budding activists. (Jodi Latremouille, 2018a)

wicihitowin

One small remembering: Judson Innes, a local teacher, from a poem called "Time":
Tender parting and elegant flow,
a silent passing above the forest floor.
Wings raised up to gain favour,
and soften the looming perch. (Jusdon Innes, 2015, p. 107)

wahkohtowin

One small conspiracy: Michael Sitka-Sage (Michael Derby, 2015, p. 14) in writing about his team's work at a nature-based school in Maple Ridge, B.C., endeavours to make space for "education as storytelling: where chatter, laughter, conversations, stories, songs and dreams are as continuous as breathing."

sakihitowin

One small sowing: In Kehte-aya Bob Cardinal and Dwayne Donald's graduate holistic curriculum studies course at the University of Alberta, we focus on developing the four-part person. We are encouraged to inquire into and share our understandings of how "wisdom teachings regarding holistic understandings of life and living [may] provide meaningful curricular and pedagogical guidance in schools today" (Dwayne Donald, 2014a, p. 2). Kehte-aya Bob teaches that holistic approaches to learning must move people from their heads to their hearts, and so must be dedicated to healing. He facilitates shifts in thinking towards more holistic ways of knowing by continually asking the question: kiikway enohte ohpinaman? (What are you trying to lift?). As Dwayne Donald (in Jodi Latremouilllle, Antonella Bell, Zahra Kasamali, Mandy Krahn, Lesley Tait, & Dwayne Donald 2016, p. 9–10) has come to see it, "holism involves honouring ourselves by honouring the various more-than-human entities that give us life. When we lift what gives us life, we simultaneously lift all our relations."

wicihitowin

One small story: Stephanie Bartlett from Calgary, Alberta, worked with her kindergarten class to create Project Engage: Living our Lives for a Sustainable Future. It includes a metal collection station, a Christmas light collection and recycling campaign, a sweater day to raise awareness around energy use, and a partnership with a local community centre re-design (Chinook Park, 2016).

wahkohtowin

One small life: Carli Molnar contemplates a teaching whereby "life cannot be postponed. Mortality is nearer than we think" (2016, p. 97). She makes a promise to a young, terminally ill student, to "trust the journey/and to live well/today" (p. 101).

sakihitowin

One small conversation: Darren Vaast and Sarah Beech (2018) year-long work on a REDress Project with Grade 9 students issues and images of missing and murdered indigenous women.

wahkohtowin

One small visit (Lesley Tait): We take teachers to visit Nose Hill in the north of Calgary. It has a new offering circle that represents all four Blackfoot Nations. For most Calgarians, it is just a familiar place to walk your dog. And yet this sparse landscape right here in the middle of the city has medicine plants. Yarrow. Sage. Wolf willow. We visit time and time again. We walk up the big hill to the wheel. Coming to know. The term "authentic" comes up over and over again. How can we speak well about this land, these relationships, our own learning? We watch her change. We listen to her speak to us and tell us stories. We contemplate her as a holder of knowledge, as a warning system, as a mathematician. We learn to speak to her in a language that she has known the longest. She doesn't ask us who is more or less "authentic." And yet . . . There is a word in Cree that means "you have gone too far." pastahowin. Meaning you have stepped outside of your knowledge. I listen to Kehte-aya Bob ask me again, kiikway enohte ohpinaman, "what are you trying to lift?"

wicihitowin

One small wondering: Jackie Seidel (2012) writes about a paperwhite's lesson plan:

> The paperwhite is not worried about or planning for the future. It is alive right now. It is living in its own time, which is the only time there is. The only relationship we can have with it is in the time we share—which is the time we are living in now. The paperwhite cannot be in some other time or some other place. It can only be right here. Where it is. Now.

Might we hold the life of the paperwhite, still, in our hearts?
Might we hold our own lives and the lives of
our students, still, in our hearts?
The time and the body of the earth, still,
in our hearts?
(n.p.)

sakihitowin

"Like Life, it is Hazy" I: "We Seek the Right Word"
David Jardine

Language itself is a form of life, and like life it is hazy [diesig]; over and over it will surround us with a haze. Again and again we move for a while in a self-lighting haze, a haze that again envelops us as we seek the right word. Hans-Georg Gadamer (2007a, p. 371)

That first phrase alludes to Ludwig Wittgenstein's *Philosophical Investigations* (1968) about which it would be oversimplifying to say that forms of language are, or are reflective of, or are based in, or are emergent from, or are, or are, or are, forms of life. These sketch out how we live, how we belong together, how and what we imagine ourselves and our being to be, and what the nature and limits of that belonging might be. It sketches out in faded form the puzzles of who is "we" and who might not be. And this even though "others" might have the same intimacies with their language as I do with mine. And this is true, too, of the Stellar's Jay that just made its way through like it does every spring in the foothills: a breathy "che" repeated fast, in clusters of 7 breaths, each one the same pitch.

It clangors with the depth of violence that comes from robbing language away, suppressing the voice, refusing the name. Language (in its myriad) does not just point to things but is a living form of the manifest of things, a myriad of habitats and nestlings, of showings and hidings, troubles, beauties, blockages and on and on, and each of these understandable only from the point of view of someone uttering, someone writing or reading. And all this, too, with gesture and the paint stroke and the lilt of melody and the uplift foot point danced and spun.

Language arts. And funny, too, how these two elders of European philosophy allude to each other without saying so in so many words, echo upon echo, easily lost in translation.

Language is thus a multivariate shape that life takes, that, also inversely, shapes life just as much as does oxygen. We are its creature as much as its creator.

Let's be a bit more audacious and see what happens if we do: Language [in this fulsome sense] is a life-form. A myriad of life-forms, in fact, teeming, supporting, battling, related, contested. It is not simply a set of designators inside a life form's orbit, but a life-form in which we are the inhabitants, here, under Raven eyes and smoke.

We are not simply the designators but the designated. We are designated, named, summoned, implicated, accused, thanked, even by the arrival of bees at the compost heap.

WAYSTATION VII
"Everyone is Hungry": A Conversation with Jackie Seidel about Bees

Introduction

David Jardine. Monday, March 25, 2019:

I think it is interesting . . . if edited a bit, esp. with your last piece, and here's the title, to quote you: "Everyone is Hungry." It is a narrative stretch of looking, decoding, watching, learning, life, buzzing, communicating (in myriad ways, UsYouMeBeeBluberries from Chile with the plastic clam shells in the recycling bin). Being indigenous and not. And noticing, intensely, specifically. And knowing some about the ways of something things. And loving knowing. And knowing of the penumbras of unknowing we live in.

Let me fiddle w. it a wee bit and see what happens. Perhaps this email makes a good introduction.

P.S., no snow here at all.

Flights Back and Forth

David Jardine. Friday, March 22, 2019:

I thought my compost heap, now thawing, was swarmed with ground hornets. nope [I don't think?]. It's bees!

Jackie Seidel. Friday, March 22, 2019

Send pictures!

David Jardine. Friday, March 22, 2019, 12:49 PM

I can't tell. Looks furry to me?

Jackie Seidel. Friday, March 22, 2019, 1:27PM

Ohh! Honey bees! That's interesting. Who has them close to you? Can you tell what they are gathering? They are hungry. Is there something sweet there?

David Jardine. Friday, March 22, 2019, 1:28 PM

Oh yes, compost. oranges blueberries, cilantro, lettuce, banana peels and on and on. there are at least 40–50 of them.

Jackie Seidel. Friday, March 22, 2019, 1:29PM

Oh! Ha. Blueberries. They are looking for sugar! Going out to check my hives soon! I'll see who is alive. Banana. They will like that too. Technically they don't eat that stuff but I think in spring they will. Do you know who has bees nearby? I would just want to sit there watching them. They may have no food left in their hive. If they are searching like this. It's amazing! Are the pussy willow out yet?

David Jardine. Friday, March 22, 2019, 1:30 PM

I don't know of anyone nearby who's got hives. maybe they are freeloaders! No Pussy Willow yet that I've seen.

Jackie Seidel. Friday, March 22, 2019, 1:34PM

Someone has them close to you. But could be up to maybe 2 miles away. But I doubt that at this time of year. They are close. And one or two bees found your compost and went back and got the others. It's not just 50 bees. They fly so fast you won't notice them coming and going. They just appear and disappear. Like magic. Could be thousands. Coming and going.

David Jardine. Friday, March 22, 2019, 1:30 PM

Could they not have a hive they made without someone close? Must take a chair out there and sit in the sun for a bit. It'll help with my tinnitus (quite lousy lately . . . need some 'real' buzzing! Hah!)

Jackie Seidel. Friday, March 22, 2019, 2:25PM

Probably not . . . swarms do not usually survive winter in Alberta . . . it does happen . . . could be in a garage wall . . . somewhere slightly warm . . . but for a colony to survive winter, they have to go into winter with about 3 pounds of bees probably (to have about 2 pounds left by spring). and a queen which they could have made one last summer . . . it is possible that they could be from a swarm but rare. I suspect someone has bees nearby. It's the most reasonable explanation. Bees do pretty well out there. The great thing is that wherever they are from, they made it through this harsh winter . . .

. . .so far . . . a ways to go before they can find enough food . . . they need pollen (protein) asap for their babies . . . the adult bees eat carbs only . . . so that's why they are there at your house . . . searching for carbs . . . so they can fly around and find baby food . . . once they start to find pollen, the queen will start laying. I bought some pollen this year . . . it arrived with UPS earlier so I will go out and put into the hives in a while.

I thought only one of my hives survived, but there are bees outside *all three* today. Although it could be only bees from one hive . . . they may be going into the other ones stealing honey and those hives may be dead. Also,

another person in Brentwood has a lot of hives around the neighborhood . . . bees could be coming from those people. So if those colonies are dead I should remove the honey frames and give them to the live bees or save them in the garage . . . I'll know soon . . stay tuned.
Tinnitus! Yuck. I have it too. Definitely go watch the bees!
Jackie Seidel, Sunday March 24, 2019, 6:33 PM
P.S. All three of my colonies are *alive* for now . . . I need to look deeper on next warm day . . . to see if there are eggs, and see what size of colonies is . . . all I know for sure is there are live bees in each, but that doesn't mean queens are alive, or that there is a sufficient colony size to maintain them until spring or do the hard work they need to do to build up their colony once spring really hits . . .
I meant to say, when you said they are 'fuzzy' in one of your initial emails . . . fuzziness is one of the distinguishing characteristics of *all* bees. It distinguishes them from wasps and flies (along with other markers from bee species to bee species). As soon as you said they are fuzzy, I knew they were bees before seeing the picture . . . you should see Bumble Bees any day at your place . . . that is prime Bumble habitat . . . I was reading that in K-Country they should be out *en masse* on the southern slopes within the next 2 weeks. Watch for them! As soon as anything appears that has pollen (pussy willows! Kinnikinick . . . do you have it there? Probably .), they will appear . . . you'll see the big queens first . . . they are hibernating alone. They mated in the fall . . . they have to establish their nests . so they will build their nest, lay eggs, collect lots of pollen to feed the babies . . . then you'll see even more very soon . . .

Snowing heavily . . . sigh.

David Jardine. Friday, March 24, 2019, 7:30 PM
Can't possibly recall when I "heard" that bees were fuzzy. I make a cleaned-up version of the attached and it could be all or part of your waystation for the jodilesleyme book?
Jackie Seidel, Sunday March 24, 2019, 8:00 PM
Hmm . . . maybe? Is it interesting to other people? I'm not sure.

Relations, Aliveness, Love | 179

The most interesting part to me is the mystery of where they come from . . .
along with the fact that
they are not indigenous here, and
neither is most of what is in your compost
(actually
none
of what is in your compost
right
now)
. . . everyone is hungry . . .

David Jardine, Friday, June 21, 2019, 4:34PM
Hope you don't mind that I broke up the lines of your last email. It was so gorgeous, reading it now, months later @Solstice and the anniversary, yesterday, of the floods.

"Like Life, it is Hazy": Part II, "It is All I Can Muster"
David Jardine

Picking up the compost at the local grocery store and making sure the plastic gets recycled seems like an utterly trivial penance and I continue to do it daily and let myself face that triviality, that utter meagerness, every single time. Any time anyone visits and we tour the joint I mention it and how tragic the whole matter is. A whole large box of still-edible red onions caught in exactly whose agony of having made it all the way here from afar and ending up sitting in the back hall right now as I write?

It is all I can muster to "help"—but it seems so meager, so small, so futile.

I was picking up the daily load last Friday and in the back of the grocery store there was a Grade 4 class, about twenty kids, talking w. the owner who just then, by coincidence, was telling the group about what I did daily. [An aside: to be back in the middle of such a gathering nearly brought me to tears. Old memories of invigoration and clarity and teaching and learning].

So, I packed the car, got the mail, and meanwhile the store owner had given the kids Macintosh apples as a treat.

As I left the parking lot where the kids and teachers were now gathered, I swung by to give the teacher my phone number, and mention that the compost heaps I keep are just around the corner if they want another short field trip—greenhouse, gardens, etc. Kids started coming up to me with their apple cores. I opened the car hatch and they started tossing them in the boxes I'd just picked up. I got to say something bland and true like "Yes, it is a simple as that" as some hurried up to finish and toss.

Got back in the car with the window rolled down, ready to go, and one utterly beautiful young girl came near, stood still and looked at me, softly, and nearly smiled, no words.

Transfixing. In retrospect, feels like another vivid dream that lasted hours, even though it was only a few seconds. Caught in her regard and she in mine.

As is my weakness, I just checked the etymology regarding 'regard': not just looking at and seeing each other, but that other sense of "kindly feeling which springs from a consideration of estimable qualities."

And So. Relations, Aliveness, Love III
Jodi Latremouille, Lesley Tait & David Jardine

One small reminder: Ian Walsh offers advice to a new teacher: "Young teacher, young teacher, you will never 'go teach.' You will always be at a place" (Ian Walsh, 2016, p. 65)

wahkohtowin

> Stopping discouragement because wherever you are is a place to practice. (Tsong-Kha-Pa, 2000, p. 191)

So, no, don't panic. Don't rush. Study. Still. You will always be at a place. The challenge we face is to find new, more careful and proper ways to write about and through this cluster of work that is already erupting. There is no "one best way" (Robert Kanigel, 2005) through the full and abundant wealth of the Earth. "Only in the multifariousness of . . . . . . voices do [we Earthly beings] exist" (Hans-Georg Gadamer, 2004, p. 295). And *sometimes* efficiency is just the thing our circumstances need, but it has lost its responsiveness, its summons, its sense of proper proportion. It has become monstrous. This cleaves around an odd reminder from David G. Smith (2006, p. 55):

> The real challenge is to face the truth that no one tradition can say everything that needs to be said about the full expression of human experience in the world and that what the global community requires more than anything else is mutual recognition of the various poverties of *every* tradition. The search to cure the poverty of one's own tradition works in all directions at once.

We don't need new buzzwords, checklists, acronyms, and yet another sleek packaged curriculum resource. "We need to let the words stand like single malt whiskey or aged cheddar, instead of always seeking the fast-food remedy" (Carl Leggo, 2006, p. 78)

A Death in the Family

David Jardine

Part One:

Daresay February 26, 2019, 7:03 AM.
Still, no word. Still. No word.

A Poem Found Near Sea Level (for Carl)
  The word still
  Is enough.
... .speaking of this "still,"
... .this "and yet,"
... .this "persisting,"
... .this "quieting,"
... .this secret source of pirated spirits deep in the woods,
all giggled together, distilled into words at sea level.
(David Jardine, 2019, p. 5, all this above being part of the dedication of
  that book to Carl Leggo, who died on March 7, 2019)

Part Two:
So, still, still word and no word. Still. So still.
Friday, March 1, 2019, 11:18 MT:
On Your Behalf (David Jardine)
Carl, Carl.

I'm breathing up on Raven wings.
On both our behalfs.
If you stretch out your eyes,
Down below the arced blacks of ink and feathers.
Up on the up on the up on the
Up winds. There. Stretch.
You'll see I'm still.
In love with you.

But I guess you knew that already.
You and me and we of once-long-and-oh-so-thinning-hair.
And thinning years.
Guess what lasts? You know. You taught me this. You've become my
   teacher once again.
Just a reminder that you gave me so often
            then, and now, oh, now, oh, so now.
To let the living happen as it will
            and as it won't.
As we all will on your behalf

What is needed is something that must be "won by a certain labor" (Sheila Ross & David Jardine, 2009) by practices and attention over lingering, intense time. The secret here, is that insight into the richness and poverty of our shared and contested circumstances and traditions is not a matter of tearing things down, not one of being merely "radical" in the common coinage of this term. We search for something more deeply radical (Latin: radicalis, "root"), a rootedness in the human and more-than-human world that seeks the conditions of its continuance and well-being.

There are ways of following leads, of treading softly, of paying attention, of being wisely aware (Lesley Tait, in Jodi Latremouillle, Antonella Bell, Zahra Kasamali, Mandy Krahn, Lesley Tait, & Dwayne Donald 2016, p. 12).

"There are other ways of making worlds" (Anna Tsing, 2015, p. 155).

wahkohtowin

Everything points to some other thing. Nothing comes forward just in the one meaning that is offered to us. (Hans-Georg Gadamer, 2007b, p. 131)

> Every word breaks forth as if from a center and is related to a whole, through which alone it is a word. Every word causes the whole ... to which it belongs to resonate. Every word [every gesture, every breath] ... carries with it the unsaid, to which it is related by responding and summoning. (Hans-Georg, Gadamer, 2004, p. 458)

In classrooms, we do not group students together to talk about a topic simply (yet not so simply) so that they can each have their say and hear what others have to say. We do it because, in relation—like the three of us authoring this writing, like the ancestors we summon and quote—each of us is able to *find out* what we have to say (its limits, its breakthroughs, its pathologies, its glimmers of insight) by having it read back to us "other-wise." Just like, in an elementary school mathematics class, subtraction helps illuminate addition in a way that wouldn't happen if they are taught out of relation, so, too, "relations" refers to our kin, our fellow human beings, our family, our colleagues, our ancestors, living and dead, listened to or read. We gather, here, and read them back and forth. We gather in conspiracies of shared breath and then email back and forth, weave (Latin *textus*). We teach, knowing full well that "everything around us teaches" (Tsong-Kha-Pa, 2000, p. 151) and that only when teaching itself, learning itself, curriculum itself, releases itself out into all its relations of responding and summoning, do each of them become viable and sustainable and true.

"Like Life, it is Hazy": Part III "We All Knew What was Happening"
David Jardine

Let's not get too cute. The full citation from Tsong-Kha-Pa above is that "everything around us teaches impermanence" (p. 151).

Last year, sitting out on the deck in the red-brown-yellow smoke haze from the fires in the B.C. interior and from Northern Alberta, it became clear. Despite monstrous hallucinations about "climate change," the real result will not be [just] some recognizable catastrophic monster event that demonstrates with clear regard.

It will be like this, *diesig*, "hazy," a slump in the light, an acridity in the air, a wee eye-sting, and half the tomatoes in the greenhouse not ripening before the hard frosts hit.

All bent. Slumped vines. Shoulder-slumped. The postures of regret and ringing ears.

"The word 'slump,' or 'slumped,' has too coarse a sound to be used by a lady. [Eliza Leslie, Miss Leslie's Behaviour Book, Philadelphia, 1839]," (this from the Online Etymological Dictionary).

Funny, that, in a way. "Too coarse a sound." Slump. This life-form of language evolves in such weird ways over the years.

All this gathered up is like a vivid dream had some years ago of walking a city street full of people—I'd swear it was downtown Dayton, Ohio, back in my Bergamo days—full of too-bright sunlight, but with large spacious white

snowflake-like drifts coming down from the sky, lilting in air like white doves. And we all knew what was happening. And we all knew what we had done. And we all knew that it was now too late.

And it was beautiful, beautiful to regard. Even our sorrow.

Things revealing themselves passing away. We've got that owl on the front cover, and in some First Nations traditions, it is a portend of death. And then this Greek prospect: The owl is Minerva's consort, an old Athenian image on coins, summoning Athena and wisdom. And it invokes an adage of Georg Wilhelm Friedrich Hegel, where the owl, in ancient Greek memory, portends the possibility of insight, of wisdom (as might a portend of death, too), but—and here is the agony, the grief of "too late" (think of the regret of death coming and finding insight too late)—it only flies at dusk, at the end of the day, the end of the age, at the ending:

> A further word on the subject of *issuing instructions* on how the world ought to be: philosophy . . . . always comes too late to perform this function. When philosophy paints its grey in grey, a shape of life has grown old, and it cannot be rejuvenated, but only recognized. The owl of Minerva begins its flight only with the onset of dusk. (Georg Wilhelm Friedrich Hegel, 1820/1991, p. 22)

This needs consideration. What if all the urgent calls for what education "ought to be" inevitably emerge "too late"? What if joy, aliveness and love come by as time slips? What if this is true, that insight only comes as something is on the verge of now-inevitably passing away? This very idea is an ecological nightmare as much as is our insight into the ecological nightmares that surround us like dusk.

What shall we do, now? What if it is too late to be simply shaken from sleep? What if the smoke haze rounds the sun in mid-day?

And so, wahkohtowin:

> The term *wahkohtowin* refers to kinship relations and teaches us to extend our relational network so that it also includes the more-than-human beings that live amongst us. Doing so helps us remain mindful that we human beings are fully enmeshed in a series of relationships that enable us to live. Thus, following the relational wisdom of *wahkohtowin*, we are called to repeatedly acknowledge the fact that the sun, the land, the wind, the water, the animals and the trees (just to name a few) are quite literally our relatives; we carry parts of each of them inside our own bodies. We are fully reliant on them for our survival, and so the wise person works to ensure that those more-than-human relatives are kept healthy and treated with the deep respect that they deserve. (Dwayne Donald, 2016, p. 10)

Lesley Tait: The footsteps of the many who walk up amongst the grasses to the top of each hill awaken the land and alert her to our presence. Each step begins again the process of attunement to the vibrations, voice, songs of this particular place. . . . .

"Songlines"
David Jardine and Jodi Latremouille

Jodi: Hi, David, I was reading [David Abram's 1996] The Spell of the Sensuous was reminded of that paper you sent us a couple of weeks ago. There is a passage about the Australian Aboriginal tradition of "songlines" or "ways through" the continent, meandering trails, auditory route maps that are composed of a melody with various verses to be sung in different locations. It speaks of the Dreamtime Ancestors, while chanting their ways across the land, depositing a trail of "spirit children" along the trail. They are described as "life cells," children not yet born; they lie in a potential state within the ground. When a woman is pregnant, the actual conception is thought to occur with the quickening, when she steps on a song couplet in the earth. So the spirit child "works its way into her womb, and impregnates the fetus with song":

> Wherever the woman find herself when she feels the quickening—the first kick within her womb—she knows that a spirit child has just leapt into her body from the earth. And so she notes the precis place in the land where the quickening occurred, and reports this to the tribal Elders. The Elders then examine the land at that spot, discerning which Ancestor's songline was involved, and precisely which stanzas of that Ancestor's song will belong to the child … In this manner every Aboriginal person, at birth, inherits a particular stretch of song as his private property, a stretch of song that is, as it were, his title to a stretch of land, to his conception site. (David Abram, 1996, p. 166–7).

I woke up this morning way too early and couldn't go back to sleep! Maybe if I send you this I can sleep again:-)

David: Well, I woke up this morning thinking of that paper and how I might either finish it or abandon it again for now. This almost reminds me of what Abram is describing—this fortuitous email just leapt! And that that leap is an ancestral one in its own way.

(full passage is from David Jardine, 2015c, p. 109–110)

Lesley Tait:... Each coming to know each other again. The first time you greet the land by her name kikawinaw askiy (mother earth) or our plant relations by their names, whether it be nîpisîy (willow), or iyinimina (blueberries), a process has begun. The process of coming to know land, time, space and relationship that was not possible before you learned their names. The process of relearning what it might mean to listen and what it is that we deem worthy of listening to. Speaking these names into the air not only begins the process of coming to know but summons the ancestors to walk alongside you. Now you notice them. Now you see them change. Now you see their first buds.

wahkohtowin

Winter
(Lesley Tait)

Renewal and preparation begin again. We are back in the place where we see our footsteps in the snow and ask that we are able to return to the place where we see our footsteps in the grass.

I choose sage over oil when anointing myself to write. Guidance around how the hands will help the words flow.

January, February, March, April begins the inane prattle
May, June, July
Repeated into students until they leave their dent
Shiny new backpacks
Children on carpets
Asked to remain in their space
Small windows not to distract them with the outside
God forbid

Adults remember the prattle
They obey the command
Tell me the months of the year . . ..
August September, October
Now tell me its origin
Silence . . ...
Silence . . ...
The ceasing of the prattle.
November, December
Said with hope

Months imported from the ancient Greeks and romans
Lots of space between here and there
Thousands of stories between here and there
kisîpîsim (keey **say** pissim)
mikisiwi-pîsim- (Mick **so** pisim)
niskipîsim- (Nisk **ih** pisim)
athîkipîsim-(ay ee **ki** pisim)

Great moon, eagle moon, goose moon, frog moon
Tethered

Here

The space between time and place disappears as I repeat and practice

sakipakawpisim (sah gee pah cow pisim)
paskahopisim (paska **hoe** pisim)
paskkowipisim (pask cow Ih(i) pisim)
ohpahowpisim (oh paw **ho** pisim)
nocihtowpisim (no chi **toe** pisim)
pinaskowipisim (pinask cow pisim)
kaskatinowpisim (kask a **no** pisim)
pawahcakinasispisim (pow wa chik i na sis pisim)

Lesley Tait, December 7, 2018. E-Mail to David, Jodi

This doesn't fit. I just need to share. I am stuck around the concept of equity in education. And how that relates to assessments. I know these are ideas everyone already understands. But sometimes I need to write to understand my own thoughts.

Assessment has long been a system used to classify and sort out or students. Insert your [preferred] term here: High achievers, low achievers, masters, proficient, requiring support, not yet meeting standards, detailed, lazy. These all indicate a sub-belief about those we are educating. That they can indeed be sorted and in fact deserve to be sorted. They are used to find out those worthy of going to university and thus succeeding. Those who needs to find trades, those who need to find low stress work, those who will excel etc. Assessment as a sieve (graphic?). Input = output of a person. Maximizing achievement gaps. Create competition for the top of the bell curve. Dance for us. Success is scarce. You can't all have it. With a promise of a reward. Please give up if you are near the bottom.

Like the teacher who proudly told me: "don't worry, I passed Sally"—

Like the teacher who said, "but their effort is a large part of assessing their skills."

Like the principal who said: "but zeros prepare them for the real world, not everything comes easy."

About 50 % of our Indigenous youth live in poverty. They work full time. They deal with racism daily. They take care of their siblings. This is the fucking real world. Don't tell me about the fucking real world.

Jodi Latremouille, December 7, 2018. E-Mail to David, Lesley

This was in a recent paper for Ellyn Lyle's book. A tiny excerpt from a poem ... this was "a confession to the academy." The idea was "I am very bad at drawing boundaries ..."

Not on other lives:

> How do I, a teacher, grade a life? Based on the size of the word-stones they hurl at others to impress me in class discussions? Based on the fact that just making it to class every day is a victory in their life? Based on a sterile, static rubric? Based on how many years they have been speaking and writing "my" English? Based on how much money their parents make? Based on how much they travel? Based on what they had for dinner last night? Based on "self-esteem?" Growth? Stagnation? Passion? Pride? How do I grade a life? (Jodi Latremouille, 2018b, p. 221)

Lesley Tait, December 7, 2018. Email to David, Jodi

> Historically, a primary social mission of our schools has to begin the process of sorting citizens into the various segments of our social and economic system by ranking them based on achievement by the end of high school. Assessment's traditional role has been to provide the evidence needed. (Rick Stiggins, 2007, p. 24)

Dance for us. Success is scarce. You can't all have it. Please give up. Your hopelessness allows me to justify everything I have done to you. I created the hopelessness. It's just the way it's done. I'm just preparing you for the real world.

Just over half of Canada's Indigenous youth graduate from high school. This is the fucking real world. Don't tell me about the fucking real world.

> To redesign social systems we need first to acknowledge their colossal unseen dimensions. The silences and denials surrounding privilege are the key political tool here. They keep the thinking about equality or equity incomplete, protecting unearned advantage and conferred dominance by making these taboo

subjects. Most talk by whites about equal opportunity seems to be now to be about equal opportunity to try to get into a position of dominance while denying that systems of dominance exist. (McIntosh, 1989, p. 12)

Success in (Aboriginal curricular initiatives) is measured by how well Aboriginal topics and students can be swallowed into the larger corpus known as education. That corpus feeds on and digests what it swallows, and eventually poops out what it cannot otherwise process. (Dwayne Donald, 2016, p. 15)

You dance, I decide your worth.

A Breath, When the Birds Will Show Us
Lesley Tait

And so . . . I do not swallow you whole or in pieces, I walk alongside you. I do not hold the knowledge. I do not hold the answers. But I watch you walk. We greet those who come to greet us. We enter into the field of play. We argue over the correct word by which to call that one plant. You were right. It was the buffalo berry. We sit together beside the river and wonder why these berries aren't eaten by the birds this year. Must be the dirt we decide. Still made dirty from the flood 5 years ago. We wonder when the birds will show us when they are safe to eat again. Soon, maybe.

Part VI
Silent Reading

Successful Assimilation Part I

Lesley Tait

I first encountered the words "successful assimilation" while reading everything I could about the significant loss of lands for the Michel First Nation band. Michel First Nation is where my family comes from. My great-grandfather was chief. My grandfather was chief after him. Trace it back far enough and I am a direct descendant of Michel Calihoo for whom the band was named. He himself was a signatory on the Treaty 6 documentation. This is not a loose and fleeting attachment. This is somehow something more.

Something significant.

Yet I myself would never be looked at by unknowing eyes as an Indigenous person. I don't have the skin tone, I don't speak the language.

In 1958, for the first and only time in Canadian history, the Canadian government involuntarily enfranchised the remaining and vastly depleted lands of the Michel Band as a whole and sold these lands to various parties. Indian Act was changed in 1958, specifically for the "legal" enfranchisement of Michel lands, then immediately changed back in 1959 after the completion of land title transfer. Between 1880 and 1958, the entire 25,600 acres of Michel reserve were lost to enfranchisement and surrender.

As such, we are a scattered people. A people without a cultural and ancestral homeland. A people without our extended family around the next corner. A people with no land on which to share our stories both with ourselves and with others. We, the Michel Nation are disconnected and disjointed from each other and our heritage.

Would this be different if we were not "landless"? This landlessness and "enfranchisement" have many far-reaching implications. The stories are not as strong as they need to be. The traditions are beginning to fade, the understandings of the land are beginning to dwindle. And if we take an idea from Thomas King (2003) that all we are is our stories, where does that leave the people of Michel? We don't live with our relatives, in the same community, like other bands, like other indigenous families. We don't have a place to come together, to celebrate, to mourn, to pass on knowledge and history. I would assert that the dispossession of our lands has led to the breakdown of my family and our connection to one another and our culture.

Or as others may view it, Successful assimilation.

So, who am I? I do not speak our language; I do not drum or chant. I cannot hoop dance. And yet I choose to identify myself as Indigenous and as a member of Michel Nation.

Am I the "assimilated Indian" the government and Frank Oliver were looking for? Are we, the people of Michel, an example of successful enfranchising?

"Learn to Read and Become Civilized," Part I
David Jardine

Something like decolonization is not going to occur by forgetting what has happened to all of us. It can only occur by transforming these Eurocentric legacies into legible threads of inheritance, legible threads of decisions made or foregone, remembered or forgotten. Those little developmentally sequenced books, so commonplace in schools, are not just "the way thing are" in Canadian schools. They are full of ghosts and voices and stories long forgotten. Like Lesley's.

Like this, too. Elio Antonio de Nebrija (1444–1522), grammarian, Spain, petitioned Queen Isabella on August 18, 1492, 15 days after Columbus first sailed:

Nebrija advocates the reduction of the Queen's subjects to an entirely new type of dependence. He presents her with a new weapon, grammar. [Nebrija] offers Isabella a tool to colonize the language spoken *by her own subjects* [and, from here, that which will allow the subjugations that will follow]; he wants her to replace the people's speech by the imposition of the queen's *lengua* - her language, her tongue. [Nebrija petitioned the Queen]: "Language has always been the consort of empire, and forever shall remain its mate. Together they come into being, together they grow and flower, and together they decline." (Ivan Illich, 1980)

> These words, rung back to 1492, make the erasures of First Nations languages make perfect, terrible sense. But then again, developmental readers work out the same logic in all who read them.
> And this, I now find, just a small step portend of The Doctrine of Discovery (see Gilder Leherman Institute of American History, 1493) to be issued as a Papal Bull, "Inter Caetera" by Pope Alexander VI on May 4, 1493:

The Bull stated that any land not inhabited by Christians was available to be "discovered," claimed, and exploited by Christian rulers and declared that "the Catholic faith and the Christian religion be exalted and be everywhere increased and spread, that the health of souls be cared for and that barbarous nations be overthrown and brought to the faith itself." This "Doctrine of Discovery" became the basis of all European claims in the Americas as well as the foundation for the United States' western expansion. In the US Supreme Court in the 1823 case *Johnson v. McIntosh*, Chief Justice John Marshall's opinion in the unanimous decision held "that the principle of discovery gave European nations an absolute right to New World lands." In essence, American Indians had only a right of occupancy, which could be abolished. (Gilder Leherman Institute of American History, 1493)

Who's forgetting? Who forgot? Who never knew til now? To my shame, the above references to Nebrija I had originally found in 2005.

This "discovery" document? 2022. After the [white] public upwell of unmarked children's graves long known behind the fence full of stuffed animals in their memory.

Raising a Reader I:
terror-memory prelude: I *Am* Reading
Jodi Latremouille

Kevin O'Leary is an affiliate of *The Learning Company*, a subsidiary of Houghton Mifflin, which publishes various popular "learn to read" series, such as Carmen Sandiego and Reader Rabbit. During an episode of the CBC series, "Dragon's Den," he said:

> I'm all for children, but I want to make a buck . . . I *am* Reader Rabbit, I *am* Carmen San Diego, I *am* Reader Rabbit. And this is what I do. People as you know, will do anything for their children to help them in math and reading scores. I made a fortune just servicing that market. I love the terror in a mother's heart when she sees her child fall behind in reading. I profited from that. (Kevin O'Leary, 2012)

David Jardine reflects:

> [T]his market logic does not work properly when one simply takes advantage of such terror and satisfies it. Such terror must be cultivated and maintained in just the right measure. Market economies are premised on the creation of dissatisfaction and the promise and semblance of just enough satisfaction to allow dissatisfaction to re-emerge once the promise is forgotten. (David Jardine, 2016d, p. 162)

Successful Assimilation, Part II
Lesley Tait

In 2015, I started a new teaching position. I was a literacy specialist for 1 year, and 98% of my students were learning English and were entering into a new culture for the first time. I also walked into a building where books exist at "levels" and are housed in plastic bags. These are objects removed from their "place." Literacy is thought to be successful if children move up the ladder from plastic level bag to plastic levelled bag. We continue to colonize these children through the good news of literacy. Learn to read and become civilized.

This school, as with many others, assumes their audience before they begin to teach. It does not matter who walks through that door, the curriculum and the aim will be same. There exists a constant low level of panic. What if they don't learn to read? What if we, as teachers, fail? Every aspect of curriculum has been disconnected from where it truly lives.

How do we step outside the panic? How do we slow down in a time of terrible trial when this is what we see every day in schools?

The current response to kids not reading is to give them books not worth reading. These plastic bags promise quick growth and increased phonemic awareness. They promise a year's growth in only 6 months. Follow the program and all will be okay. They, in fact, promise successful assimilation. These words now sit very heavily on my shoulders and they are uncomfortable.

WAYSTATION VIII
Mom's poem
Sheila Ewasiuk

Laurier was my friend

I met him at Villeneuve school
an off reserve school
4 miles from my home

my home of many siblings and full of my parent's love

Laurier was my friend
We played marbles
ran races
laughed
he always waited for me at recess
saved me a seat on the bus

Laurier was no longer my friend

told by his mother that I was an Indian
no longer could he play with me
Laurier was my friend
I still miss him
Sheila Ewasiuk

Lesley: I remember mom telling me this story a few times when I was a child.
   I think she told me as a warning.
   I always knew we were never to tell people who we were.
   She was protecting me.

"Learn to Read and Become Civilized," Part II:
David Jardine

Books exist at
"levels"
and are
housed in plastic
bags. move up the ladder from
plastic levelled
bag to plastic
levelled
bag.

> The good news of literacy:
> Learn to read and become civilized.
> (Lesley Tait, 2016b, p. 18)

John Gray clearly voices modernity's self-understanding: "Modernity is a single condition, everywhere the same and always benign. As societies become more modern, so they become more alike. At the same time, they become better" (John Gray, 2003, p. 1).

In [Jean] Piaget's work, the founder of the contemporary sort of developmentalism that overtook schools, "the child is the real primitive among us, the missing link between prehistorical men and contemporary adults" (Jean Jacques Voneche & Magali Bovet, 1982, p. 88)

The child is the real primitive.

The primitive is the real child.

The thinkers of the Enlightenment . . . never doubted that the future for every nation in the world was to accept some version of Western institutions and values. A diversity of cultures was not a permanent condition of human life. It was a stage on the way to a universal civilization. (John Gray, 2001, p. 2)

With developmentalism, we get a new twist on [the advances of colonialism]: "we" . . . are not just "the best" amongst others in the world. "We" are that *towards which* the world is heading *in its natural and inevitable progress towards maturity [/civility]*. "We" [fully developed non-primitives] are not just *in the world* [as the best, most civilized, and so on] but are its natural *end* (see Francis Fukuyama, 2006), and the failures of the world to continue to (naturally) develop *into what we already are* must be dealt with pre-emptively [as one would with a child]. In education [we] are always at great pains to understand *in advance* what students' futures might be. (David Jardine, 2012, p. 66)

Education seems like a preparation for something that never happens because . . .it has *already happened*. There *is* no future because the future *already is*. (David G. Smith, 2006, p. 25)

Learn to read and become civilized.

Part of the tough joy, here, is that we refuse to hold our breaths, to hold our tongues, to let little insights remain marginalized or trivialized.

We sing up into the air right here, in the face of this pointed story that we are living out whether we know it or not.

This rush and ravage and muddy amnesia, this fragmentation and standardization and market-economic levelling and foreclosing is not the real world or "just the way things are," even if we experience it to be thus.

It is just how the world happens to have turned out.

It can be otherwise.
We can be other-wise.
It can be otherwise.
We can be other-wise

Raising a Reader II: First Reading: Terror-Memories
Jodi Latremouille

Mother: Ok, so, I was raised to believe that reading was very valuable, and I lived under the myth that I was a strong, fast reader from an early age. As the oldest of two daughters, I was an overachiever, perfectionist, ambitious child. I am told that when I was 4 years old, I was painstakingly writing stories about Little Red Riding Hood, cats in doll's clothes, and sisters playing by the lake. I would yell into the kitchen, "Mom, how do you spell 'kitty'? ... Mom, how do you make a 'k'?" At age eight, I read *Children: The Challenge* (Rudolf Dreikurs & Vicki Stolz, 1987), thick, green tome, filled with case studies and in-depth parenting advice and psychological analysis. I then proceeded to critique my parents' parenting skills and offer advice about how they might best deal with their "challenging child."

I love and cherish these old stories, as they are part of my identity as a creative, thoughtful, and intellectual individual. I have come to believe that my strength in reading is deeply interwoven with my success in the academic world and life in general. I have also come to believe through research and experience that readers are more physically fit, have greater vocabularies, greater empathy, and reap the benefits of increased success in academic environments and our text-based world. For you see, textual knowledge is a valuable commodity.

So, when I became a mother, and friends and family gushed over my oldest daughter, Marie, telling me that she was so much like me, her mom, my myth started to slowly become her myth. She had no idea, of course. But when she reached the magic age of four, I started to notice....

Marie was a bright, articulate 4-year-old, and she too loved to hear stories, to trace out letters, to practice writing her name. Her vocabulary was expanding intensely, often to the point where strangers would marvel at her command of language.

The myth was intensifying...

So, I started to push.

I pulled out the phonics readers and started pointing out sight words and three-letter words as we were reading books together. I even signed out some Level 1 Readers from the library and began pointing to each word, haltingly and awkwardly sounding out every syllable. At first, Marie had no idea what I was up to, and participated willingly, but she must have wondered why her mom had forgotten how to read! Soon, however, she stopped choosing the phonics books at storytime, and when I pulled them out, she would tense up and pull away from me. Finally, I asked her what was wrong. "Mom, I hate those books!" When I asked why, she said, "The stories are so boring!"

So, we just read beautiful books again.

For a while.

A year later, when Marie was in kindergarten, and the weekly alphabet worksheets started coming home, my anxiety once again surfaced. She was now nearly 6 years old and although she still had a great relationship with words, and she loved to point out signs that she could read, and write the names of all her family members, she still wasn't what I would have called a "reader." So, this time around, I tried to be more subtle, more sneaky. I didn't bring out the phonics books or levelled readers, but as we were reading, I would point out words here and there, or identify simple words and ask her to sound them out as we were reading. Marie continued to resist, protesting every time I tried to get her to read, turning her head away from the book. I would stop when she asked me to, but after a few days, the pressure would mount, and I would find a way to sneak some reading in, with the same result.

At the beginning of Grade 1, I renewed my resolve to refrain from pressuring Marie to learn to read. But one day in late September, I caved once again. We had just finished reading a beautiful book, and I noticed as I closed it that the title was a simple, three-word sentence. I turned to Marie and said, "Let's read this title! Can you sound it out?" I thought she might be ready this time. After all, she was nearly 7 years old, which I was told was well in the age range of beginning readers. She looked at me with tears in her eyes, and said, "Mom, I'm just not ready! Don't you get that? I feel stupid! It's too hard for me and I don't want to do it!"

My heart broke.

We talked a little bit about how reading is difficult, and wonderful, and that it would happen when she was ready. I told her I would back off completely, agreeing to follow her lead. So far, I have not broken that promise. It hasn't been easy, I must admit.

The next day, I spoke with our childcare provider, Holly, about what had happened. She said that Marie had been reluctant to practice reading with her as well, and that she had expressed no interest in any form of reading, even with attempts to disguise it and to "make learning fun!" through online games and phonics activities. She did, however, mention that when Louise, Marie's 4-year-old sister, played those online early reading games, that Marie's entire demeanor was transformed, and she would put on a big, fake smile, look over Louise's shoulder, and say in a sing-song, falsetto voice,

"Oh, my, isn't this just so much fun, Louise? Isn't reading fun?"

Raising a Reader, Part III: re-memory Interlude: lovely, difficult work
Jodi Latremouille

David Jardine (2016d, p. 162) concludes:

> The hidden complicities of those who love and foster terror and then magically appear just in time to alleviate it—this is a story as old as the hills. Reading and understanding that story allows me to begin stepping away from its allure. It allows me to interrupt the panic-manipulation and to return to the lovely, difficult work of learning to read with children.

"They Did Not Do This to Themselves"
David Jardine

Kevin O'Leary. I love the terror because it allows me to create the lure of what I sell, sell it, profit, and then further stimulate the very terror I meant to cure. Market Logic. Now insinuate this market logic of producing and marketing right into the heart of our image of knowledge itself:

And then they arrived. The little shiny books. We opened the box in the middle of a reading time, and the children swarmed around.
"Sunshine books," some called out.
"There's Sunshine books over here!"
We were pleased. The children recognized the series from their Grade 1 year and seemed anxious to have a go at this year's set.
Our pleasure was short-lived. Slowly, terribly, the children became fretful, furtive-eyed,
near-panicked.
"I can't find a book at my level," one said. "Help me find my level." "We don't know what you mean. What's a 'level?' What are you talking about?" They showed us the colour-coding on the books' covers, clearly identifying the successive stages of difficulty for all the books in the series. One child burst into tears. Confident readers became uncertain.
"Is it okay to read this one?"
"Is this the right level?"
"Who's got the second purple book?"
(David Jardine, Patricia Clifford, & Sharon Friesen, 1999, p. 328–9)

The feeling of community, the respect for the myriad aspects of that community, the understanding of the roiling differences involved in each child's taking the other to task in long conversations over Odysseus' woes and the fairness to monsters tending their sheep—the myriad reasons why any one of us might have picked up this book, this time—all this disappeared within a day of this bright and blinding arrival. And let us be blunt about this. When these books arrived, what we and the children experienced was not simply the imposition of the safeties and securities of colour-codedness (no irony intended, but the squirm is palpable). We have schooled these children well enough by Grade 2 that imposition was no longer needed.

"They did this to themselves." (p. 330)
They did *not* do this to themselves.
They *learned to do it to themselves.*
They were *taught* to do this to themselves.
I taught them whether I meant to or not.

Doing it to themselves is becoming an "independent learner." One of the great mechanisms of market logic is that one must stimulate the desire for precisely that which I have to sell and that my continuing provision of that from which I will profit can now be attributed to those who want this product, not to my occluded stimulation of that want and subsequent provision of its (never quite sated) relief.

They did not do this to themselves.

Raising a Reader IV:
Second Reading: Heartful Re-Memories
Jodi Latremouille

My Four Directions Teachers
(Kehte-aya Bob Cardinal, oral teachings, 2014;
with Dwayne Donald, course handout, 2014b).

Thunder Being from the West

Teaches Mental Knowing: To speak respectfully and honour

the life journeys of others.
Key principles: Learning about oneself and caring for others through cognitive, psychological, and spiritual insights.
Asks: "How can this incident help you to understand and strengthen your mental capabilities to achieve balance, self-knowledge, and empathy?"

Grandmother Mouse from the South

Teaches Spiritual Knowing: To be humble, loving, nurturing and giving.
Key principles: Awareness of other wisdom traditions, respect for ceremony and Elders.
Asks: "In what ways are your own spiritual and cultural identity connected to this incident?"

Buffalo from the North

Teaches Physical Knowing: To utilize all and not waste any gifts.
Key principles: Respectful, embodied relationships, communication built on trust.
Asks: "How can the incident be understood as a struggle to embody safety, trust, respect, and walking alongside others to give strength?"

Bear from the East

Teaches Emotional Knowing: To foster patience, compassion and knowledge of the past.
Key principles: Conflict resolution, empathy, understanding emotions.
Asks: "What can you learn from attending to emotions involved in this incident?"

Eagle

Teaches a Connected, Unified Understanding: To have a balanced perspective.
Key principles: Strength, courage, humility and vision.

Asks: "How might this incident be understood in holistic and balanced ways?"

I: The Gift of Reading

Mother: As a child, I experienced the implications of the educational myth that reduces literacy to the technical skill of "decoding" (Emilia Ferreiro, 2003, p. 18). My early technical abilities in reading and writing were highly and publicly prized, whereas my growing ability to read the world (Paulo Freire, 2000) to be a reader "in the full sense of the word" (Emilia Ferreiro, 2003, p. 17), nurtured through diverse learning experiences and careful encouragement by my parents, was undervalued in the school context.

Schools continue to "teach a technique" (p. 14) rather than teaching reading, in the sense of fostering an ability to read the world through all of the diverse languages it presents. These technical skills of reading and writing are commodities, in that they produce high marks for students, a valuable "market-exchange item" (David Jardine, Patricia Clifford, & Sharon Friesen, 2003, p. 208) in the economy of life.

Buffalo: Culture is an enactment of a Creation story. Your growing abilities as a reader "in the full sense of the word" (Emilia Ferreiro, 2003, p. 17) were actually promoting and strengthening the development of your decoding skills, providing you with an important context within which to learn to read. The decoding didn't actually come first!

As you came to believe in the value of the commodities of high marks and school achievements, your value as a human being was misplaced within these skills. Do you want your daughter to de-value her growing skills as a reader of the world?

Mother: Even with my many years of experience in questioning the logic of fragmentation and the Christian Creation story of individualism, self-reliance, order and control, in moments of insecurity, I would indeed find myself caught up in the myth.

Eagle: Thomas King (2003, p. 26) wondered, "Do the stories we tell reflect the world as it truly is, or did we simply start off with the wrong story?" Dwayne Donald notes that, in regarding culture as a re-enactment of a Creation story (personal communication, October 11, 2014), you may be able to re-story the raising of a reader as "a shared activity, [. . .] a world that begins in chaos and moves towards harmony, [. . .] a world determined by co-operation" (Thomas King, 2003, p. 25). Like any other form of learning, "learning to read is a relational activity" (David G. Smith, 1999, p. 71); the most powerful way to take care of your daughter's reading is to take care of your relationship with her.

Mother: I found it easy to tell other parents that the technical reading would happen in its own time, but when my own child's learning was at stake, I found myself sliding back down into the panic of scarcity, competitiveness and insecurity. When "[t]here is so much to 'cover,' there is so little time, students are in constant competition for marks and their value as market-exchange items" (David Jardine, Patricia Clifford, & Sharon Friesen, 2003, p. 208) then everything in my power must be done to keep my child from falling behind, from losing that ever-so-important "edge." In my panic I clamped down harder on my reluctant reader; I pushed harder, trying to convince my young daughter that she was ready to read, to keep up.

Bear: In your impatience, you have risked your daughter's love of reading. You have tried to guarantee her place in a world storied by competition, scarcity, and chaos. Although there are no guarantees no matter what approach you take, placing an undue emphasis on technical training actually is the more uncertain approach (Emilia Ferreiro, 2003, p. 25) to reading "in the full sense." Despite the false promise of the levelled readers, they suppress the truth that the experience of reading is inherently difficult, wonderful, satisfying, complex, and magical.

Grandmother Mouse: Your job as a teacher is to "re-teach [your child her own] loveliness" (Galway Kinnell, 2002). Your job is to remind her of her sacred place in the wonders of language, not the language of fragmented, technical leveled readers, but the languages of the world.

What you are giving her is not a prize or a form of currency.

It is a gift.

II: Wording the World (in Her Own Time)

Mother: I hear anecdotes about how all readers are different. I hear a story told by a father of three children: The first one was actively and confidently reading simple books at age five; the second carefully observed, took notes, copied words, and agonizingly sounded out letters for 2 years, until she was finally reading competently at age seven; the third child blatantly refused to read the words in a book until age eight, at which time he took off, and by age ten was reading novels cover to cover. I remember my own mythical memories of precocious reading, and wonder: Where does Marie's path to reading lie in the multiplicities of all of these stories?

Thunder Being: Marie is none of these children. And Marie is not you. Listen to her more carefully now, as she expresses herself in the world. She loves gymnastics, drama, nature, climbing trees, and thinking mathematically. She has an impressive, expressive vocabulary, and the thinks critically about the world in ways that astound and amaze you. Her sense of humour is clever and highly nuanced. She is curious and full of life. She loves reading the world. And someday, you must trust that she will come to love reading words.

Mother: But what if . . . (breathe, now) . . . she doesn't? Will I still be willing to accept her openly and unconditionally . . . if she never comes to love reading? And what if . . . (breathe, again) . . . she never learns how to read? I know that I have no evidence or good reason to believe that this is true; however, perhaps like every parent of what I might call a pre-reading child, I secretly harbor that niggling, nagging, nibbling fear.

Thunder Being: No need to panic. Love her without knowing what the outcome will be (Deborah Osberg & Gert Biesta, 2008, p. 320). If you are going to accept Marie's own personal relationship with reading, you will need to be open to the (however unlikely) possibility that she might choose to partially or completely refuse the invitation into the world of reading or take it up in a way that you did not expect or even desire. Listen carefully to your child's voice as she comes into her own preferences, excitements, interests and talents, as she reveals her own weaknesses, limitations, roles and chosen responses to the world. Remember:

> The bud
> stands for all things,
> even for those things that don't flower,
> for everything flowers from within, of self-blessing.
> (Galway Kinnell, 2002)

Can you imagine your child turning out in ways that you never could have imagined, in ways that you would not desire for her? You will be a true teacher if you treat her, not as a projection of your own desires and fears, but with an open heart, "as a subject of mystery-producing wonder and awe" (Dwayne Huebner, 2008, p. 8) in you. What can you learn about yourself from raising a reader?

III: Reading as Ceremony

Mother: It is possible for adults to treat the process of learning to read as a form of ceremony. We may naturally conduct ourselves in ways that show our love of the worded world, fulfilling our shared responsibility in an orientation towards its renewal (Hannah Arendt, 1969, p. 193). As adults, we start by pointing out objects, actions and people to our youngest ones, identifying them through their appearances, relations and patterns. These namings then evolve into conversations about the world, in which the concepts become even more abundant.

As I look at beautiful picture books with my young children, they ask questions about the characters, the words, the stories' connections to their own learning. We stop, come back, ponder, and ruminate over things that we dearly love, and for which we are jointly responsible. We each become more in the face of their loveliness. In the study of things, like literature, "[w]e love them and we love what we become in our dedication to them" (David Jardine, Patricia Clifford,

& Sharon Friesen, 2003, p. 208). My children, too, come to love themselves in the face of literature. They write things down, draw pictures, do dramatic re-enactments; they live the words through play. And through this play, the words become bigger, more evocative, more exciting, more than they could ever be in isolation from the world.

So . . . why did I feel the need to "make reading fun"?

Grandmother Mouse: In your haste, you have lost touch with the abundance, joy and great responsibility that are embedded in the ritual of learning to read. In stripping the technical act of decoding of its much deeper ceremony of reading, you have been forced to re-layer it with the false promises of "fun" and rewards.

If "[c]reativity should always be a form of prayer" (Ben Okri, 1997, p. 27), how might you prayerfully and gently invite your children into the contemplative work of reading, to nurture them with its abundance? In giving this gift of literacy to your children, how might you properly lead your children into the ceremony of reading; how might you become someone that you yourself may once again love in your dedication to it? How might you demonstrate to your daughter the possibilities of who she is, and who she might become in her own love of reading?

Mother: As my daughter explores the world of literature, I notice that "[t]he play soon becomes its own sustenance" (Okri, 1997, p. 23). It seems almost ridiculous to now come face to face with my underlying belief that I needed to instill a love of reading in Marie, simply because she was not yet sounding out the words on the page. When I tried to separate the act of reading from its world of meanings and reduced it to nothing more than sounding out the letters, I was in essence selfishly withholding my own deep love of reading from her. I was sapping her of her own strength to become an active agent of her own learning. She recognized this; her refusal to take up reading in this way was not mere stubbornness; she was demanding more of me as a teacher. She was holding me accountable.

Eagle: "No child needs to be motivated to learn. To learn is their trade. They can't stop learning because they can't stop growing. All objects (material or conceptual) to which adults give importance capture the attention of children" (Emilia Ferreiro, 2003, p. 23) Having successfully isolated the decoding from its abundant, deeper relationship to literacy, you left her with nothing that would nourish her. Of course you would feel the need to lie to her by disguising this technical, gaunt, isolated notion of reading as "fun." And, of course your child would see through the farce: she is already a good reader!

Mother: Oh my . . .
   She read me like a book (ahem), as the saying goes.
   My child.
   My reader.

. . .re-memory postlude: for you see, in fact, I am Reading . . .

David G. Smith remembers:

Technically and pedagogically, teaching young children to read is not a particularly difficult task. Put children and their natural curiosity together with a competent reader (parent, teacher, peer) with the time and inclination to watch over the children as they come into contact with books, magazines, stories, comics, signs and so on, and almost unawares youngsters will confidently declare: "I can read." (David G. Smith, 1999, p. 71)

Raising a Writer
David Jardine

Translating Water: Final Pedagogical Reflection

once upon a time ther was a rain drop and it gope on a bird then the sun trd into a watrvapr the radrop fad his bovrsrs and trnd into a fofe white cloud and then it trnd in too a havie plak kloub and then it trd in bake to the sam radrop and gropt on the sam bird.
   Name Eric

Below is a translation which opens this water-text out into a field of "conventionality" and allows its meaning to become visible and audible while, at the same time, betraying its frailty, this young boy and his ear for the soundings of words and their meaning—6 years old at the time, writing at the computer—now slipped away into adulthood:

Once upon a time there was a raindrop.
And it dropped on a bird.

The sun turned into a water vapour.
The raindrop found his brothers
And turned into a fluffy white cloud.
And then it turned into a heavy black cloud.
And then it turned back into the same raindrop
And dropped on to the same bird.
Eric Jardine

I cite it here to be read out loud. It is my chance to mourn anew the sound of translating water and its passing (full passage is from David Jardine, 2014, p. 54).

WAYSTATION IX
I Provide a Pre-emptive Waystation
Eric Jardine

I provide a pre-emptive waystation. Readers should know what they are getting themselves into by reading this work. The text is atypical. The prose is flowery and poetic by design. The structure is loaded with side-trails and embedded passages from older articles that exist adjacent to primary themes in the text. In short, the text is somewhat hard to read. And lacking an answer to the question of how to read this text, some readers might set it aside and pursue other, easier things.

But that misses the point. Writing often includes an implicit philosophy of reading. Pick up a manual on how to 'write well' and you'll get told that short direct sentences, active voice, and logically sequential sentences make excellent writing.

These bits of advice are not wrong. Following them will make your work easier to read. I tell these same steps to my students, who often don't know how to write clearly in the first place.

But implicit in the textbook definition of how to write well is the assumption that good writing is the same as writing that is easy for the reader to digest. The philosophy of writing in the standard vein is that writers do the heavy work; readers reap the benefits by being able to read without thinking or effort.

I am personally and professionally highly sympathetic to this approach. I appreciate its emphasis on simplicity and clarity. But it is not the only approach out there. Aesthetics change over time—tone differs, preferred words emerge and fall. These changes reflect, in turn, changes to society at large.

Like changes in grammar, word choice, and syntax, the relationship between the reader and the writer is fluid. Pick up any classic text and the first few lines are likely to be more of a chore than the modern reader is used to.

I have Bertrand Russell's *A History of Western Philosophy* on my office shelf. The first two lines of the introduction are:

> The conceptions of life and the world which we call "philosophical" are a product of two factors: one, inherited religious and ethical conceptions; the other, the sort of investigation which may be called "scientific," using this word in its broadest sense. Individual philosophers have differed widely in regard to the proportions in which these two factors entered into their systems, but it is the presence of both, in some degree, that characterizes philosophy. (Bertrand Russell, 1972, p. xiii)

The passage is dense, but clear with some work on the reader's part.

My point is that good writing, important writing, need not necessarily be based around the idea that the writer does the work and the reader reaps the benefits. That is one philosophy of writing—one that fits our contemporary proclivities, perhaps—but it is not the only approach.

It is not the approach that my father, Jodi, and Lesley take here. This book, instead, is deliberately designed to make the reader work, as that work is a part of the fun, experience, and benefit one gets from reading the text, in part or in whole.

The text is written as three peoples' poetic rumination. Reading it requires that the reader, too, ruminate on the words, ideas, and prose of the text. You cannot come away from the book simply by reading the words and knowing what the others think—indeed, as expressed quite well on the opening pages, no text is so simply unidimensional. Even if the text was written in a way that minimizes the work required of the reader, good readers would still come away with unintended new ideas, counter points, misinterpretations and reimaginations. Good reading is never meant to be work free.

I write these words to say that readers need to expect that hard work will invariably be required of them. There are a lot of ideas in this book—ideas both subtle and complex—but they only emerge if readers work and meet the writers halfway.

—Eric Jardine

Part VII
Breath Again

Breath Again
David Jardine

Re-citing something all over again is an interesting act. To watch walking again. To greet anew and wonder. Read now, after what has happened in between since the last appearance. Migratory bird returned now that the airs have clear a bit, for now, from the smoke that, we wail, will probably return as the new normal:

> And so ... I do not swallow you whole or in pieces, I walk alongside you. I do not hold the knowledge. I do not hold the answers. But I watch you walk. We greet those who come to greet us. We enter into the field of play. We argue over the correct word by which to call that one plant. You were right. It was the buffalo berry. We sit together beside the river and wonder why these berries aren't eaten by the birds this year. Must be the dirt we decide. Still made dirty from the flood 5 years ago. We wonder when the birds will show us when they are safe to eat again. Soon, maybe. (Lesley Tait)

"Like Life, it is Hazy": Part IV, "Too Late"
David Jardine

David G. Smith, Sat, Jun 1, 2019 at 10:58 PM:

> Read your "hazy" piece. Very good. Yes, the fact that it may be "too late" for any effective remediation of our earthly condition is extremely sobering and poses the question of how we shall now live with this new realization. You and I might barely escape the inescapable fires (both a metaphor as well as literal reality) but Eric's children won't. We should meditate on this together.

David W. Jardine, Sun. June 2, 2019 at 5:58 AM

> The emotions that went with that vivid dream were incredible and were a link between all the folks wandering around the streets. The depth of the sorrow, remorse, guilt, resignation, full knowledge of what was occurring . . . amazing.

David G. Smith, Friday, July 5, 2019 at 1:24PM

> Philosophy may always be (too) late but it can also be profoundly prophetic.

David W. Jardine, Sat. June 6, 2019 at 5:58 AM

> Even those women we dread sitting next to on buses or trains, their bodies swelling with messy secrets, the odour of complaint on their breath, may be prophets. Whether we listen or not won't stop them from telling our story in their own. (Bronwen Wallace, 1989, p. 48).

Sharp Exhale: When Will the Birds Show Me? I
David Jardine

A happenstance drifted by in the orbit of writing a response to "Watching my Mother Die—Subjectivity and the Other Side of Dementia" Nancy Moules (and Andrew Estefan, 2018) had written about her mother slowly no longer remembering her, no longer recognizing here. I still haven't worked it out adequately, yet, but it is the closest I've come to glimpsing this land. Just a broken-up journal-scrawl sketch, then, found in part of my response, "To Be Dying Under their Wings is a Weird Miracle":

> ..... this very same sort of memory/forgetting ... . driving into south Calgary on Saturday along hwy. 22 .... all the construction, with many of the old, familiar signposts and figures and trees and fields torn up. .... had the feeling, not simply that I didn't quite know where I was, but that I knew exactly where I was, but that this place doesn't remember me being there at all. Like I'd been forgotten, erased from tree-memory, earth-memory, or something ... . after all those drive-bys, all that attention and devotion .... right there in the midst of me lamenting its shifts and remembering its shapes, it forgets .... me, trying to be so in touch with the place and feeling its perishings, and having it spurn like that .... it's not just that I've lost something, but that something has lost me. This happened to me a lot when I was young. The town I grew up in had these repeated ravagings of the living grass and field and bird and flat dirt path surroundings to make way for spiking population growth .... and it wasn't just that places I remembered were gone, but that the places that remembered me were gone .... could no longer remember. That I had become forgotten by the land itself .... a small version semi-inverse of a First Nations lament that I can hardly stand to have quite so near .... (David Jardine, 2019, p. 147)

Perhaps recitation will help.
   Great moon, eagle moon, goose moon, frog moon
   Tethered
   Here

Lesley Tait

Again:
   Great moon, eagle moon, goose moon, frog moon
   Tethered
   Here

Lesley Tait

Some gut cry above the chanted repeat is needed but writing sometimes isn't easily accommodating.

What, then?

An Email Conversation on Writing, February 2020

Lesley Tait and Jodi Latremouille

Lesley: Writing is kind of like standing up in front of everyone and proclaiming, "I know something," and even further, writing things down seem like shouting "I am an expert" and "everyone should listen to what I say because it is true because it is written." I think about writing like exploring. I don't have a plan and I am not sure where I might end up but it sure might be fun. It also doesn't mean I am right, or knowledgeable, or an expert. It's just me thinking about stuff I want others to think about. Maybe I'm right, maybe I'm wrong. Who am I to say? No one. I am no expert, no Elder, no knowledge keeper. I have listened to Kehte-aya Bob say enough times, "I am no one, I know nothing, I am nobody." I feel the same. I am nobody and I know nothing. AND . . . I can say that and still feel like I have something to say. One does not negate the other. I can know nothing and something all at the same time. Who are you to tell me I can't? Who are you to tell me I should see myself and that other should see me as an expert. I'm not. Have I said that enough? I'm not. So why write? Because how else I am supposed to know who am I or what I think. And to some degree, what I think others should think.

If I didn't hope that someone might eventually read my words and think differently about something, then maybe I would think twice about doing it?

Maybe. Maybe not.

So I write.

Jodi: I write to proclaim, "I am here. This is what here is to me. This is how I feel it, live it, love it. Do you feel me? Can you hear me? Please touch me. Am I alone? I hope not." I want to know I am not a figment of my own imagination. Yes I am nobody. But also everybody. In what ways am I nothing and everything at the same time? And when I hear a call back, I know both of those things can be true at the same time. Like, when I bawl my eyes out at seeing a tiny vole get squished under a shoe at a family campout. On purpose. By my little relative who wants to be somebody and feels like nobody at the same time. Who is told he is the most important thing in the whole goddamn world, then treated like he is nothing. And who doesn't have the words to ask, love me! And my dad who did a tiny little serious burial ceremony for my daughters and niece and nephew. I have had the most incredibly, shockingly, unexpectedly, and multiply weird and unsettling in so many random and unconnected ways, randomly devastating morning, and you just made it so much better. Thank you.

We are here.

Something happens to you as you read the words written by others. They become intertwined with the fabric of you. They carefully wrap themselves around your neurons, heart muscles and bones of your body, ensuring their survival with you. (Lesley Tait, 2014, p. 94)

Lesley: "Please touch me. I am not alone." Crushed it.

Lesley: Also . . . maybe you think like me. Maybe you don't. But if you did . . . we could talk about it then I could have some company in this place I am. Is it all arrogant . . . to think I have something to say . . . something someone or anyone might give a **t**iny little shit about? Arrogance at its best, is it not?

How can we be humble and still choose to write. Maybe one does negate the other?

Jodi: Right . . . like, what is so important that our words need to be preserved outside the context of the intimate conversation? If they were so important, they would be passed on by others. With their own colourings and flavours and their own agreements and disagreements. Which brings us back to Kehte-aya Bob and I am nobody. I am only somebody in relationship.

Lesley: Relationship. How did I miss that? Of course that has to play a role. I only share my first thoughts with trusted people. Cause they might get it. If they don't, they will know what I might have been trying to say and won't judge me too harshly. Judgement sounds like a heavy word.

They already know me, so they likely already know my thoughts. Maybe my thoughts can't live outside of people knowing me? Meaning you shouldn't read my writing unless you know me personally? I am only somebody in relationship. My words are only something if they exist in relationship to the reader.

Kinda shrinks the reading pool a bit doesn't it?

But . . . then if you know me . . . and you read what I write . . . why bother writing it why don't I just tell you?

Oral writing if you will:

It is not writing. Not poetry, not prose. I am not a writer. Yet it is in my throat, stomach, arms. This book that I am not able to write. There are words that insist in silence. Words that betray me. The words make me sleep. They keep me awake. (Kristiana Gunnars, 1989, section 1)

But writing helps me figure out my thoughts. ;Back to my beginning argument here. A stunning turn of events that I have ended up where I started.

Sharp Exhale: When Will the Birds Show Me? II
David Jardine

Maybe ALL CAPS WILL HELP with this broad low sorrow that I'm sensing all around me? No?

 . . . .. they are nothing but the upper cases, holding letters to be used with old printing presses.

Maybe Judson Innes (2016, p. 110) can help:

Alone now, they wind through tangles, relentless,
and re-emerge into one.

Call up to the creators; we are here, we are here.
What of those who occupy the spaces in between,
and linger along the precipice?

"Like Life, it is Hazy": Part V, "Like the Green Signals"

David Jardine

David W. Jardine, Sun. June 2, 2019, 6:41 AM
Thinking of those apple cores and that huddle of children, that girl's still face, still, regarding.

Remembering it is like an awful forge:

How their deaths quicken the air around them, stipple their bodies with a light like the green signals trees send out before their leaves appear. (Bronwen Wallace, 1989, p. 40)

All this almost helps. An awful forge:

Remembrances of the Land and Rocks in my Pocket

Lesley Tait

> The music of the land rose up in all its many textures, each tree, each cliff, each place he'd passed, until finally the song of home added its voice to the others. His cave called out from the blanketing shrubs and pillows of moss at its mouth, and Chiro followed the familiar sound back into the sheltering earth. (Ari Berk, 2012)

The hands of my children are continually picking up rocks and stones. Their fingers grip tight to their latest treasure. Each groove and bump is felt as their small fingertips run over the surface. Soon their hand is overturned, and an open palm allows their eyes to examine each facet of its being. These are not necessarily the prettiest rocks or the biggest, but simply stones that somehow meet their unknown needs at that particular moment in time.

After this through examination, these same hands unceremoniously shove these stones into pants pockets, coats pockets and when all other options are full, their mother's pockets. These stones then find their way into all aspects of our home. They become bath toys, decorations for a Christmas centrepiece, pets for various stuffed animals and toppings for delicious mud pies.

I have watched my children lament over the loneliness of a solitary stone, create entire stone families, and stop mid-sentence to address the needs of a distant rock calling out to them. To them, these stones are precious. They have the ability to feel, be lonely, cold and afraid. They can also be comforted and feel love.

It is easy to dismiss these activities and attachments as childish; to view these understandings as make believe or simply the games of children. It is more difficult to see them for what they are; deep and true understandings of the world and our land. Rocks are grounding. They provide us with a weight and gravitas and pull us back the earth in a way that does not first surround us with a protective layer. Rocks are foundational and markers of meaning. They seek to remind us of our long-forgotten relationship with the land

This is how my children travel through the world; attentive, wisely aware and hands at the ready, in search of a stone needing saving in their pocket.

"Like Life, it is Hazy": Part VI, With Apologies to J. Y and A. G.
David Jardine

Howl Moon
My mind has been destroyed by madness
Generation Hysteria, dragging my self
Under smoky air.
Angel-headed hipster having burned up
heavenly connections, shh-boomer, there she goes!

Burned up even the starry dynamo
into smoky air. Nice going.
Night Machineries without enough owls to keep
the measures right.

Without the supernatural darkness of cold-water
clean enough
To drink.

Passed through university
with radiant cool eyes.
Hallucinating with precise citations.

Clear air. Clear air.
Drips from my pen.
(No, it doesn't).
Become an unintended scholar of war.

A bent grey skull
Slumped over a clock of meat sunk and run
downdying in mid-smoky air.

WAYSTATION X
"Hush, child . . ." A Conversation with Kiera and Taylor Nyeste

Jodi: Kiera and Taylor wanted to join the kids' climate strike on March 15, 2019. They got together with a small group of four girls, and spent their morning making posters, with slogans such as "There is no Planet B," and "Make Earth Cool Again," out of salvaged wood and cardboard. People driving by on the main street would honk their horns and wave, which encouraged the girls to jump up and down with their signs, cheering.

The movement grew, and for the next global protest on September 20, 2019, there were eleven children on the corner. When they marched again on September 27, 2019, they were joined by over forty protesters from all generations, backgrounds and social locations. A person walked by, and asked me what we were doing. When I explained, she said, "How cute, your little girls are doing a little protest!" I replied, "And yet, how important and timely it is!"

When we returned home after a day of protesting, dragging our sore, blistered feet and bedraggled signs, Kiera asked me, "Mom, what's the point of all this effort? What if it doesn't do anything?"

I had no words.

Taylor replied, "That's not the point. The point is that we are doing something good. Right now."

"hush, child . .". (Latremouille, 2014a, p. 31)

Yes, it looks bleak. But you are still alive now. You are alive with all the others, in this present moment. And because the truth is speaking in the work, it unlocks the heart. And there's such a feeling and experience of adventure. It's like a trumpet call to a great adventure. (Joanna Macy, 2014, par. 11)

My Forgetting, Their Remembering
David Jardine

And then this, cited here again, originally written, my oh my, over 20 years ago after my first return from Alberta back to Southern Ontario where I was raised:

> How things smell, the racket of leaves turning on their stems, how my breath pulls this humid air, how birds songs combine, the familiar directions of sudden thundery winds, the rising insect drills of cicada tree buzzes that I remember so intimately, so immediately, that when they sound, it feels as if this place itself has remembered what I have forgotten, as if my own memory, my own raising, some of my own life, is stored up in these trees for safekeeping. Cicadas become archaic storytellers telling me, like all good storytellers, of the life I'd forgotten I'd lived, of deep, fleshy, familial relations that worm their ways out of my belly and breath into these soils, these smells, this air. And I'm left shocked

that they know so much, that they remember so well, and that they can be so perfectly articulate. (David Jardine, 2016c, p. 83–4)

Energeia
David Jardine

Aristotle was able to think a motion [an "animateness"] .... something like life itself, like being aware, seeing, or thinking. All of these he called 'pure *Energeia.*' (Hans-Georg Gadamer, 2007a, p. 213) In an alternate translation, Sheila Ross (2006, p. 108) renders part of this passage as "something like aliveness itself" and she links it directly to the sort of whiling or "tarrying time" (p. 108) requisite of interpretive work. (David Jardine, 2018b, p. 5).

They begin to move closer . . . . and I begin to comprehend, just barely, a great aliveness. (Richard Dawson, 2013/2015)

the feel of live
movement in space
between here and there
Lesley Tait

And so, wicihitowin:

The life-giving energy that is generated when people face each other as relatives and build trusting relationships by connecting with others in respectful ways. (Dwayne Donald, 2016, p. 10)

These others, we ponder, could be more-than-human. They could be the teachers and students in a classroom. But they could also be the haunting figures in that story told that morning, or that trickle of water down the driveway. When treated properly, these things can flourish in our love for them, and they will add their energies to ours and this burgeoning aliveness is something we have witnessed countless times in schools, in grades from Kindergarten to Grade 12, and in undergraduate classes and graduate ones and Ph.D. dissertations. It grows. It sustains. It draws us into its orbit and measures us with the very enlivening it gives us as a gift. Our teaching practices, which, when they work in the spirit of wahkohtowin, to face each other honestly, build and connect, in respectful ways, "as relatives," have this cadence, this heartbeat of working together gathered around a livewire topic (Latin *topos*, place), sharing energies that may begin to take on a life of their own, "over and above our wanting and doing" (Hans-Georg Gadamer, 2004, p. xxviii). Here, in these conspiratorial relationships, we began to face each other across layered ecological, political and historical divides (Dwayne Donald, 2010), breathing life into possibilities for new ways to live well together. This facing, this common breath, requires us to let go of our deep adhesion to being insiders and outsiders (Dwayne Donald, 2009, p. 2). Now we are storytellers. But more than that, we can begin to see that it is not only the human people who want to share their stories. And it is not only the human people who long to let go of being insiders and outsiders.

More on Whiling Time and Aliveness
David Jardine

This mention of tarrying time or whiling time—staying with something, returning to it, mulling ... so many words swirl around this phenomenon, but there is something about it that is often mis-characterized. Such whiling stillness:

> is not a function of lackadaisical, meandering contemplation, least of all passive in any way, but is a function of the fullness and *intensity* of attention and engrossment. (Sheila Ross, 2006, p. 109)

> Rocks are grounding. ;They provide us with a weight and gravitas and pull us back the earth in a way that does not first surround us with a protective layer. ;Rocks are foundational and markers of meaning. They seek to remind us of our long-forgotten relationship with the land. This is how my children travel through the world; attentive, wisely aware and hands at the ready, in search of a stone needing saving in their pocket. (Lesley).

Hans-Georg Gadamer (2007a, p. 189) called this attentiveness "the readiness ... . to be "all ears" [*ganz Ohr zu sein*]." But such alive and enlivening readiness can atrophy. It can be forgotten, ignored, marginalized or subjectified. Things—rocks, leaves turning on their stems, the words writ just right in a text—teach us to be all ears and require of us that we be all ears, both of these at once. Both cause and effect. Readiness to experience aliveness is a practice that needs practiced in order to become practiced in it. *Hands at the ready* are a way to "reteach a thing its loveliness" (think of the brow caress of the sow in Galway Kinnell's [2002] "Saint Francis and the Sow") and, in the very same affectionate gesture, *learn of such loveliness* from the very act of reteaching:

> Readiness needs to be sought, cultivated. It needs to be taken care of properly and repeatedly and relentlessly. Readiness takes work, it takes energy, *energeia*, "aliveness" . . . . and it not only takes it. It *produces* it. And when it works, it hits the still spot between give and take and begins to glow. The joy . . . . in being "all ears" *creates* joy. "As in love, our satisfaction [in this joy] sets us at ease because we know that somehow its use at once assures its plenty" (Lewis Hyde, 1983, p. 22). (David Jardine, 2019, p. 104)

Such is the paradoxical nature of "aliveness," the life-giving energy that is generated when we face each other and build. It gives and takes. We learn and teach, all in one gesture of a ready hand on a brow. The hand teaches the stones and learns from them, not just about stones but about hands and readiness. "The way we treat a thing can sometimes change its nature" (Lewis Hyde, 1983, p. xiii).

> to put a hand on its brow
> . . . .
> and retell it in words and in touch
> it is lovely

(Galway Kinnell, 2002, n.p.)

But then, things can teach us about our treatment and our nature.
Stones can lay their hands on our brows.
Stones can lay their hands on our brows.
Stones can lay their hands on our brows.
Even stones.
Ohh. Breath sharp exhale. I just might be lovely

They can do this and we have to learn to let them. Paradox literally means "beyond belief"—beyond theories of learning and subjectivity and objects and your perspective and my perspective. Despite all that educational muddle-talk, stones leap out, Raven swoop over. This belies many beliefs about teaching and learning that education often tries to articulate:

This experience is immediate and intimate, but it takes repeated practice and hard study to release and realize this immediacy, and even then it is not released once and for all. As the exigencies of every life rise up, so, too, rises up the tendency to retrench, harden and once again conceal. This "un-concealing" can be, therefore, frustrating at first. It can seem like deliberate obfuscation or weird otherworldliness. But, with practice, the path will clear, the ears pop:

> Why did he tell us to practice and find out for ourselves? Some people really worry about this. "If the Buddha really knew," they say, "he would have told us. Why should he keep anything hidden?" This sort of thinking is wrong. We can't see the truth in that way. We must practice, we must cultivate, in order to see. (Ajahn Chah, 2005, p. 111)

And, rest assured, as with any practice worthy of our while, days will

pass and amnesia and somnolence and distraction will rise up, and the exhausting acceleration of the world will make panic seem normal—"it'll grind you up." But when you return to the joyful practice, *it will be right where you left it,* patiently having waited for your return. (David Jardine, 2016a, p. xxvii)

"This is How the Story Should be Told"
Lesley Tait

Blackfoot Elder Saa'kokoto told me a story. His grandfather used to gather and call together his relations. First grandfather and son would remove all the furniture from the small living room. Everything would move until the room was bare, with only the old wooden floors left behind. One by one, relatives would gather in this bare room and would join the forming circle. The room would fill with laughter as they began to visit and recount stories since they had last seen each other. When it was time, the conversation would cease and the work would begin.

Grandfather would tell a story. The person next to him would tell the same story. Around it would go, this same story. Each time it was told, there were slight variations. Eventually it would return to the starting place. After listening to all his relations tell the story, grandfather would say, "This is how the story will be told" and it would be told once more.

wicihitowin

It is no wonder that love ensues in those long, delicious conversations that can happen in a classroom when the wind picks up under the wings, like the Ravens on the thermals in the smoky air foothills, summer 2018.

Lesley Tait: We have studied together, we have practiced together, we learned together. I am only me because of others. It took me 10 years to tell people I was from Michel First Nation. It took me another four to say it with pride. Another two to think that that might mean something to the field of curriculum studies. So, yes I can tell people that I am a mother to two daughters, that I live in moh-kîns-tsis (Calgary) but come from Treaty 6 territory, that I love reading and have a Master's degree. But I can tell the both of you, and mostly only through words on a page, that I am aware of how being Nehiwayak (Cree) and living on Niitsitapi (Blackfoot) territory asks for learning, thought and care. Or how I wondered about the words "colonization" and "decolonization" for an entire day.

And so, I bring teachers to the river. We sit along its banks in snow deep enough to nearly bury us whole. Here, we begin to recount stories about water. Some ancient, some new. Stories of falling in, stories of noticing how the plants are changing and disappearing, stories of how this place came to be.

Our conversations slow down and begin to glow, in loving the place within which we have come upon each other—Pythagoras, shadows, ravens, wetlands, paperwhites, loomed owls, rocks and pockets.

sakihitowin

"To know the world, we have to love it" (Wendell Berry, with Bill Moyers, 2013, n.p.):

If I can? When I'm able? Later in my career once I'm certified, or have tenure? Should the circumstances allow? If I have the time? The funding? The permission? The right school? The right kids? No. Love is not an outcome of the right circumstances but a *cause* of right circumstance. (David Jardine, 2019, p. 202)

No. Not exactly. It is outcome *and* it is cause.

Jodi Latremouille: In Merritt, where I grew up, we live on nearly an acre of land in town inherited from my husband's grandparents, a massive flat, bare dustbowl that used to be a rocky riverbed. In the summertime, my husband likes to mow the weeds and I mourn as the topsoil blows away in the parched heat. I keep planting rye and clover to try to build up the barren earth, and I can see green patches of hope starting to sprout up and keep down the dust. When we moved in there were two scraggly maple trees on the property, and one lonely plum tree, about 3 feet tall. It was a moonscape, littered in garbage and old broken bottles. We spent three summers picking broken glass out of the weeds, so it would be safe for our kids to walk barefoot. I have been nurturing a small orchard of courageous little fruit trees for 10 years now. I research local plants and trees to try to build the land back up, to fulfill what I see as my responsibility to help it recover from past human abuses.

Notice how it is getting more and more difficult to see to which section these excepts might properly belong. wahkohtowin? wicihitowin? sakihitowin? This increasing difficulty simply means that we are, in however small a way, succeeding in our efforts.

It used to be believed that trees would compete with each other for sunlight and nutrients, and that the tallest, strongest trees would eventually overshadow the other, smaller trees, thus making it difficult for them to flourish under the canopy.

Lesley (Aside): Capitalism at its best—in the forest! But scientific research by Suzanne Simard (2012) demonstrated how the larger, stronger trees are actually communicating with the baby trees under their canopy through their mycelial networks and send carbon dioxide and nutrients to nourish other trees. And they are finding that this communication occurs amongst different species. Like our in-breaths. Like what is needed to learn the ways of a place well enough to be well.

Jodi Latremouille: I was raised on a rural hobby farm, by parents of French, Syrian, and English heritage. They understood what it meant to live directly in relationship with the land, the elements, the plants, animals and other beings. My father Vern is a mushroom gatherer, huckleberry picker, fisherman, hunter, carpenter, mechanic, inventor, search and rescue volunteer, a botanist, trapper. If I had to go and survive in the wilderness for a year, I would go with him. I recently asked my father about his experience growing up in Little Fort BC, north of Kamloops, and his ways of walking on the earth. He talked about his family's relationship with Indigenous peoples in that region. He said, "My parents might be called pioneers. We had to live with the land and learn its ways. We learned from the Indigenous people who lived here and learned to survive on the land long before us; they taught us as guests here, in this place" And Vern's email in response: "I am honoured, you elevate me to a place which I will attempt to aspire to," following with a lovely little wink-and-smooch emoji (V. Latremouille, personal communication w. J.L., June 22, 2018).

"You Need Accuracy" IV: An Appreciation of a Modern Hunting Tradition and a Grouse's Life Unwasted

David Jardine

So, in appreciation, I want to betray my age and what struck me most in Jodi's writing, that the lives of these Great Beings should not be wasted, and that, in understanding this, we understand something of ourselves and our own frail passings. Our lives, too, should not be wasted.

I end, therefore, with a wee bit more of Vern Latremouille's email which betrays, as does Jodi's work, a great and trembling intimacy in the hunt:

> So far nothing to pack or skid yet this fall. Been close to two three-point Bull Moose and got within 50 feet of a bedded Bull and cow. [The] bull . . . . . . was up and gone before we could shoot, a big guy. The cow walked to within 30 feet of us. Mixed feelings on chasing a big productive guy like that this late in the season, could be tough. Probably leave him for another year and try for him early. He's probably getting old like me anyway and past his prime so will give him this last hurrah before we meet.

And I end with a photo of another painting by Anita McComas, "Moonlight Reflections" (www.anitamcomas.com) that I sent Vern after we met for the first time at Jodi's PhD defense in 2019:

This is the affection we co-authors feel, too, scurrying back and forth, writing, composing ourselves over these thoughts and words.

Some [Edited] Introductory Words for Two Little Earth-Cousins
David Jardine

> Out from behind his oxygen mask
> As if he were just my good old, familiar little earth-cousin.
> from Jodi Latremouille (2014b), "My Treasured Relation"

Cancer really is one of "those" words.

Two days ago, an old friend, Fernando, died of it, and the funeral is this Thursday, January 23—lung cancer come down hard and fast, as it often does.

And then there's me at 8 years old and my mother, 1958, undergoing a radical mastectomy.

Drawn living room curtains for weeks, drawn cheeks, a big wicker laundry basket full of neighbors' tiny presents, one to be opened each day, smells of soaps and lotions and other notions, meant to help stretch out time's lingering,

I guess, and to show wee affections without words, without "that" word.

Easy to recall how many had to disappear from view, unable to be present to such things.

Understandable in its own sad way. Makes my own skin lesions over the past couple of years seem quite silly in comparison, not only because they are less severe and the suffering is near nil (although hearing "that" word chills nevertheless), but because, at the level of our living and dying, cancer is always incomparable

An old hermeneutic saw: "the individual case . . .. is not exhausted by being a particular example of a universal law or concept." (Hans-Georg Gadamer, 2004, p. 39)

Without tough disciplined thinking and writing, phrases like "childhood leukemia" can lose their function of "responding and summoning" (Hans-Georg Gadamer, 2004, p. 458) and simply repel. Of course, be repel if need be. Of course.

"Childhood Leukemia" too easily becomes a hard category of illness, and our responses to it becomes subjectivized into nothing but "moist gastric intimacy" (Jean Paul Sartre, 1970, p. 4).

Remaining true to the intimacy of this "special case" (Hans-Georg Gadamer, 2004, p. 39) dear Shelby, is an especially difficult form of research that requires generosity, patience, perseverance, discipline, stillness and wisdom (6 aspired to "perfections," [Sanskrit: *paramitas*] in Buddhist practice [see Tsong-Kha-Pa, 2000, 2003, 2004]).

All clustered, of course, around impermanence.

"We will have to hold firmly to the standpoint of finiteness" (Hans-Georg Gadamer, 2004, p. 99), both in the topics we consider and in the expended breath of our consideration itself. Why? Because the topic of a hermeneutic study is finite as is our insight into it.

"Future generations will understand differently" (p. 340) and therefore, the purpose of a hermeneutic inquiry is to "keep [the topic] open for the future" (p. 340).

In reading *My Treasured Relation*, I'm blessed with the meeting of these two little earth-cousins and the cuddle of writing I found them in. It that makes me remember that I, too, and however near or distant, am a third earth-cousin in this inevitably fatal round.

Interpretive work is meant to be read interpretively. It is meant to be suffered. Read this and let yourself be third.

"It Must Be Read as Carefully as Mushrooms"
David Jardine

It must be read as carefully as mushrooms that always just might be poisonous even if delicious, just might be nourishing even if acrid. We are in a fix—pedagogically, ecologically, in body and mind and otherwise—and it's going to take some doing to even start undoing this fix. (David Jardine, 2015a, p. xvi)

Read . . . . slowly and repeatedly. That is what these matters need [and deserve]. If you read . . . . too fast, the pull of the gravity and imminence of our circumstances will only increase [panic will ensue, things will become illegible, you'll be vulnerable to cynical manipulations. Read slowly, the [panic-]pull starts to lessen and we can then slowly start to see where we are, what has happened to us and our kin, what we have done, what we might now do. Hurry will only lead to panic that is distracting and of no use. It will only tighten the knots and the tangle and the confusion. [It will only lead to more panic and increases in the hurry meant to lessen the panic but that in fact increases it]. (p. xvi)

This work asks for love and takes care of that very same love, all at the same time, along with the blushing of it and with the coupling of hard-nosed and hard-won composure, the tears and the embarrassment all. Let the tears come and then sit up. Stop. Think. Write. Carefully. With all the care that this work musters and measures and needs. Get the citations in line. Don't quote the wrong page. Get the years right. You need accuracy. Don't let yourself get poisoned in the rush of things. Don't let yourself forget to listen for the old voices in the air. Like this from yet another Elder writing of another Elder:

It was a memorable and energizing [wicihitowin] event, the 7th Provoking Curriculum Studies Conference. Ted Aoki was very much present at that meeting, asking (after my paper praising him): "Who is this Ted Aoki? I'd like to meet him." (William Pinar, 2018, p. xv)

We read this, knowing Bill Pinar, and having known Ted's wisdom and self-effacing humor. Lesley (Tait, 2014, p. 94) remembers how "watching Maxine Greene on the screen created a deep wish within me. I want her to be my grandmother. Could her spirit and essence help guide me? With time and thought, I realized, she already was." We consider Bill Doll, the shock of white hair and arching laugh, now stilled yet rattling and ringing still. We are sustained still by the clear cold water of Cynthia Chambers' (see, for example, 1999, 2008) work, reminding, refreshing and startling all at once, pored over and over again with such affection, even at this great distance of years. We know this having been gifted with the counsel of Kehte-aya Bob Cardinal.

My heart is broken,

open.

(Rick Fields, 1990, p. xiv)

Our hearts.

WAYSTATION XI
Await.
Meredith McLeod

Don't ever apologize for crying for the trees burning in the Amazon or over the waters polluted from mines in the Rockies. Don't apologize for the sorrow, grief, and rage you feel. It is a measure of your humanity and your maturity. It is a measure of your open heart, and as your heart breaks open there will be room for the world to heal. That is what is happening as we see people honestly confronting the sorrows of our time. (Joanna Macy, 1996, p. 175)

Photo by Danielle Bertoia. Merritt, BC. September 27, 2019.

This picture. It must be read as carefully as mushrooms. Don't rush. Sit squat. Await

So Where Are We, Now?

Jodi Latremouille, Lesley Tait & David Jardine

> "To be patient in an emergency is a terrible trial." (Wendell Berry, with Bill Moyers, 2013, n.p.).

> "As your heart breaks open there will be room for the world to heal" (Joanna Macy, 1996, p. 175).

What do we seek?

> Research that acknowledges the tangled messiness of the heart's desires and demands, research [and teaching] that honors the tangled mysteries of the heart's dynamic beating like a winter storm that compels us. (Carl Leggo, 2006, p. 77)

Where do we turn? Again and again, to treasured relations.

My Treasured Relation Jodi Latremouille

I have always wanted to write about my cousin Shelby, but whenever I try, the words just don't seem to do justice to my cousin who never grew up. I want to make him live again in this story. But mostly, I would just really like to not cry today.

Shelby was born to my aunt, with too much life ahead of her, and so he was raised by my silent-stoic, gentle grandfather, Dave and Leona, the asthmatic, arthritic heart-young grandmother, with more love in her than those sick lungs could handle.

This little boy was never formally diagnosed, as he never got the opportunity to spend much time in school, but looking back now, I know that he did indeed have certain cognitive delays, which I did not, and still cannot, name. Nor do I want to. Socially constructed deficiencies are not lovable. To me, he was just Shelby, even though on that level beyond the one that we talk about, we all knew that he didn't function in quite the same way we all did.

Shelby was diagnosed with something, though. He was diagnosed with leukemia at the age of 5. His childhood years were a blur for all of us.

Waiting and hoping,
trips to Vancouver through the Fraser Canyon- and later, over the Coquihalla,
stays at the Ronald McDonald house,
fundraising projects,
months in isolation units,
missed school,
missed life,
hours and hours stalking and thrashing in the shallow end of the backyard pool:
daring us to venture near him.
A wheelchair-bound, abbreviated trip to Disneyland,
Make-A-Wish dream visits with Hulk Hogan and Trevor Linden,
Birthday pizzas delivered by none other than
Raphael the Teenage Mutant Ninja Turtle,
and a failed autologous bone marrow transplant.

We were told that Shelby was going to receive a "miracle cure," a treatment that my 11-year-old brain understood in the following terms: the doctors would take a massive needle that would suck the bone marrow from his spine, purge it of cancer cells with radiation, and return it back to his body with another massive needle, with the expectation that the healthy bone marrow would regenerate and grow, filling his spine with healthy bone marrow. My sister and I have always wondered if our matching needle phobias were inspired by bearing witness to our cousin's medical treatments.

I learned the language of platelets and prednisone and blood counts and spinal taps and we-still-have-hope and in/remission/out and chemo and things-are-not-looking good and be-nicer-he's-sick and making time count.

No, wait a minute
Time counted us
by appointments
and remissions
and birthdays
and good days
bad days
and
one
more

> day.
> We counted everything
> Except time.

I now understand this "miracle cure," autologous bone marrow transplant, the way the doctors and all the adults in the room did, as what it was in those days, as more of a "last ditch experimental treatment." Shelby spent 3 months in complete isolation while the bone marrow was being purged of cancer cells. In order to visit him, we had to wash our hands to the elbow with stinging, sharp-smelling disinfectant soap, walk through the sliding door into the closet-sized "isolation chamber," wash our hands again for several minutes, don plastic shoe coverings, plastic clothing, and face masks, then enter through a second sliding door, careful, fearful, not to get too close. We could touch his hand, but hugs were out of the question. We just couldn't risk it. He was my alien-cousin, a lovable monster descended from another planet, participating in an experimental study, peering out from behind his oxygen mask. Then I would hear his muffled, cheerful gravelly voice, saying "Hi, Jode!" as if he were just my good old, familiar little earth-cousin. At age ten, he was much more subdued, resigned to the treatments, than he had been in the early years.

> 6-year-old tornado.
>
> "I am a DINOSAUR and I am going to SMASH YOU!"
>
> Pierced.
>
> "I am a LION and I am going to EAT YOU!"
>
> Swearing.
>
> "SHIT! I HATE YOU!"
>
> Despising his cruel saviours.
>
> "I am JAKE THE SNAKE and I am going to do a D.D.T. right on your HEAD!"
>
> Restrained.
>
> "I am going to ride my snowmobile all the way back to Merritt and you will never find me again!"

My sister and I spent many hours with Shelby through the years, his contracted playmates, and I think our company probably was one of the reasons my grandmother was able to maintain some semblance of sanity. He was a challenging kid to begin with, prone to temper tantrums and boiling-over fits of anger. And having to be stuck with needles, of varying diameters, on a daily basis, was, and still is, unfathomable to me. Anyone who had to go through all of that would, understandably, be just a little "on edge." My mother would send us over to Grandma's house every day after school until we became too busy with our extracurricular lives; in the later years we would squeeze in weekend sleepovers and pool parties when we could. The two girls would play Duck Hunter and Super Mario Brothers for hours and hours on end, while Shelby wrestled in the background with his stuffed animals and Teenage Mutant Ninja Turtle figurines, shouting out the play-by-play, occasionally jumping off the couch and squashing us flat-out under his roly-poly body, making us gasp under his weight, begging to be freed, to breathe again.

On the day of my 8th birthday party, all of my friends had come over to celebrate. Of course, Shelby was invited. It was a glorious spring day at the "Fox Farm," our 5-acre mountainside hobby farm, perfect for badminton on the lawn and hikes up the mountain to the magical forest. My father had installed a rope swing in the woods about 200 metres above the house. All of the kids were taking turns. One of the less experienced "city slickers" lost his grip and launched himself into space, then landed softly, unbelievably, gracefully, like a ski-jumper on the steep landing slope, sliding down the leaf-strewn mountainside straight into an anthill. One girl forgot the only safety rule (to launch yourself *away* from the tree in a circular trajectory), and flew straight out from the tree, then straight back in, smashing into the tree trunk. We watched her float in slow-motion horror, and then cringed in sympathy, shielding our eyes and turning away, wincing at the inevitable "thud." We turned back and peeled our hands from our eyes to watch her loosen her grip and slither listlessly off the rope into a weeping heap at the base of the tree. Only two casualties this time. Not bad.

Shelby was down at the house, as it was too difficult for him to hump all the way up the sidehill to the rope swing. I am pretty sure that what we did that day was my idea. One of us ran down to the house to grab a bottle of ketchup. We chose a "victim," smeared the ketchup on her, and started hollering. "Shelby, help! Tracy fell off the rope swing and she's bleeding!" I heard him, out of sight near the house, yelling, "What? Oh no! I'm coming, Jode!" And we were all snickering and jeering, until we saw him emerge over the hill, panting and crying, wheezing, tripping over sticks, stumbling up, knees dirty, nose running.

Distraught.

Our laughter froze instantly to silence. He had brought a tea towel. I didn't know what he thought he was going to do with that. I guess . . . I suppose . . . that was the funny part. It was just a joke.

For his 10th birthday, our family bought him a funny little voice-activated yellow plastic sunflower in a funny little plastic green pot that danced a herky-jerky hula, its funny little happy sunglassed face bobbing along to the Mini Pops singing their funny little-kid version of "Karma Chameleon."

That flower was cool, man. Totally rocked that song.

In order to get it into the room we had to unwrap and open up the package, then wipe down every single surface with the disinfectant, including the batteries. The nurses brought it in for him, as that day he was having a "bad immune system day." We smiled through the window as he tried it out, grinning from cheek to soft, chubby cheek. We could see him laughing through the glass, and in my head I could hear his hoarse, breathless chortle. My mom picked out that flower for him. I am sure she thought it would cheer him up. It did; she nailed it out of the park. He loved that flower. All the days of his life. Because you should never grow out of silly little things.

>
> Shelby finally did make his escape.
> We were called in to visit him in the hometown Merritt hospital.
> I knew it was bad,
> because any self-respecting version of Hope would have bundled him up in her
> arms and magically swooped him all the way back up and over
> the winter-blizzard highway
> to Vancouver Children's Hospital.
> Bloated, drained, cushioned by crisp white pillows
> and our false cheerfulness.
> Distracted by niceties and pain.
> We, the kids, protected, excluded.
> Unaware but still knowing.
> Just a short visit.
> Tired. Ready. Calm. Barely 11 years old.
> Selfless. Raspy.
> "Have fun skiing tomorrow, Jode."
> Big, soft, squishy, forever hug.
> We knew things were bad when we were allowed to hug him.
> Wait, hold it, hold on, for him.
> Cry in the backseat on the way home.
> Look out the foggy window at the hazy, unending night.

Shelby died on a blowing-snow January night, at the age of 11. I was 12 years old.

I got my first menstrual period the day of the funeral. What a day for firsts. I wasn't particularly afraid or ashamed, as some young girls were back in the days before moms were supposed to be a girl's best friend and talk about, oh, about just absolutely everything! I had read about it in a book somewhere and had some "samples" stashed in my bathroom cupboard. I was just, oh, just annoyed, awkward and lonely. I just wasn't ready to grow up, not just yet.

Shelby's neighbour
and best friend in the whole entire world,
a mature young woman-ish,
kind, gentle 12-year-old
Robyn,
who didn't have to be his friend,
with two perfect, large fake front teeth
that got knocked out years ago in a biking accident
riding down "Suicide Hill" by our neighbourhood school,
who felt-penned a massive "Hulkamania!" poster for Shelby's best-day-ever
and who probably got her period (light-years) months before me,
and who I imagined would know
exactly how
to handle her newfound womanhood
gracefully,
(She didn't. She told me so years later.)
was beside herself after she returned from viewing his body.
His Vancouver Canucks jerseyed,
Google-eyeballed Disneyland-Goofy capped,
painless body.

"That's the first time in his life that he has ever been alone."

She wanted to wait with him in that room until the service began.

Our great-aunt was asked to perform the eulogy, and my narrow little 12-year-old self was disappointed in the choice, expecting that she just way too stuffy and stodgy to do my hilarious, ridiculous, lovely little cousin justice. My mom had written the eulogy—oh, it was just so perfect—and I didn't want it spoiled by someone who didn't know him just the way we did. I think back now and realize that my pin-curled aunt was probably the only one in the entire jam-packed room of 300 people who was tightly wound enough to hold it together for the entire speech.

And she re-called him to a "T."
A "D.D.T.," that is:
"I know that Shelby is up there in heaven,

riding his snowmobile
and doing D.D.T.'S on all the angels."

Shelby was the exception. To everything. He was the beautiful little monster who reflected back to us who we really were. We were rude, wild, loud, unfiltered, imaginative, hungry, hurting, scared-cruel dreamers.

That is what love does.
It makes us want to do justice.
Without justice we are merely co-existing.
Waiting for the reward.
Labelling.
Judging- and moving on.
I will never move on.
I want to make him live again.
My treasured teacher.
My relation.
Alien-cousin.
Brother.
Heart-swelling baby dinosaur.
Lion.
Hulk.

Part VIII
Where do we Turn?

Where do we Turn?
Jodi Latremouille, Lesley Tait & David Jardine

> Imagine. Death's swerving halt sets things in motion. Death enlivens—memory, presumption, desire, hope, imagination, expectation, regret, anger, and grief, yes grief. Precisely its eventful finality makes it an unfinished swerve, back and forth, and sidelong into surroundings, multiple. (David Jardine, 2019, p. 133)

> Their living, in death, gets tossed up into thin air and scattered outwards, an energy out beyond the thicknesses of a body, lying, stilled. It is getting these grave gravities back in motion again, back "in play" that is the work of undergoing grief—back in motion, Aristotle's *energeia*, that very thing that grief can drain faster than it fills up, "aliveness." (p. 132)

Thus, we turn to life writing (Cynthia Chambers, Erika Hasebe-Ludt, Carl Leggo, & Anita Sinner, 2012), Indigenous métissage and literary métissage (Dwayne Donald, 2016; see Jodi Latremouillle, Antonella Bell, Zahra Kasamali, Mandy Krahn, Lesley Tait, & Dwayne Donald, 2016) as we seek ways to "address the complicated issues of living ethically and with empathy among all our relations" (Erika Hasebe-Ludt, Cynthia Chambers, & Carl Leggo, 2009, p. 14). We turn to our Elders, our Knowledge Keepers, Our Ceremonialists, our Ancestors. We ask for guidance about lifting a curriculum that tells our shared story. Not the Indigenous story, not the settler story, but our shared story.

We turn to the stones in our pockets:

> Rocks are grounding.
>   the mythic image
>   bone become stone
>   carrying life. (Jackie Seidel, 2014, p. 40)

"Yet the 'teaching rocks' are somewhat careful about sharing their counsel … Like a stranger, they will not sit down and tell you everything immediately," [Leroy] Little Bear says. "Only when the rocks begin to know you will they tell you their story" (Don Hill, 2008).

"Cultivate love for those who have gathered to listen." (Tsong-Kha-Pa, 2000, p. 64) Learn some of the miracles. Survive. Weave your transformations in your life as well as in your work. Live. Stay alive. Don't go under, don't go mad. Keep sowing. Time will reap. Weave your songs by whatever means you can. (Ben Okri, 1997, p. 14)

> Shared earth stories.
> So many stories.
> Gifts that are not ours to hold.

"We Do Know What to Do" David Jardine

Preamble

> We need to take afflictions as the path. This is very important because if we are unable to take them as the path, no matter how good our practice may be, we will be overcome by the afflictions. (Thrangu Rinpoche, 2011, p. 182)

> If we do not look at the essence of the afflictions, they will grow strong and stronger. The remedy is not to reject, block or suppress the emotion—as scientists these days say, repressing your disturbing emotions will lead to illness in your body. This, however, does not mean that we should just follow our afflictions and go wherever they lead us. Instead, we need to look at the essence of the afflictions. (p. 190)

> "The essence of the afflictions is naturally empty." (Thrangu Rinpoche, 2011, p. 183). This: there is no stubborn, self-existent "thing" *to which* I might acquiesce [it is, instead, just arising causes and conditions and habits and weaving circumstances, personal, historical, cultural, inherited, perhaps even things I've personally fallen for far too often, thus strengthening the semblance of its solid reality and inevitability—called, in Buddhism, "reification"], therefore the seemingly self-existent "I myself" that rises to the bait becomes visible as itself "empty" of self-existence and full only of dependently co-arising, here, now. (David Jardine, 2016, p. 228)

The bait and the one that rises to it are intertwined. They rise up together and if this is not looked at carefully, each strengthens the other in the semblances of permanence in the sense of the other one being the cause for my arousal, and this self of mine then glories in the sense of efficacy and power and feeling of sheer *aliveness* that ensues in thus meeting the enemy that, in great part, my rising up has created.

This, of course, is war consciousness at its best. Finally, in all this swirling, the feel of something solid and permanent and "real":

> Like trying to grab cornstarch dissolved in water, the faster and harder and more desperately we try to seize these matters and cling to something hard and permanent the more substantial they *feel* and the more is aggravated our desire to grip even tighter. (David Jardine, 2012, p. 219)

The illusory *feel* of substantiality is *caused* by the gripping and then too easily attributed to what the gripping has caused—the *feeling* of solidity and resistance—as the cause of me needed to grip. This cycle only inflates unless I let go.

The grip of ecological sorrowfulness can distort and delude.

It is in the nature of reifying war consciousness to accelerate, propagate, enlarge, distend and, of course, then, in a great act of profound psychopathological obliviousness, project. "If it wasn't for *that* I wouldn't be doing *this*." If it wasn't for "them," "us" would be fine. The grip blames what it grips blitheringly unaware of how its own grip plays a part in what it then fears.

The grip of ecological sorrowfulness can distort and delude.

This is a closed circle and, once I'm inside of it, what is thinkable, speakable, is already set out in advance. But more than this, I come to believe that my only relief can come from defeating that which now grips me in its/my grip. Refuge is imagined as "overcoming," semi-automatic weapons on the state house steps readied to *increase* the triggered grip.

Small wonder that Ajahn Chah's (1987, n.p.) adage, "take the feeling of letting go as your refuge" (see David Jardine, 2012, p. 217–230) might just cause the gripping outrage to increase.

And So

And so, Wednesday, April 8, 2020, CTV news online. Potentially 800 000 cases of COVID-19 in Alberta, Canada. "Most likely" (CTV News Edmonton, 2020). Shall I read this, about Alberta's "war" against the COVID-19 virus invasion? Exactly what *for*? I feel myself drawn towards it, even though the work of surrounding myself with actions and affections that are more local, more careful and step-by-step, are things that need my attention and devotion.

Still, this headline draws. It draws me toward, but also draws me away. It strengthens me and weakens me all at once.

But let me tell the truth, here. After the first few seconds of some hospital hallway story or that, I turn it off, not because I don't "care," but because, well, I don't care to subject myself to something quite so however—unintentionally manipulative *to no end*—well, only to the end of blurring and draining the work of surrounding myself.

I'm drawn towards and then repelled. I'm recalling Phil Ochs' (1967) lines in the song *Crucifixion*:

Tell me every detail, I've got to know it all,
And do you have a picture of the pain?

Moth-Nature

All this helps me understand moths and feel for them. The lure that can burn you up. Oh, look! [click] Another frontline worker is Skyping in! [click] Oh dear, dear, dear! [click click click]. Remember, here, that it is my own fraught Moth-Nature that I'm mocking inside myself, as well as how the screeching candlelight of relentless media sources know full well about this Nature and how widespread it is, how easy it is to stimulate and arouse, how profitable all that can surely be:

"That tough balance between being drawn into it for the sake of burning it off and being simply inflamed by that approach and deepening the error of it" (David Jardine, 2016a, p. 231).

Oh, were I as wise as the things I can sometimes write. That, by itself, is the strangest of things, to be able to glimpse the tough balances that are thoughtful and wise and might ask the best of me, while all the while having neck muscles betray me with no noticeable effort, getting me leaning into the latest "Look at that! Look at that!" news that is, in reality, nothing "new" at all.

Closer.

Closer.

Pfft!

On Collective Stress Disorder

The grip of ecological sorrowfulness can distort and delude.

I made up a term when teaching practicum classes full of student teachers who I would then visit with regularly in their placement classes in local elementary schools. It was meant to indicate a commonly experienced thing in the work of teaching (and, of course, far beyond that). I expect that many who are more emotionally wise than I am have known this far before I figured out anything about it. It's like this.

Small things in the day-to-day work of living in a classroom can each cause a low-level bit of annoyance, stress, distraction, exhaustion and the like. Sometimes, when I get too tired or distracted, the collective stress of *all* the small things can come to be visited on *any one of those things*, leading to a distorted sense of what is happening here and now with this particular one thing, how much attention it needs, how important it is, what it really *is*, how I might properly act, and so on.

Collective stress disorder:

> "You must not allow them to linger but must immediately disperse them as though they were drawings on water. Do not let them be like drawings on stone" (Tsong-kha-pa, 2000, p. 347–8).

There is a thread, here, that needs to be out in the open, though. *Who benefits*, who *profits* if I fail to remain composed and able to ask this question and not just fall for it into panic and fear and exhaustion and retreat? Who [click] profits [click]?

"What is Localism's Answer?"

I was reminded of this long-ago thing about collective stress disorder when I was reading a recently published conversation between Tim DeChristopher and Wendell Berry (2020) in *Orion Magazine*. It was revealing to read once I got over a certain knee-jerk reaction that felt very personal. Briefly put, I'm quite able to find every encouragement I have attempted, every act I do or word I write, to be utterly meaningless and trivial when placed in the grand scheme of global troubles.

This placement is, in part, what this conversation circled like an exhausting drain.

I won't recapitulate all the turns of this conversation (https://orionmagazine.org/article/to-live-and-love-with-a-dying-world/), because there is just one thread, for now, that interests me. It has to do with the small ways in which we might act, think, be careful and encouraging in these ecologically sorrowful times, "no matter how small or unnewsworthy" (Wendell Berry, from Tim DeChristopher & Wendell Berry, 2020), and how we, how I might prevent huge world events from visiting themselves upon those small ways and asking them to live up to that hugeness.

Wendell Berry is responding to Tim DeChristopher saying that, even with concerted local actions and legal mineral rights "they're going to suck the oil out of there whether you sign the papers or not":

> *WB:* Those are the people who have the wealth and power, and there's no easy, immediate answer to that, except to live so far as you can in opposition. You've got to live and love. You've got to find the answers in your heart.
>
> *TD:* But that gets more complicated every day, to learn how to live and love with a dying world and a broken society. Exponentially tougher when you're talking about farmers in Honduras who can't grow anything anymore because of how dramatically the climate has changed. Or farmers in Syria, who are forced off of their land because of the drought and watched their country be destroyed by civil war as a result of that mass migration. We're just at the beginning of that. We will see hundreds of millions more of those sorts of refugees forced into migration and—
>
> *WB:* You realize, don't you, that you've won this argument?
>
> *TD:* What is localism's answer to refugees? To those whose homeland is not livable anymore? Whether that place is underwater, has turned to desert, was destroyed by American imperialism and our desire for more resources?
>
> *WB:* You've won this argument. The argument for despair is impenetrable, it's invulnerable. You got all the cards. You got the statistics, the science, the projections on your side. But then we're still just sitting here with our hands hanging down, not doing anything. (DeChristopher & Berry, 2020)

I'm out this morning, April 26, 2020, to plant the first peas in the garden still trudged with some snow, but this conversation lingers like a moth. Like a flame.

What is localism's answer? Be careful. The grip of ecological sorrowfulness can distort and delude. What *seems to be the answer*, but not really said in so many words, is this:

Localism, to be a place of real repose, must become answerable to the very worst case that might be visited upon it. Every single pea, every single grace of sunlight, every breath of relief from this long, long winter, must bear the full weight of all imaginable of the world's woes if I am to take any true and settling refuge in it. Otherwise it is false, naive, and useless.

Need a bigger flame?

WB: David Kline just published a book called The Round of a Country Year. One of the remarkable things is that it's a happy book. David's family, his neighbors, they're cooperating all the time, and nobody's overworked.

TD: So, take that community as an example. That happy community that is working sustainably in that way. Now let's say, even a small fraction of the 80 million Bangladeshis whose homes are less than 10 meters above sea level, who are losing their homes right now, every day—a small portion of them, just a few hundred thousand, show up at that community. How do they respond? What is that community's response to that mass migration?

. . ..

I see folks like David Fleming, who are explicit that a local economy requires barriers to entry. He's pretty explicitly opposed to immigration. And when we look at the pattern of migration, the military has an answer, the xenophobes have an answer. (Tim DeChristopher & Wendell Berry, 2020)

And again:

TD: When it became clear that all those people in Bangladesh are going to lose their homes, India built a border fence all the way around Bangladesh. A 1900-mile, partially electrified border fence. Over the past decade, there's been a proliferation of border fences, between rich and poor areas, across the world. The military's answer is genocide—we're going to make sure these people die right where they're at. So, if we're going to live in love in this time in history, we need to have a better answer.

"We Do Know What to Do"

WB: Well, here we are, wasting time. What are we doing here? Why aren't we out somewhere else doing something else? Why are we just sitting here talking?

TD: Because we don't know what to do. That's what I'm trying to say. It's really complicated to live in love, at this time.

WB: We do know what to do. We need to take care of the responsibilities that we've got. The effective boundaries of responsibility are your own limits. There's so much you can do, and you ought to do it. That's all. But to sit here and hypothesize the worst possible thing that could happen and decide what we're going to do about it, or what the Amish are going to do about it, seems just a waste of time. (Tim DeChristopher & Wendell Berry, 2020)

There is, here, a profound and vital admission of inadequacy in the face of the woes of the whole wide world. I need to take care of the responsibilities that I have, and the *effective* boundaries of that are my very own limits of flesh and bone, of age and the slippages of time.

Letting even a small glimpse of the full suffering of the world visit itself on this aging hand handling peas *seems* like a globally aware ecological consciousness, but, in fact, it is too easily no more than an act of *hubris*. It can be a refusal to recognize that "effective boundaries of responsibility are [my] own limits." It is subjecting my *effective boundaries* to paralyzing unboundedness. The grip of ecological sorrowfulness can distort and delude.

I must accept my own boundedness, my limitedness, even if it makes me cry out.

Small potatoes.

Small peas planted.

Small compost heaps set up against the apocalypse.

Garden tended under smoky skies.

Accepting this is its own form of suffering that can *then* bear itself out in witness of small things done fully, done as well as possible, peas planted, a bit of writing in an effort to comfort and commiserate and instruct *myself* as much as anyone:

WB: It was the Shakers who were sure the end could come anytime, and they still saved the seeds and figured out how to make better diets for old people. Thomas Merton was interested in the Shakers. I said to him,

> "If they were certain that the world could end at any minute, how come they built the best buildings in Kentucky?"
> "You don't understand," he said. "If you know the world could end at any minute, you know there's no need to hurry. You take your time and do the best work you possibly can."[4]

That was important to me. I've repeated it many times. (Tim DeChristopher & Wendell Berry, 2020)

Imagine the shame of doing rushed and shabby work that exhausts you and spends your love, your affection, your care and limited energies *as if believing that my rushing can outrun the steady, clear-eyed stalk of time and the earthly way of things.*

No. Such denial sometimes, sometimes *unwittingly*, hides in the grandiosities of ecological awareness is foolish, childish, animal-body-threat-based war consciousness. It leads to limp and impotent rifles on the steps. Go home. Exercise what frail and fragile freedom you actually have. Be strong and well-practiced enough to be patient in an emergency (Wendell Berry, with Moyers, 2013)

We do know what to do.

I do know what to do. Go out, today. Plant peas. Split some more wood for a winter that might never come. Split for another year I might never see. The pitch-crack sound and smell remain beautiful as ever. The Ravens still gather for a look.

Enjoy doing it. Be *pleased* by the sun after all these feet of snow. Maybe then write a bit, finish up this here little thing that has been lingering for a while. Post it in the hope that it might raise a smile, that it might do some small good.

So, yes. Take the feeling of letting go as your refuge and *get on with it*, because getting paralyzed is the most unbecoming of luxuries. We do know what to do:

> under the tough old stars--
> In the shadow of bluffs
>   I came back to myself,
> To the real work, to
>   "What is to be done."
>
>   (Gary Snyder (n.d.), from "I Went into the Maverick Bar")

WAYSTATION XII
Heartland
Kiera Nyeste

We are Back in the Place Where We See Our Footsteps in The Grass
Jodi Latremouille, Lesley Tait & David Jardine

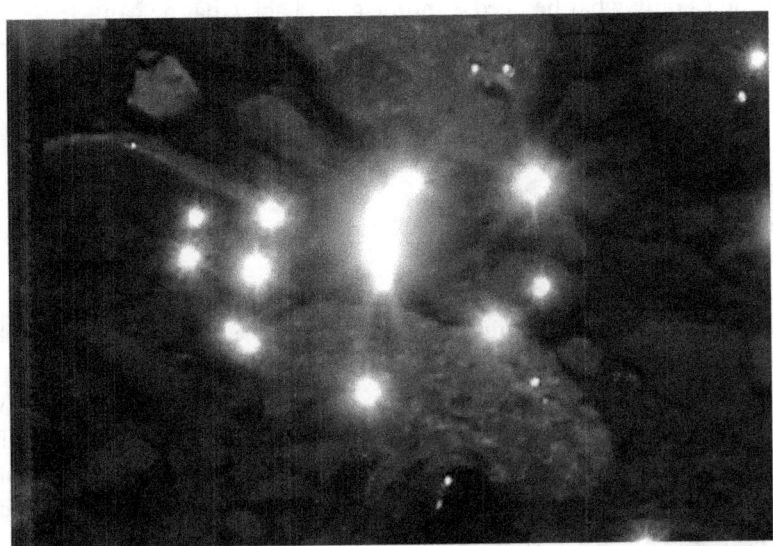

David Jardine: Back in place. We dream momentary classroom gatherings the radiant length of a shutter-click in the driveway runoff of bowing teachers, students alight and circling. Beauty as fleet as all that. Relations as fleet as all that. Aliveness that fleet-footed. Love like a lit bow, arrowed. That fragile.

Lesley Tait: Renewal and preparation begins again. We are back in the place where we see our footsteps in the grass and ask that we are able to return to the place where we see our footsteps in the snow:

> People [like smaller trees from larger trees] receive nourishment from particular places and the inhabitants of those places, as they learn the skills necessary to live in those places. And as they learn and practice the skills necessary to live in that particular place, they become who they are. (Cynthia Chambers, 2008, p. 117)

Lesley Tait: We stand on the blood and the bones of our ancestors. Our creations stories are born from this land and give birth to the hills, mountains, lakes, rivers and animals that sustain us. Our identity is born[e] on the land:

> Immerse yourself in meaningful, rich and deep work with students and you will forget about finishing it. Teacher, you are never finished, but you are also never

unfinished. What matters most is what you do with the very next moment in front of you. (Megan Liddell, 2016, p. 176)

Jodi Latremouille: My father walks softly in the bush, he gives thanks for his kills, he takes only what he needs, and he gives back what he can.

Ask the questions that have no answers.
Invest in the millennium. Plant sequoias.
Say that your main crop is the forest
that you did not plant,
that you will not live to harvest. (Wendell Berry, 1991)

David Jardine: The water's now well down the driveway in the full mix of things, still-ripple and shining in the mixes of road gravel and horse shit and boot
prints in the slush and sloosh. It's why the dogs scurry back and forth when we walk the road. So much dissolved to solve in every whiff. Two great fur saints following the paths of deliquescence. So, there go the Ravens, my dears, again caught and uncaught on the warm Spring-air foothill uplifts. To be dying under their wings is a weird miracle. (2018c, p. xiii)

Lesley Tait: Her small hand reached out and grasped onto mine.
Shhh. Relax my love.
Listen. Listen to the beat, feel it in your heart. Hear the whispers of your grandparents.
Her small little body became weighted in my lap and we began to sing.

References

Abram, D. (1996). *The spell of the sensuous: Language in a more-than-human world.* Pantheon.

Abram, D. (2010). *Becoming animal: An earthly cosmology.* Vintage.

Abram, D., & Jardine, D. (2000). All knowledge is carnal knowledge: A conversation. *Canadian journal of environmental education,* (5), 167–177.

Aho, K. (2018). Neurasthenia revisited: On medically unexplained syndromes and the value of hermeneutic medicine. *Journal of applied hermeneutics,* Article 6. Retrieved from https://jah.journalhosting.ucalgary.ca/jah/index.php/jah/article/view/174/pdf.

Air Quality Health Index. (2017, November). British Columbia-Air quality health index-provincial summary. Government of Canada. Retrieved from https://weather.gc.ca/airquality/pages/provincial_summary/bc_e.html.

Alberta Education. (2006a). Social Studies Kindergarten to Grade 6 Programs of Study. Alberta Education. Retrieved from https://education.alberta.ca/social-studies-k-6/programs-of-study/.

Alberta Education. (2006b). Social Studies Grade 10 to 12 Programs of Study. Alberta Education. Retrieved from https://education.alberta.ca/social-studies-10-12/programs-of-study/.

Albrecht, G., Sartoire, G. M, Higginbotham, N., Freeman, S., Kelly, B., Stain, H., Tonna, A., & Pollard, G. (2007). Solastalgia: the distress caused by environmental change. Published in *Australasian psychiatry,* 2001, 15, Suppl. 1: S 95–98. Abstract available online through the US National Library of Medicine/National Institute of Health at: https://www.ncbi.nlm.nih.gov/pubmed/18027145.

Allen, P. (2020). Heart-breaking photo of nursery children forced to play in isolation chalk squares sparks outcry in France after schools reopen. *Daily Mail*, May 13, 2020. Retrieved from https://www.dailymail.co.uk/news/article-8314697/Heart-breaking-photo-children-forced-play-isolation-zones-sparks-outcry-France.html.

Aoki, T. (1987). In receiving, a giving: A response to the panelist's gifts. *Journal of Curriculum Theorizing, 7*(3).

Arendt, H. (1969). *Between past and future*. Penguin.

Basso, K. (1996). *Wisdom sits in places: Landscape and language among the Western Apache*. University of New Mexico.

Bastien, B. (2004). *Blackfoot ways of knowing: The worldview of the Siksikaitsitapi*. University of Calgary.

Battiste, M., & Bouvier, R. (2013). *Decolonizing education: Nourishing the learning spirit*. Purich.

Beard, G. (1881). *American nervousness, its causes and consequences: A supplement to nervous exhaustion (neurasthenia)*. G. P. Putnam's Sons.

Berk, A. (2012). *Nightsong*. Simon & Schuster Books for Young Children.

Berry, W. (1983). *Standing by words*. North Point.

Berry, W. (1986). *The unsettling of America*. Sierra Club.

Berry, W. (1987). *Home economics*. North Point.

Berry, W. (1988). The profit in work's pleasure. *Harper's magazine*, March 1989, 19–24.

Berry, W. (1991). Manifesto: The mad farmer liberation front. In Context: A Quarterly of Humane Sustainable Culture (Reclaiming Politics: Participating in Public Life), 30(3), 62. Retrieved from https://www.context.org/iclib/ic30/berry/.

Berry, W. (with Moyers, B.) (2013). Wendell Berry: Poet and prophet. Interview by Bill Moyers. Moyers & Company. Retrieved from http://billmoyers.com/episode/wendell-berry-poet-prophet/.

Blenkinsop, S. (2012). Four slogans for cultural change: An evolving place-based, imaginative and ecological learning experience. *Journal of moral education*, 41(2), 353–368.

Bly, R. (2008). Advice from the geese. Retrieved from http://www.poets.org/poetsorg/poem/advice-geese.

Brady, I. (2009). Foreword. In M. Prendergrast, C. Leggo, & P. Sameshima (Eds.), *Poetic inquiry: Vibrant voices in the social sciences* (pp. xi–xvi). Sense.

British Columbia Ministry of Education. (2016). Curriculum 10–12 drafts. British Columbia Ministry of Education. Retrieved from https://curriculum.gov.bc.ca/curriculum/10-12#ss.

Calgary Board of Education. (2015). Collaborative online resource environment. [Password protected resource bank]. Retrieved from https://www.albertacore.ca/access/home.

Calgary Catholic School District. (2015). Instructional media centre. [Password-protected resource bank]. Retrieved from http://www.cssd.ab.ca/staff/.

Canada's History. (2015). Shashi Shergill: Recipient of the 2015 Governor General's History Award for Excellence in Teaching. Canada's History. Retrieved from http://www.canadashistory.ca/awards1445/governor-general-s-history-awards/award recipients/2015/shashi-shergill.

Caputo, J. (1993). *Against ethics: Contributions to a poetics of obligation with constant reference to deconstruction*. Indiana State University.

Carruthers, M. (2005). *The book of memory: A study of memory in medieval culture.* Cambridge University.
Carson, R. (1962). Silent spring. Houghton-Mifflin.
Chah, A. (1987). Our real home: A talk to an aging lay disciple approaching death. *Access to Insight.* Retrieved from http://www.accesstoinsight.org/lib/thai/chah/bl111.html.
Chah, A. (2005). *Everything arises, everything falls away.* Shambhala.
Chambers, C. (1999). A topography for curriculum theory. *Canadian journal of education*, 24 (2), p. 137–150.
Chambers, C. (2008). Where are we? Finding common ground in a curriculum of place. *Journal for the Canadian association of curriculum studies,* 6 (2), 113–128.
Chambers, C., & Blood, N. (2009). Love thy neighbour: Repatriating precarious Blackfoot Sites. *International journal of Canadian studies,* 2009 (39–40), 253–279.
Chambers, C. M., Hasebe-Ludt, E., Leggo, C., & Sinner, A. (2012). *A heart of wisdom: Life writing as empathetic inquiry.* Peter Lang.
Chinook Park. (2016). Project engage: Living our lives for a sustainable future. Calgary Board of Education.
City of Merritt. (2016). Welcome to Merritt. Retrieved from http://www.merritt.ca/.
Collins English dictionary. (2012). Greenwash. William Collins Sons & Co. Retrieved from http://www.collinsdictionary.com/dictionary/english/greenwash.
CTV News Edmonton. (2020). Alberta could see up to 800,000 COVID-19 infections in 'most likely' scenario. Retrieved from https://edmonton.ctvnews.ca/alberta-could-see-up-to-800-000-covid-19-infections-in-most-likely-scenario-1.4886693.
CTV News Vancouver. (2019, May 9). Nicola lake bracing for floods with more rain in forecast. The Canadian Press. Retrieved from http://bc.ctvnews.ca/nicola-lake-area-bracing-for-floods-with-more-rain-in-forecast-1.3405983.
David Suzuki Foundation. (2016). Blue dot. Retrieved from http://bluedot.ca/.
Dawson, R. (2013/2015). From the liner notes to his CD *The glass trunk.* Domino Records.
Daybreak Kamloops. (2015, November 15). Millie Mitchell, long-time B.C. activist, passes away. Daybreak Kamloops. CBC News. Retrieved from http://www.cbc.ca/news/canada/british-columbia/millie-mitchell-long-time-b-c-activist-passes-away-1.2998321.
DeChristopher, T., & Berry, W. (2020). To live and love with a dying world. *Orion Magazine.* March 2, 2020.Retrieved from https://orionmagazine.org/article/to-live-and-love-with-a-dying-world/.
Derby, M. (2015). *Place, being, resonance: A critical ecohermeneutic approach to education.* Peter Lang.
Doll, W. (2002). Ghosts and the curriculum. In *Curriculum visions* (pp. 23–70). Peter Lang.
Donald, D. (2003). *Elder, student, teacher: A Kanai curriculum métissage* (Unpublished master's thesis). University of Lethbridge.
Donald, D. (2009). Forts, curriculum and Indigenous métissage: Imagining decolonization of Aboriginal-Canadian relations in educational contexts. *First nations perspectives,* 2 (21), 1–24.
Donald, D. (2010). Dwayne Donald: On what terms can we speak? Vimeo. University of Lethbridge Faculty of Education. Retrieved from https://vimeo.com/15264558.

Donald, D. (2012). Indigenous Métissage: A decolonizing research sensibility. *International Journal of Qualitative Studies in Education, 25*(5), 535–555.

Donald, D. (2014a). EDSE 501–601 (800). Holistic approaches to learning: A curricular and pedagogical inquiry. Course outline. Faculty of Education, Department of Secondary Education. University of Alberta.

Donald, D. (2014b). Four directions teachings- Kehte-aya Bob Cardinal: Reflection on a critical incident. Course handout. EDSE 501–60 (800): Holistic approaches to learning: A curricular and pedagogical inquiry. Faculty of Education, Department of Secondary Education. University of Alberta.

Donald, D. (2016). From what does ethical relationality flow? An Indian Act in three artifacts. In D. Jardine & J. Seidel (Eds.), *The Ecological heart of teaching: Radical tales of refuge and renewal for classrooms and communities* (p. 10–16). Peter Lang.

Donald, D. (2019). Place. In J. Wearing, C. Deluca, T. Christou & B Bolden (Eds.), *Key concepts in curriculum studies: Perspectives on the fundamentals* (p. 156–162). Routledge.

Dreikurs, R., & Stolz, V. (1987). *Children: The challenge.* Penguin Group.

Earth Charter International Council. (2000). The Earth Charter: A declaration of fundamental principles for building a just, sustainable, and peaceful global society in the 21st century. Earth Charter Commission. Retrieved from www.earthcharter.org.

Eliade, M. (1968). *Myth and reality.* Harper and Row.

Evernden, N. (1999). *The natural alien: Humankind and environment.* 2nd edition. University of Toronto. (Original work published in 1985).

Ewasiuk, J. (1988). Time for tea. In *Rolling Along* (p. 98–100). Northgate Writing Society. Self-published book. Quality Color.

Ferreiro, E. (2003). *Past and present of the verbs to read and write: Essays on literacy.* M. Fried (tr.). Groundwood.

Fields, R. (1990). [Untitled Poem], cited in the Introduction to C. Ingram (1990). *In the footsteps of Gandhi: Conversations with spiritual social activists* (p. xiv). Parallax.

Fisher-Wirth, A., & Street, L. G. (2013). *The ecopoetry anthology.* Trinity University.

Foucault, M. (1980). Colin Gordon, ed. (1980). *Power/knowledge: Selected interviews & other writings, 1972–1977.* Pantheon.

Foucault, M. (1990). *Politics philosophy culture: Interviews and other writings, 1977–1984.* Lawrence Kritzman, ed. Routledge.

Freire, P. (2000). *Pedagogy of the oppressed.* Continuum International.

Friesen, S., & Jardine, D. (2009). On field(ing) knowledge. In S. Goodchild & B. Sriraman (Eds.), *Festschrifte in celebration of Paul Ernest's 65th birthday.* S. Goodchild and B. Sriraman the Montana Monographs in Mathematics Education Series (p. 149–175). Information Age.

Fukuyama, F. (2006). *The end of history and the last man.* The Free Press.

Gadamer, H. G. (1970). Concerning empty and ful-filled time. *Southern journal of philosophy,* Winter 1970, p. 341–353.

Gadamer, H. G. (1977). *Philosophical hermeneutics.* D. E Linge, trans. University of California Press.

Gadamer, H. G. (1984). The hermeneutics of suspicion. *Man and world, 17,* p. 313–323.

Gadamer, H. G. (1994). *Heidegger's ways.* MIT.

Gadamer, H. G. (2001). *Gadamer in conversation: Reflections and commentary*. R. Palmer, ed. and trans. Yale University.

Gadamer, H. G. (2004). *Truth and method*. 3rd ed., J. Weinsheimer & D. G. Marshall, trans. Continuum.

Gadamer, H. G. (2007a). Hermeneutics and the ontological difference. In R. E. Palmer (Ed. & Trans.), *The Gadamer reader: A Bouquet of the later writings* (pp. 356–371). Northwestern University.

Gadamer, H. G. (2007b). Aesthetics and hermeneutics. In R. E. Palmer (Ed.), *The Gadamer reader: A Bouquet of the later writings* (p. 124–131). Northwestern University.

Gadotti, M. (2003). Pedagogy of the earth and culture of sustainability. Paper presented at the *International conference of the transformative learning centre*, p. 17–19. October 2003. Ontario Institute for Studies in Education.

Gilder Leherman Institute of American History. (1493). *The Doctrine of Discovery, 1493. A Spotlight on a Primary Source by Pope Alexander VI*. Retrieved from https://www.gilderlehrman.org/history-resources/spotlight-primary-source/doctrine-discovery1493#:~:text=The%20Bull%20stated%20that%20any,and%20that%20barbarous%20nations%20be.

Giroux, H. (2017, November 2). *Disposability in the age of disasters: From dreamers and Puerto Rico to violence in Las Vegas*. Truthout.org. Retrieved from http://www.truth-out.org/news/item/42450-disposability-in-the-age-of-disasters-from-dreamers-and-puerto-rico-to-violence-in-las-vegas.

Gleick, J. (1987). *Chaos: The Making of a New Science*. New York: Penguin Books.

Global News Okanagan. (2017, September 28). BC wildfires map 2017: Current location of wildfires around the province. *Global News*. Retrieved from https://globalnews.ca/news/3585284/b-c-wildfires-map-2017-current-location-of-wildfires-around-the-province/.

Grant, S. (2017). Gifford Pinchot: Bridging two eras of national conservation. Connecticut History Organization. Retrieved from https://connecticuthistory.org/gifford-pinchot-bridging-two-eras-of-national-conservation/

Gray, J. (2001). *False dawn: The delusions of global capitalism*. The New Press.

Gray, J. (2003). *Al Qaeda and what it means to be modern*. The New Press.

Griffin, S. (1996). *The Eros of everyday life: Essays on ecology, gender and society*. Doubleday.

Grondin, J. (1995). *Introduction to philosophical hermeneutics*. Yale University.

Gruenewald, D. A. (2003). Foundations of place: A multidisciplinary framework for place-conscious education. *American education research journal*, 40(3), 619–654.

Gruenewald, D. A. (2008). The best of both worlds: A critical pedagogy of place. *Environmental education research*, 14(3), 308–324.

Gunnars, K. (1989). *The prowler*. Red Deer College, section 1.

Hanh, T. N. (1995). *The long road turns to joy: A guide to walking meditation*. Parallax.

Haraway, D. (2016). *Staying with the trouble: Making kin in the chthulucene*. Duke University.

Harrison, G. (1970). Beware of darkness. 1972 From his CD *All things must pass*. Harrisongs.

Hasebe-Ludt, E., Chambers, C. M., & Leggo, C. (2009). *Life writing and literary métissage as an ethos for our times*. Peter Lang.

Heavy Head, R. (2015, February 15). Narcisse Blood last dance. Retrieved from https://www.youtube.com/watch?v=eX_Z5W1R2r8.

Hegel, G. W. F. (1820/1991). *Elements of a philosophy of right*. A. Wood, ed., H. B. Nisbet, trans. Cambridge University.

Heidegger, M. (1968). *What is called thinking?* Harper and Row.

Hermes, W. (1997). Too Many Stories: Are we getting paralyzed by narrative overload? *Utne reader*. Retrieved from https://www.utne.com/media/too-many-stories-narrative-glut/.

Hill, D. (2008). Listening to stones: Learning in Leroy Little Bear's laboratory: Dialogue in the world outside. *Alberta Views*. Retrieved from https://albertaviews.ca/listening-to-stones/.

Hillman, J. (2005). Senex and puer: an aspect of the historical and psychological present. In J. Hillman (2005). *Senex and puer* (p. 30–70). Spring.

Hillman, J. (2006a). Segregation of beauty. In J. Hillman (2006). *City and soul* (p. 187–193). Spring.

Hillman, J. (2006b). Aesthetic response as political action. In J. Hillman (2006). *City and soul* (p. 142–145). Spring.

Hillman, J., & Shamdasani, S. (2013). *Lament of the dead: Psychology after Jung's Red Book*. W.W. Norton & Company.

Hillman, J., & Ventura, M. (1992). *We've had a hundred years of psychotherapy – and the world's getting worse*. HarperOne.

Hogan, L. (1995). *Dwellings: A spiritual history of the living world*. W.W. Norton & Company.

Hongzhi, Z. (1991). *Cultivating the empty field*. T. D. Leighton & Wu, Y. trans. North Point.

hooks, b. (2003). *Teaching community: A pedagogy of hope*. Routledge.

Huebner, D. E. (2008). *The lure of the transcendent: Collected essays by Dwayne E. Huebner*. Hillis, V. (Ed.). Routledge.

Hyde, L. (1983). *The gift: Imagination and the erotic life of property*. Vintage Books.

Illich, I. (1980). Vernacular values. Retrieved from http://www.preservenet.com/theory/Illich/Vernacular.html#EMPIRE.

Illich, I. (1998). The cultivation of conspiracy. A translated, edited and expanded version of an address given by Ivan Illich at the Villa Ichon in Bremen, Germany, March 14, 1998.

Illich, I., & Sanders, B. (1988). *ABC: The alphabetization of the popular mind*. North Point.

Innes, J. (2015). Time. In D. Jardine, C. Gilham, & G. McCaffery, G. (2015). *On the pedagogy of suffering: Hermeneutic and Buddhist meditations* (p. 107). Peter Lang.

Innes, J. (2016). From "A pocket of darkness" and "time." In J. Seidel & D. Jardine (Eds.), *The ecological heart of teaching: Radical tales of refuge and renewal for classrooms and communities*, p. 110. Peter Lang.

Jacobs, J. (2000). *The nature of economies*. Random House Canada.

Jardine, D. (1990). On the humility of mathematical language. *Educational theory*. 40(2), 181– 192.

Jardine, D. (1992a). *Speaking with a boneless tongue*. Makyo.

Jardine, D. (1992b). Reflections on hermeneutics, education and ambiguity: Hermeneutics as a restoring of life to its original difficulty. In Pinar, W. & Reynolds, W. (Eds.), *Understanding curriculum as a phenomenological and deconstructed text* (p. 116–130). Teacher's College.

Jardine, D. (1997). The surroundings. *JCT: The journal of curriculum theorizing*, 13(3), 18– 21.

Jardine, D. (2000a). Foreword by D. G. Smith. In*"Under the tough old stars": Ecopedagogical essays*. Psychology / Holistic Education.

Jardine. D. (2000b). "Littered with literacy": An ecopedagogical reflection on whole language, pedocentrism, and the necessity of refusal. In *"Under the tough old stars": ecopedagogical essays* (p. 47–68). Psychology / Holistic Education.

Jardine, D. (2000c). Reflections on education, hermeneutics and ambiguity: Hermeneutics as a restoring of life to its original difficulty. In *"Under the tough old stars": ecopedagogical essays* (p. 115–132). Psychology / Holistic Education.

Jardine, D. (2008). On the while of things. *Journal of the American association for the advancement of curriculum studies.* February 2008. Retrieved from https://ojs.library.ubc.ca/index.php/jaaacs/article/view/187670/1857697676.

Jardine, D. (2012). *Pedagogy left in peace: On the cultivation of free spaces in teaching and learning.* Continuu.

Jardine, D. (2013). "Time is [not] always running out." *Journal of the American association for the advancement of curriculum studies, 9,* p. 1–32.

Jardine, D. (2014). Translating water. In J. Seidel & D. Jardine (Eds.), *Ecological pedagogy, Buddhist pedagogy, hermeneutic pedagogy: Experiments in a curriculum for miracles* (p. 45–54). Peter Lang.

Jardine, D. (2015a). Introduction: how to love black snow. In M. Derby, *Place, being, resonance: A critical ecohermeneutic approach to education* (pp. xv–xviii). Peter Lang.

Jardine, D. (2015b). "You need accuracy": An appreciation of a modern hunting tradition. *One world in dialogue: A peer reviewed journal and focus newsletter, 4*(1). Alberta Teachers' Association Social Studies Council.

Jardine, D. (2015c). Quickening, patience, suffering. In David Jardine, Graham McCaffrey, & Chris Gilham (2015). *On the pedagogy of suffering: Hermeneutic and Buddhist meditations* (p. 109–110). Peter Lang.

Jardine, D. (2016a). *In praise of radiant beings: a retrospective path through education, Buddhism and ecology.* Information Age.

Jardine, D. (2016b). "Under the tough old stars." In *In praise of radiant beings: A retrospective path through education, Buddhism and ecology* (p. 63–70). Information Age.

Jardine, D. (2016c). Birding lessons and the teachings of cicadas. In *In praise of radiant beings: A retrospective path through education, Buddhism and ecology* (p. 83–88). Information Age.

Jardine, D. (2016d). "I love the terror in a mother's heart." In Seidel, J. & Jardine, D. (Eds.), *The ecological heart of teaching: Radical tales of refuge and renewal for classrooms and communities* (p. 161–2). Peter Lang.

Jardine, D. (2018a). "To know the world, we have to love it." In C. Leggo & E. Hasebe-Ludt (Eds.), *Canadian curriculum studies: A métissage of inspiration/imagination/ interconnection* (p. 224–5). Canadian Scholars' Press.

Jardine, D. (2018b). "Asleep in my sunshine chair." *Journal of applied hermeneutics.* Retrieved from https://www.academia.edu/36423073/_Asleep_in_My_Sunshine_Chair._

Jardine, D. (2018c). Advice in this liquid midst. Preface. In E. Lyle (Ed.), *The negotiated self: Exploring reflexive inquiry to explore teacher identity* (p. vi–xiv). Brill Sense.

Jardine, D. (2019a). *Asleep in my sunshine chair. DIO.*

Jardine, D., Bastock, M., George, J., & Martin, J. (2008). "Cleaving with Affection": On grain elevators and the cultivation of memory. In Jardine, D., Clifford, P., & Friesen, S., eds.

(2008). *Back to the basics of teaching and learning: "Thinking the world together"* (p. 11–58). 2nd Edition. Routledge.

Jardine, D., Clifford, P., & Friesen, S. (1999). "Standing helpless before the child." A response to Naomi Norquay's "Social difference and the problem of the 'unique individual': An uneasy legacy of child-centered pedagogy." *Canadian journal of education*, 24(3), 321–331.

Jardine, D., Clifford, P., & Friesen, S., eds. (2003). *Back to the basics of teaching and learning: "Thinking the world together."* Mahwah, NJ: Lawrence Erlbaum and Associates.

Jardine, D., & Smith, D. G. (2019). "Catastrophism becomes the perfect after-play." In D. Jardine 2019, *Asleep in my sunshine chair* (p. 77–86). DIO Press.

Jensen, D. (2002). *Listening to the land: Conversations about nature, culture, eros*. Chelsea Green.

Jensen, D. (2004). *Walking on water: Reading, writing, and revolution*. Chelsea Green.

Jensen, D., & Draffan, G. (2003). *Strangely like war: The global assault on forests*. Chelsea Green.

Judd, A. (2017, August 9). B.C. wildfires status Wednesday: More than 360 wildfires this season are human-caused. *Global News*. Retrieved from https://globalnews.ca/news/3657702/b-c-wildfires-status-wednesday-more-than-360-wildfires-this-season-are-human-caused/.

Kalman, D. Z. (2020). Shul in the time of coronavirus. *Tablet magazine*. Retrieved from https://www.tabletmag.com/jewish-life-and-religion/300624/shul-in-the-time-of-coronavirus.

Kanigel, R. (2005). *The one best way: Fredrick Winslow Taylor and the enigma of efficiency*. The MIT Press.

Keller, C. (1988). *From a broken web: Separation, sexism and self*. Beacon.

Kimmerer, R. W. (2013). *Braiding sweetgrass: Indigenous wisdom, scientific knowledge, and the teachings of plants*. Milkweed Editions.

Kincheloe, J., & Steinberg, S. R. (2012). Indigenous knowledges in education: Complexities, dangers, and profound benefits. In S. Steinberg & G. S. Cannella (Eds.), *Critical qualitative research reader, Vol. 2* (pp. 341–361). Peter Lang.

King, T. (1990). (Ed.). *All my relations: An anthology of contemporary Native fiction*. McClelland & Stewart.

King, T. (2003). *The truth about stories: A Native narrative*. Dead Dog Café Productions.

Kinnell, G. (2002). Saint Francis and the sow. Retrieved from http://www.poetryfoundation.org/poem/171395.

Klein, N. (2014). *This changes everything: Capitalism vs the climate*. Alfred A. Knopf Canada.

Knufken, D. (2010). The top 25 greenwashed products in America. *Business pundit*. Retrieved from http://www.businesspundit.com/the-top-25-greenwashed-products-in-america/.

Latremouille, J. (2014a). *Feasting on whispers: Life writing towards a pedagogy of kinship*. (Unpublished Master's thesis). University of Calgary.

Latremouille, J. (2014b). My treasured relation. *Journal of applied hermeneutics*. Retrieved from https://journalhosting.ucalgary.ca/index.php/jah/article/view/53238.

Latremouille, J. (2015). A modern hunting tradition. *One world in dialogue: A peer reviewed journal and focus newsletter*, 3(2), 9–11. Alberta Teachers' Association Social Studies Council.

Latremouille, J. (2018a). Environment. In D. G. Krutka, A. M. Whitlock, & M. Helmsing (Eds.), *Keywords in the social studies: Concepts and conversations* (pp. 66–77). Peter Lang.

Latremouille, J. (2018b). Writing from the heart-mind: Cultivating not-knowing towards an "earthly pedagogy." In E. Lyle (Ed.), *Fostering relational pedagogy: Self-study as transformative practice* (pp. 211–228). Brill.

Latremouille, J. (2020). An ecological pedagogy of joy. In S. Steinberg & B. Down (Eds.), *SAGE handbook of critical pedagogies* (pp. 1–25). Sage.

Latremouillle, J., Bell, A., Krahn, M., Kasamali, Z., Tait, L., & Donald, D. (2016). kistikwânihk êsko kitêhk: Storying holistic understandings in education. *Journal of the Canadian association for curriculum studies,* 14(1), 8–22. Video link: https://jcacs.journals.yorku.ca/index.php/jcacs/article/view/40294.

Leavy, P. (2013). *Fiction as research practice: Short stories, novellas, and novels.* Left Coast.

Leggo, C. (2006). Learning by heart: A poetics of research. *Journal of curriculum theorizing,* Winter, p. 73–96.

Le Guin, U. (1985). She unnames them. *The New Yorker.* Retrieved from https://www.newyorker.com/magazine/1985/01/21/she-unnames-them.

Leopold, A. (1949). *A Sand County almanac.* Retrieved from http://www.umag.cl/facultades/williams/wp-content/uploads/2016/11/Leopold-1949-ASandCountyAlmanac-complete.pdf.

Liddell, M. (2016). Thoughts on being neither finished nor unfinished. In J. Seidel & D. Jardine (2016). *The ecological heart of teaching: Radical tales of refuge and renewal for classrooms and communities* (p. 175–176). Peter Lang.

Little Bear, L. (2000). Jagged worldviews colliding. In M. Battiste, ed. (2000). *Reclaiming Indigenous voice and vision* (pp. 77–85). UBC.

Loy, D. (2010). *The world is made of stories.* Wisdom.

Lui, W. C., & Lo, I. (1990). *Sunflower splendor: Three thousand years of Chinese poetry.* University of Indiana.

Lukacs, M. (2017). Neoliberalism has conned us into fighting climate change as individuals. *The Guardian.* Retrieved from https://www.theguardian.com/environment/true north/2017/jul/17/neoliberalism-has-conned-us-into-fighting-climate-change-as-individuals?CMP=share_btn_fb

Macy, J. (1989). Awakening the ecological self. In J. Plant (Ed.), *Healing the wounds: The promise of ecofeminism.* Between the Lines.

Macy, J. (1996). The greening of the self. In A. Kotler (Ed.), *Engaged Buddhist reader.* (p. 171–180). Parallax.

Macy, J. (2007). The greening of the self. In World as lover, world as self: Courage for global justice and ecological renewal, pp. 148–158. Parallax.

Macy, J. (2014). Joanna Macy on how to prepare internally for whatever comes next. *Ecobuddhism.* Retrieved from www.ecobuddhism.org/wisdom/interviews/jmacy.

Martin-Woodhouse, T. (2017, July 22). Evacuation order lifted for much of 100 Mile House. *Global News.* Retrieved from https://globalnews.ca/news/3617551/evacuation-order-lifted-for-much-of-100-mile-house/.

Martusewicz, R. (2005). Eros in the commons: Educating for eco-ethical consciousness in a poetics of place. *Ethics, place, and environment,* 8(3), 331–348.

McIntosh, P. (1989). White privilege: Unpacking the invisible knapsack. *Peace and freedom,* July-August 1989, pp. 10–12.

McLeod, N. (2007). Cree narrative memory: From treaties to contemporary times. Purich.

Merriam-Webster. (2016). Environment. Retrieved from http://www.merriam-webster.com/dictionary/environment.

Molnar, C. (2016). Hypoplastic left heart syndrome. In J. Seidel & D. Jardine (Eds.), *The ecological heart of teaching: Radical tales of refuge and renewal for classrooms and communities* (p. 89–99). Peter Lang.

Momaday, N. S. (1997). *The man made of words: Essays, stories, passages*. St. Martin's.

Moules, N. J., & Estefan, A. (2018). Editorial: Watching my mother die - Subjectivity and the other side of dementia. *Journal of applied hermeneutics*, Editorial 3. Retrieved from https://journalhosting.ucalgary.ca/index.php/jah/article/view/57328/pdf.

Murphy, S. (2014). *Minding the earth, mending the world: Zen and the art of planetary crisis*. Counterpoint.

National Geographic. (2016). Environment. *National geographic society*. Retrieved from http://www.nationalgeographic.com/environment/.

News 1130. (2017, August 1). Over 300 buildings gone as B.C. wildfires expected to grow amid smoky conditions. *The Canadian press*. Retrieved from http://www.news1130.com/2017/08/01/more-than-300-buildings-destroyed-by-persistent-wildfires-across-b-c/.

Nishitani, K. (1982). *Religion and nothingness*. University of California.

Nixon, R. (2011). *Slow violence and the environmentalism of the poor*. Harvard University.

Ochs, P. (1967). Crucifixion. From P. Ochs (1967), *The Pleasures of the Harbor*. Compact Disc. A&M Records.

OED. (n.d.). Online Etymological Dictionary. Retrieved from www.etymonline.com.

Okri, B. (1997). *A way of being free*. Orion.

O'Leary, K. (2012). Dragon's Den. Produced by the Canadian Broadcasting Company. Series 6, Episode 19, first aired March 14, 2012. Retrieved from www.cbc.ca/dragonsden/pitches/ukloo.

Ontario Ministry of Education. (2011). The Ontario Curriculum grades 1–8 and kindergarten programs. Environmental education: Scope and sequence of programs. Queen's Printer for Ontario.

Oreskes, N., & Conway, E. (2011). *Merchants of doubt: How a handful of scientists obscured the truth on issues from tobacco smoke to global warming*. Bloomsbury.

Orr, D. (1991). What is education for? Six myths about the foundations of modern education, and six new principles to replace them. *The Learning Revolution*, 27(4), 52–55. Retrieved from http://www.context.org/iclib/ic27/orr/.

Osberg, D., & Biesta, G. (2008). The emergent curriculum: Navigating a complex course between unguided learning and planned enculturation. *Journal of curriculum studies*, 40(3), pp. 313–328.Pal, A. (2005). Wangari Maathai interview. *The progressive*, 69(5), 5.

Palmer, P. (1989). *To know as we are known: Education as a spiritual discipline*. Harper Collins.

Parks, V. D. (1966). Lyrics from the song "Wonderful," music by Brian Wilson. Licensed to YouTube by UMG (on behalf of EMI); EMI Music Publishing, UMPG Publishing, BMI - Broadcast Music Inc. Retrieved from https://www.youtube.com/watch?v=RSTJJKffsPI.

Pelden, K. (2007). *The nectar of Manjushri's speech*. Shambhala.

Peterson, R. T. (1980). *A field guide to the birds east of the Rockies*. 4th Edition. Houghton Mifflin.

Pinar, W. F. (2006). Foreword: The lure that pulls flowerheads to face the sun. In D. Jardine, S. Friesen, & P. Clifford, *Curriculum in abundance* (pp. ix–xxii). Lawrence Erlbaum & Associates.

Pinar, W. F. (2012). *What is curriculum theory?* Taylor & Francis.

Pinar, W. F. (2018). Revealing interrelationality, unearthing histories. In C. Leggo & E. Hasebe-Ludt (Eds.), *Canadian curriculum studies: A métissage of inspiration/imagination/interconnection*. (p. xv). Canadian Scholars' Press.

Pullen, L. (May 18, 2017). State of emergency issued near Merritt. *Global News*. Retrieved from https://globalnews.ca/news/3462952/state-of-emergency-issued-near-merritt/.

Racette, S. (2017). Pieces along the trail: Material culture histories and Indigenous studies. In C. Anderson & J.M. Obrien (Eds.), *Sources and methods in Indigenous studies* (pp. 223–239). Routledge.

Ramesh, R. (2009, October 7). Maldive ministers prepare for underwater cabinet meeting. *The Guardian*. Retrieved from https://www.theguardian.com/world/2009/oct/07/maldives-underwater-cabinet-meeting

Richardson, L. (1994). Writing: A method of inquiry. In N. Denzin & Y. Lincoln (Eds.), *Handbook of qualitative research* (pp. 516–529). Sage.

Richardson, L. (2001). Getting personal: Writing-stories. *International Journal of Qualitative Studies in Education*, 14(1), 33–38.

Roosevelt, T. (1912). A confession of faith. Speech given at Progressive Party Convention. August 6, 1912. Chicago, IL. Retrieved from http://www.theodore-roosevelt.com/images/research/speeches/trarmageddon.pdf.

Ross, S. (2006). The temporality of tarrying in Gadamer. *Theory, culture & society*, 23(1), 101–123.

Ross, S., & Jardine, D. (2009). Won by a certain labour: A conversation on the while of things. *Journal of the American association for the advancement of curriculum studies*, 5. Retrieved from http://www.uwstout.edu/soe/jaaacs/Vol5/Ross_Jardine.htm.

Russell, B. (1972). *The history of western philosophy*. Simon and Schuster.

Sale, K. (2000). *Dwellers in the land: Bio-regional vision*. University of Georgia.

Sartre, J. P. (1970). Intentionality: A Fundamental Idea in Husserl's Phenomenology. *Journal for the British Society for Phenomenology*, 1, #2, pp. 3–5.

Seidel, J. (2012). The paperwhite's lesson plan. In *Undivided: The online journal of nonduality and psychology*, 1(3). Retrieved from http://undividedjournal.com/2012/11/29/the-paperwhites-lesson-plan/.

Seidel, J. (2014). Reading the stones. In J. Seidel & D. Jardine (Eds.), *Ecological pedagogy, Buddhist pedagogy, hermeneutic pedagogy: Experiments in a curriculum for miracles* (p. 39–44). Peter Lang.

Seidel, J. (2016). Meditations on contemplative pedagogy as sanctuary. In J. Seidel & D. Jardine (Eds.), *The ecological heart of teaching: Radical tales of refuge and renewal for classrooms and communities* (pp. 66–71). Peter Lang.

Seidel, J. & Jardine, D. (2012). EDER 693.01 L21. Hermeneutics and Inquiry in the Classroom. Fall 2012. *Course outline*. Werklund School of Education. University of Calgary.

Seidel, J., & Jardine, D. (2014). "Introduction: We are here, we are here. " In J. Seidel & D. Jardine (Eds.), *Ecological pedagogy, Buddhist pedagogy, hermeneutic pedagogy: Experiments in a curriculum for miracles* (p. 1–6). Peter Lang.

Seidel, J., & Jardine, D. (2016). The path and the goal. In J. Seidel & D. Jardine (Eds.), *The ecological heart of teaching: Radical tales of refuge and renewal for classrooms and communities* (pp. 247–250). Peter Lang.

Sekida, K. (1976). *Zen Training: Methods and Philosophy*. New York NY: Weatherhill.
Seuss, T. (1971). *The lorax*. New York, NY: Random House Books for Young Readers.
Shepard, P. (1996). *The others: How animals made us human*. Washington, D.C.: Island.
Shepard, P. (1998). *Nature and madness*. Athens, GA: University of Georgia.
Sheridan, J. (2001). Mythic ecology. In *Canadian Journal of Education*, 6(2), 194–205.
Sheridan, J., & "He Who Clears the Sky" Longboat, D. (2006). The Haudenosaunee imagination and the ecology of the sacred. In *Space and culture*, 9(4), 365–381.
Simard, S. (2012). Do trees communicate? Retrieved from https://www.youtube.com/watch?v=iSGPNm3bFmQ.
Simpson, L. Betasamosake. (2014). Land as pedagogy: Nishnaabeg intelligence and rebellious transformation. *Decolonization: Indigeneity, education & society*, 3, p 1–25.
Sinclair, M. (2017, February 7) National Centre for Truth and Reconciliation. Senator Murray Sinclair on reconciliation [video]. YouTube. https://www.youtube.com/watch?v=wjx2zDvyzs.
Smith, D. G. (1988). Children and the gods of war. *Phenomenology + pedagogy*, 6(1), 25–29.
Smith, D. G. (1991). Hermeneutic inquiry: The hermeneutic imagination and the pedagogic text. In E.C. Short (Ed.), *Forms of curriculum inquiry* (pp. 187–209). State University of New York.
Smith, D. G. (1999). *Pedagon: Interdisciplinary essays in the human sciences, pedagogy and culture*. Peter Lang.
Smith, D. G. (2006). *Trying to teach in a season of great untruth: Globalization, empire and the crises of pedagogy*. Sense.
Smith, D. G. (2012). Foreword: Spiritual cardiology and the heart of wisdom. In C. Chambers, E. Hasebe-Ludt, C. Leggo, & A. Sinner (Eds.), *A heart of wisdom: Life writing an empathetic inquiry* (pp. xi–xviii). Peter Lang.
Smith, D. G. (2014). *Teaching as the practice of wisdom*. Bloomsbury.
Smith, D. G. (2016). Foreword. In J. Seidel & D. Jardine, (2016). *The ecological heart of teaching: Radical tales of refuge and renewal for classrooms and communities*. (p. xvi–xix). Peter Lang.
Smith, D. G. (2020). *Confluences: Intercultural Journeying in Teaching and Research: From hermeneutics to a changing world order*. IAP.
Snyder, G. (n.d.) I Went to the Maverick Bar. Online: https://www.poetryfoundation.org/poems/47754/i-went-into-the-maverick-bar.
Snyder, G. (1980). *The real work*. New Directions.
Snyder, G. (1990). Survival and sacrament. In *The practice of the wild* (p. 175–185). Counterpoint.
Solnit, R. (2016). Standing Rock protests: This is only the beginning. *The Guardian*. Retrieved from https://www.theguardian.com/us-news/2016/sep/12/north-dakota-standing-rock-protests-civil-rights.
Somerville, M. (2012). The critical power of place. In S. R. Steinberg & G. S. Canella (Eds.), *Critical qualitative research reader* (pp. 67–81). Peter Lang.
Steinberg, T. (2012). *Down to earth: Nature's role in American History*. 3rd Edition. Oxford University.
Steingraber, S. (2010). *Living downstream: An ecologist's personal investigation of cancer and the environment*. Da Capo.
Stiggins, R. (2007). Assessment through the student's eyes. Educational Leadership, 64(8), 22–26. Snowflake.

Styres, S.D. (2017). *Pathways for remembering and recognizing Indigenous thought in education: Philosophies of lethi'nihstenha Ohwentsia'kekha* (Land). Toronto, ON: University of Toronto Press.

Sumedho, A. (2010). *Don't take your life personally*. Totnes, Devon, UK: Buddhist.

Tait, L. (2014). In Seidel, J., Jardine, D., Bailey, D., Gray, H., Hector, M., Innes, J., Jones, C., Kowalchuk, T., Mal, N., Meredith, J., Molnar, C., Rilstone, P., Savill, T., Sirup, K., Tait, L., Taylor, L., & Vaast, D., Echolocations. In J. Seidel & D. Jardine (Eds.,) *Ecological pedagogy, Buddhist pedagogy, hermeneutic pedagogy: Experiments in a curriculum for miracles* (p. 91–110). Peter Lang.

Tait, L. (2016a). Remembrances of the Land and Rocks in my Pocket. In J. Seidel & D. Jardine (Eds.), *The ecological heart of teaching: Radical tales of refuge and renewal for classrooms and communities* (p. 166–7). Peter Lang.

Tait, L. (2016b). Successful Assimilation. In J. Seidel & D. Jardine (Eds.), *The ecological heart of teaching: Radical tales of refuge and renewal for classrooms and communities* (p. 17–18). Peter Lang.

Taylor, F. W. (1911). Scientific management, comprising shop management, the principles of scientific management and testimony before the special house committee. Harper & Row.

Theodore Roosevelt Conservation Partnership. (2017). Our issues. Retrieved from http://www.trcp.org/what/sportsmens-access/.

Think Earth Environmental Education Foundation. (2016a). It's time to Think Earth! Think Earth Foundation. Retrieved from https://thinkearth.org/curriculum/document/1125-summary-of-unit-objectives.

Thrangu, K. (2011). *Vivid Awareness: The Mind Instructions of Khenpo Gangshar*. Shambhala.

Trungpa, C. (2004). The Collected Works of Chögyam Trungpa, Volume 3: Cutting Through Spiritual Materialism - The Myth of Freedom - The Heart of the Buddha - Selected Writings. Shambhala.

Tsing, A. L. (2015). *The mushroom at the end of the world: On the possibility of life in capitalist ruins*. Princeton University.

Tsong-Kha-Pa. (2000). *The great treatise on the stages of the path to enlightenment (Lam rim chen mo)*. Volume One. Snow Lion.

Tsong-Kha-Pa. (2003). *The great treatise on the stages of the path to enlightenment (Lam rim chen mo)*. Volume Three. Snow Lion.

Tsong-Kha-Pa. (2004). *The great treatise on the stages of the path to enlightenment (Lam rim chen mo)*. Volume Two. Snow Lion.

Vaast, D., & Beech, S. (2018). REDress Project. Retrieved from https://twitter.com/ypoitraspratt/status/98486125592718540.

van Gelder, S. (2017). Earth democracy – an interview with Vandana Shiva. *YES! magazine*. http://www.yesmagazine.org/issues/what-would-democracy-look-like/earth-democracy-an-interview-with-vandana-shiva.

Voneche, J., & Bovet, M. (1982). Training research and cognitive development: What do Piagetians want to accomplish? In S. Modgil & C. Modgil (Eds.), *Jean Piaget: Consensus and controversy* (pp. 83–94). Holt, Rinehart and Winston.

Wagamese, R. (2016). *Embers: One Ojibway's meditations*. Douglas & McIntyre.

Wagner, C. (2016, November 17). Tighter regulations proposed for local fishing spots. *Merritt Herald*. Retrieved from https://www.merrittherald.com/tighter-regulations-proposed-local-fishing-spots/.
Wallace, B. (1989). *The stubborn particulars of grace*. McClelland and Stewart.
Walsh, I. (2016). Advice to a new teacher. In J. Seidel & D. Jardine (2016). *The ecological heart of teaching: Radical tales of refuge and renewal for classrooms and communities* (p. 65). Peter Lang.
We Movement. (2017). Our beliefs. Retrieved from https://www.we.or/we-movement/ourbeliefs/me.
Weinsheimer, J. (1987). *Gadamer's hermeneutics*. Yale University.
Wiebe, R., & Johnson, Y. (1999). *Stolen life: The journey of a Cree woman*. Random House Canada.
Wittgenstein, L. (1968). *Philosophical isnvestigations*. Blackwell's.
Wrege, C. D., & Greenwood, R. (1991). *Frederick W. Taylor: The father of scientific management: Myth and reality*. Irwin. Currently out of print. The text of Chapter 9 is available online at: johntaylorgatto.com/chapters/9d.hFtm.
Yates, F. (1974). *The art of memory*. University of Chicago.
Zwicky, J. (2013). *Songs for relinquishing the earth*. Brick.

Complicated Conversation

A BOOK SERIES OF CURRICULUM STUDIES

Reframing the curricular challenge educators face after a decade of school deform, the books published in Peter Lang's Complicated Conversation Series testify to the ethical demands of our time, our place, our profession. What does it mean for us to teach now, in an era structured by political polarization, economic destabilization, and the prospect of climate catastrophe? Each of the books in the Complicated Conversation Series provides provocative paths, theoretical and practical, to a very different future. In this resounding series of scholarly and pedagogical interventions into the nightmare that is the present, we hear once again the sound of silence breaking, supporting us to rearticulate our pedagogical convictions in this time of terrorism, reframing curriculum as committed to the complicated conversation that is intercultural communication, self-understanding, and global justice.

The series editor is

> Dr. William F. Pinar
> Department of Curriculum Studies
> 2125 Main Mall
> Faculty of Education
> University of British Columbia
> Vancouver, British Columbia V6T 1Z4
> CANADA

To order other books in this series, please contact our Customer Service Department:

> peterlang@presswarehouse.com (within the U.S.)
> orders@peterlang.com (outside the U.S.)

Or browse online by series:

> www.peterlang.com

www.ingramcontent.com/pod-product-compliance
Lightning Source LLC
Chambersburg PA
CBHW061706300426
44115CB00014B/2585